Gettin' Our Groove On

African American Life Series

A complete listing of the books in this series
can be found online at http://wsupress.wayne.edu

Series Editors

Melba Joyce Boyd
Department of Africana Studies,
Wayne State University

Ronald Brown
Department of Political Science,
Wayne State University

Gettin' Our Groove On

Rhetoric, Language, and Literacy
for the Hip Hop Generation

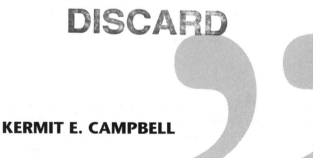

KERMIT E. CAMPBELL

Wayne State University Press   Detroit

Library of Congress Cataloging-in-Publication Data

Campbell, Kermit Ernest, 1960–
Gettin' our groove on : rhetoric, language, and literacy for the hip hop generation /
Kermit E. Campbell.
p. cm. — (African American life series)
Includes bibliographical references and index.
ISBN 0-8143-2925-X (pbk. : alk. paper)
1. African Americans—Languages. 2. American literature—African American authors—
History and criticism. 3. African American music—History and criticism. 4. English
language—United States—Rhetoric. 5. Popular culture—United States. 6. African
Americans in literature. 7. Black English—United States. 8. Literacy—United States.
9. Hip-hop—United States. I. Title. II. Series.
PE3102.N42C36 2005
427'.089'96073—dc22
2005001639

∞The paper used in this publication meets the minimum requirements of the American
National Standard for Information Sciences—Permanence of Paper for Printed Library
Materials, ANSI Z39.48-1984.

For credits, see Permissions Acknowledgments, page 195.

In memory of my father,
from whom I learned the virtue of wordplay,
of signification

And for my mother Laverne and my wife Betsy,
who have made my journey
an adventure and reward

There is obviously no unrhetorical "naturalness" of language to which one could appeal; language itself is the result of purely rhetorical arts. The power to discover and to make operative that which works and impresses, with respect to each thing, a power which Aristotle calls rhetoric, is at the same time, the essence of language.

Friedrich Nietzsche, Friedrich Nietzsche
on Rhetoric and Language

"Rap" is as old as the African beating on a log like the one in which sailors keep their records, as old as the dictum that denied slaves drums because they were "rapping" to each other after hours, drumming up rhythmic resistance. When the rappers say "word," it is old. Our speech carries our whole existence.

Amiri Baraka, "The Language of Defiance"

The soul of a people is embodied in the language peculiar to them. . . . It is significant that peoples throughout history have often stubbornly held on to their native language or dialect because they regarded it as a badge of their identity and because they felt that only through it could they express their inner beings, their attitudes and emotions, and even their own concepts of reality.

Cleanth Brooks, The Language of the American South

True *Hiphop* is a term that describes the independent collective consciousness of a specific group of inner-city people.

KRS-One, Ruminations

Contents

Acknowledgments

Earlier versions of chapters 2, 3, and 5 were presented at conferences of the International Society for the History of Rhetoric, the Modern Language Association, College Composition and Communication, and the International Association of World Englishes. I gratefully acknowledge members of these organizations for the opportunity to share with them my ideas while yet in their formative stages.

With the help of a Colgate University Research Council Grant, I was able to pay the fees for the music licenses required to quote excerpts from rap lyrics and other recorded music. In most cases, such licenses were extremely difficult if not impossible to acquire, but I am grateful that the folks at Universal Music Publishing, Hal Leonard Corp., and Wixen Music Publishing were willing to work with me on this critical part of the book. I understand that the music business is what it is, but it is gratifying to know that some in the industry are supportive of what we academics do.

I want to give a heartfelt thanks to my editors at Wayne State University Press: Kathryn Wildfong, my initial contact at the Press who expressed great interest in the work when so many others had not, Jane Hoehner for picking up where Kathryn left off with persistent enthusiasm and steadfast guardianship over my project, and series editor Dr. Melba Joyce Boyd for her many thought-provoking comments and questions about the book, all of which led me to think more deeply about the focus of my writing. Likewise I owe others a debt of gratitude for feedback they gave me at some stage in the process: my mentor Andrea Lunsford for her encouragement and input on a complete draft of the manuscript, and my dear colleague Beverly Moss for her comments on chapter 5 when it was being considered for publication in the journal *College Composition and Communication*. Although the essay didn't appear there, the comments helped me to revise the piece for inclusion in the present volume. Thanks to colleagues Thomas Miller and Linda Ferreira-Buckley for helping me early on in the process with crafting the book proposal, and to Shannon Hasselman, one of my students at the University of Texas, for clarifying for me students' reactions to the course material alluded to in chapter 4 and for hipping me to the term "Bunco" in the Watts Prophets' epigraph.

Much appreciation goes to Madison Searle for having shown great interest in my work while I was at Texas, keeping me abreast of news relevant to my project, and engaging me in many enlightening conversations about music. For her tireless clerical assistance and goodly advice about a host of matters, I want to thank my department's administrative assistant, Trudy King, who sadly passed away shortly before the publication of this book. Many, many students have passed through my writing course on Hip hop. From some of them I have gained an especial insight and inspiration that somehow found its way into the creative process of this work. From others, well . . . let's just say the dirt is off my shoulders. Special thanks go to the students in the Black Pulp Fiction class for hangin' with me and making my first and only time teaching it memorable.

Finally, this book wouldn't be what it is without Hip hop, so I would like to take this opportunity to send a shoutout to Hip hoppas across the globe for doing your thing and making the world take note. I want to send a shoutout also to a few of my peops from around the way: to my peoples in the 713 (and 281)—we done lost some good ones, but our collective soul lives on; to my compadre in San Marcos, Jaime Mejia— thanks for the strong support and for having my back all these years; and to the rest of ya'll at home and abroad—peace, love, and happiness.

I knew that the great lack of most of the big-named "Negro leaders" was their lack of any true rapport with the ghetto Negroes. How could they have rapport when they spent most of their time "integrating" with white people? I knew that the ghetto people knew that I never left the ghetto in spirit, and I never left it physically any more than I had to. I had a ghetto instinct; for instance, I could feel if tension was beyond normal in a ghetto audience. And I could speak and understand the ghetto's language.

Malcolm X, *The Autobiography of Malcolm X*

I'd made my choices. I was running away from Pittsburgh, from poverty, from blackness. To get ahead, to make something of myself, college had seemed a logical, necessary step; my exile, my flight from home began with good grades, with good English, with setting myself apart long before I'd earned a scholarship and a train ticket over the mountains to Philadelphia.

Your world. The blackness that incriminated me. Easier to change the way I talked and walked, easier to be two people than to expose in either world the awkward mix of school and home I'd become. . . . To succeed in the man's world you must become like the man and the man sure didn't claim no bunch of nigger relatives in Pittsburgh.

John Edgar Wideman, *Brothers and Keepers*

Speaking standard English to whites was our way of demonstrating that we knew their language and could use it. Speaking it to standard-English-speaking blacks was our way of showing them that we, as well as they, could "put on airs." But when we spoke standard English, we acknowledged (to ourselves and to others—but primarily to ourselves) that our customary way of speaking was inferior. We felt foolish, embarrassed, somehow diminished because we were ashamed to be our real selves. We were reserved, shy in the presence of those who owned and/or spoke *the* language.

Barbara Mellix, "From Outside, In"

So, if you want to really hurt me, talk badly about my language. Ethnic identity is twin skin to linguistic identity—I am my language. Until I can take pride in my language, I cannot take pride in myself. Until I can accept as legitimate Chicano Texas Spanish, Tex-Mex and all the other languages I speak, I cannot accept the legitimacy of myself. Until I am free to write bilingually and to switch codes without having always to translate, while I still have to speak English or Spanish when I would rather speak Spanglish, and as long as I have to accommodate the English speakers rather than having them accommodate me, my tongue will be illegitimate.

I will no longer be made to feel ashamed of existing. I will have my voice.

Gloria Anzaldua, *Borderlands/La Frontera: The New Mestiza*

1

Who You Callin' "Igno"? In Defense of the Black Vernacular Voice

In the heat of the national Ebonics debate back in '96 and '97, seem like every black person (and quite a few overzealous white folks, too!) with a mainstream rep, a microphone, and editorial space claimed the right to speak on Ebonics and the proposal by the Oakland Unified School District (OUSD) to incorporate Ebonics into their English-language curriculum. And the mainstream press loved it—ate it up, in fact, cuz for one rare moment some of the staunchest conservatives and the most bleeding-heart liberals were lockstep in condemnation of both.[1] With such a united political front, the American public was thus sold, no questions asked. Never mind that they (most of them outspoken critics on the left and right) didn't know diddly about linguistics or English education. Why, the real experts—linguists, educators, and teachers (though not all in agreement on the relevance of Ebonics to formal instruction in standard English)—couldn't even get a word in edgewise in most newspapers, magazines, and on radio and television programs across the country. And now that *the experts* have spoken by way of scholarly articles and books published in the last five years,[2] I wonder just how many of those self-proclaimed pedagogues have since taken into account the linguistic facts concerning black vernacular speech.

For all the public uproar over Ebonics, as a term and a concept, it was in fact old news to the linguistics community. I myself am no card-carrying member of that community, but I have studied enough linguistics to know a thing or two about Ebonics. I'm aware that, for one, the term

1

was in circulation long before it surfaced in the OUSD proposal and before the mainstream media went ballistic with its inflammatory and, at times, racist remarks. While in graduate school at Ohio State University in the late '80s, I stumbled upon the term in Robert L. Williams's *Ebonics: The True Language of Black Folks*. The expression intrigued me at the time but seemed a relic of '60s radicalism, reminding me of the days when sistas and brothas copped aliases for themselves like Mahogany, Coffee, and Ebony to signify a mighty and proud blackness.

Williams and others in attendance at a 1973 education conference in St. Louis, so the story goes, invented the term *Ebonics* because they wasn't satisfied with those previously used by white researchers (such as Negro Nonstandard English and Black English). They wanted something less dependent on an association (a largely negative one) with standard English for its legitimacy, so they combined "ebony" and "phonics" (standard English words, no less) to create *Ebonics*. But beyond the folks at the conference, the term never really caught on— until the OUSD proposal went prime time. (Now just about every Tom, Dick, and Jane has heard of Ebonics, think they know what it is, and is ready to damn you as unpatriotic for advocating the use of it.) In the linguistics and educational literature I reviewed between 1989 and 1993, I found no mention of the term.[3] While linguists had generally dropped the "nonstandard" referent to working-class African American speech, by the late '70s (if not earlier) they had universally adopted terms like *Black Vernacular English, Black English Vernacular,* and some time later, *African American Vernacular English*. By the mid- to late '80s, the African American vernacular had become a household word thanks in part to African American literary scholars Houston Baker, Jr. (*Blues, Ideology, and Afro-American Literature: A Vernacular Theory*) and Henry Louis Gates, Jr. (*The Signifying Monkey: A Theory of Afro-American Literary Criticism*). Their theories of African American literature based on a critical understanding of the black vernacular publicly legitimized black language like no linguistic study before them. Or so I thought. I guess theories about the aesthetics of black vernacular speech in the academy make a lot more sense than the practical uses of it in schools and other public spaces. Maybe Ebonics opponents just didn't see the connection between the African American vernacular in the novels of Toni Morrison and Alice Walker (*it sounds so quaint on the page coming out of the mouths of southerners and slaves*) and Ebonics in the speech of kids in inner-city neighborhoods and on school playgrounds (*it sounds so vile coming out the mouths of urban youth and, god forbid, their suburban white peers*). Surely, that must be it. In fact, in *Beyond Ebonics: Linguistic Pride and Racial Prejudice*, John Baugh reveals that among scholarly uses of the term there are at least "four divergent definitions of Ebonics" in circulation.[4] Maybe folks weren't clear just which definition of Ebonics OUSD was referring to. Please! Most of these folk didn't know what Ebonics was, period. And judging from their ad hominem caricatures of young Ebonics speakers, they really didn't and don't care to know.

Be that as it may, for most Black Vernacular English speakers it ain't about what you call it no way. It's about what you do with it, about making language—words, phrases, sentences, sounds—resonate with the tenor of your own voice and unique sensibility. Now, I'm not suggesting that speakers of African American Vernacular English can be defined by a single voice or register, black or otherwise. For as Jacqueline Jones Royster stated so poignantly some years ago, "I claim all my voices as my own very much authentic voices, even when it's difficult for others to imagine a person like me having the capacity to do that."[5] Like her, I do not deny the authenticity of any of my voices (academic/professional, formal standard English—what some see as white middle-class speech—southern, Christian, black vernacular, and so forth), but I refuse to be ridiculed by others into claiming only one of these voices (especially the second) as my own, be it for public or private consumption. Middle-class aspirations and an academic career have rubbed off on me, fo sho, but all hell or Texas gotta freeze over befo you see me copping out on a genuine respect and love for my native tongue. Limiting myself to one homogenized, so-called American voice, as some would have it, would be tantamount to self-negation . . . or self-hatred. And after many years of monitoring my speech, making sure I sounded like I wasn't from a one-horse, southern town and later a poor black neighborhood in the big city, I seek affirmation of the self, of my vernacular voice, and the voice of my peoples.

That's from the heart, you know. But I don't expect a lot of folks to feel me. So for those who yet insist that Ebonics is some grave blight on our national character, I offer in what follows a further defense, more from the dome—that is, a reasoned analysis and critique of some supposedly rational arguments declaiming the legitimacy of the black vernacular voice.

After my defense, in the second chapter of the book, I make the case that the vernacular is more than just language—invariant be's, double negatives, and inverted semantics—it is rhetoric, a highly developed discursive system that claims the oral tradition of rap as its centerpiece. Digging through the crates of African and African American expressive artifacts, I pick up pieces of the vernacular rhetorical tradition from the West African griot to African American street-corner rappers, Spoken Word poets, and Hip hop artists. Though as Henry Louis Gates, Jr., points out, signifying is an integral cog in this rhetorical wheel, rap or rappin' is its power, its driving force. "Can't Knock the Hustle?"

and "The Players (Book) Club," the third and fourth chapters in the book, are also reflections on vernacular tradition, particularly that of the ghetto hustler and the expressive culture that makes his/her ethos legendary. From toasts like Stag-O-Lee, the Signifying Monkey, and Dolomite to today's gangsta and pimp raps, the hustling ethos and the literary genre of ghetto realistic fiction have emerged. While gangsta and pimp rap lyrics are oftentimes gratuitously violent and misogynistic, they are also at times quite complex in their attempts through the spoken word to instantiate the self in an increasingly amoral world. Parents and government authorities worry nevertheless about the effect of this instantiation, about it likely influencing Junior to go gangsta or little Kimi to be promiscuous like her gangstress namesake. As I suggest in the final piece, "They Got Game: African American Students, Hip Hop, and Literacy," parents, political leaders, and the like may have some cause for concern, not about their children turning into violent criminals and sex fiends but about their suburban world being turned upside down. If anything, rap is exposing suburban youth to the rich African American vernacular rhetorical tradition, to the game that urban youth have in spite of the dominant culture's damaging characterization of them and their "degenerate" surroundings. Because Hip hop has breathed new life into language learning and literacy for many urban and suburban youths, it demands to be recognized. And I propose that we do just that in a place where it is most fitting—the writing and rhetoric classroom. Institutions of higher education are a prime battleground for knowledge, but teachers and students must be engaged in battle not just against ignorance and illiteracy but against the assumption of literate knowledge and the values that sustain it in mainstream culture.

Nuff said! Let's get this show started, aiight!

No Disrespect, but Who Do You Be Poppin' Collars at Me?

Enter stage left . . . the Right Reverend Jesse Jackson. Naturally, he had something to say in the glare of the national Ebonics spotlight. Blinded by the light, as it were, the brotha basically told us well-trained and highly experienced scholars and teachers that we didn't know jack about teaching English—that by recognizing the legitimacy of the black vernacular, the school board in Oakland was *teaching down to our children.*[6] Now don't get me wrong, I ain't tryna to bad mouf the reb'en—oops, I mean reverend—but what he know about teaching English or about linguistics? I mean, he cool on affirmative action, welfare, and workers rights and all that, but English, come on! Well, at least the good reverend was conscientious enough to modify his stance once he got hipped to what school board officials were really aiming to do—that is, to acknowledge the relevance of Oakland students' first dialect in teaching them standard English.

That's more than I can say about some other high-profile black folk who bum-rushed the national stage to denounce Ebonics. A student in my Rhetoric of Black Nationalism course at the time of the Ebonics controversy gave me a list she gleaned from the Internet containing public comments several black celebrities (besides Jackson) made about the Oakland decision. Reportedly, Maya Angelou, Arsenio Hall, and Kwesi Mfume (not to mention those not on her list like Shelby Steele, Eldridge Cleaver, and even my man Henry Louis Gates, Jr.)[7] all publicly denounced the school board's action, stating, in general, that allowing Ebonics into the classroom would send a damaging message to African American schoolkids (one that goes something like this: we not capable of learning standard English like e'rybody else—that is, like white kids).

Arsenio Hall, for instance, was quoted as saying the following: "Be no fan of Ebonics. Malcolm X didn't need it. Martin Luther King didn't need it. Maya Angelou didn't need it. It's absurd. I think it creates awful self-esteem in Black kids to tell them they need something extra that other Americans don't need. It sends out an awful signal."[8] If, in fact, Arsenio Hall did seriously say this (you never know with them comedians), that, in particular, Malcolm X didn't need Ebonics, the brotha clearly ain't up on his Malcolm. He need to peep the paragraphs from Malcolm's autobiography. And he also need to listen to brotha Malcolm's 1963 speech, "Message to the Grassroots." Be a whole lotta Ebonics in dat speech, Money. Granted it was delivered to a predominantly black inner-city audience, where, I'm sure, Malcolm felt at liberty to use what he calls the "ghetto's language," but, the fact is, Malcolm spoke both vernacular and standard varieties and was proud of it. As evidence, check out the portion of the autobiography that follows what I cited in the chapter's first epigraph.

> There was an example of this that always flew to my mind every time I heard some of the "big name" Negro "leaders" declaring they "spoke for" the ghetto black people. After a Harlem street rally, one of these downtown "leaders" and I were talking when we were approached by a Harlem hustler. To my knowledge I'd never seen this hustler before; he said to me, approximately: "Hey, baby! I dig you holding this all-originals scene at the track . . . I'm going to lay a vine under the Jew's balls for a dime—got to give you a play . . . Got the shorts out here trying to scuffle up on some bread . . . Well, my man, I'll get on, got to go peck a little, and cop

me some z's." And the hustler went on up Seventh Avenue. I would never have given it another thought, except that this downtown "leader" was standing, staring after that hustler, looking as if he'd just heard Sanskrit. He asked me what had been said, and I told him. The hustler had said he was aware that the Muslims were holding an all-black bazaar at Rockland Palace, which is primarily a dancehall. The hustler intended to pawn a suit for ten dollars to attend and patronize the bazaar. He had very little money but he was trying hard to make some. He was going to eat, then he would get some sleep.

The point I am making is that, as a "leader," I could talk over the ABC, CBS, or NBC microphones, at Harvard or at Tuskegee; I could talk with the so-called "middle class" Negro and with the ghetto blacks (whom all the other leaders just talked *about*).[9]

Somehow Arsenio missed this extraordinary point about Malcolm's style of leadership. Though Martin Luther King, Jr., was a very different type of orator than Malcolm, a case could also be made for his style of speaking. King's grammar and vocabulary may be fairly standard, but his pronunciation, every scholar recognizes, is reminiscent of the black vernacular style of preaching in the South. Even a northerner can sense it when King says in his "I've Been to the Mountain Top" speech, "Mine eyes I have seen the glory of the coming of the Lord."

As for the other Ebonics detractors, I was somewhat surprised by Angelou's denouncement since her *I Know Why the Caged Bird Sings* was one of the first autobiographical novels in which I took note of the literary use of black vernacular speech. And the third installment in her autobiographical series, *Singin' and Swingin' and Gettin' Merry Like Christmas,* would often playfully trip off my tongue in those days. One example of vernacular use in *I Know Why the Caged Bird Sings* is the words she cites from a cotton picker who stops by the Angelou family's general sto:

"Sister, I'll have two cans of sardines."
"I'm gonna work so fast today I'm gonna make you look like you standing still."
"Lemme have a hunk uh cheese and some sody crackers."
"Just gimme a couple them fat peanut paddies."[10]

What's even more troubling about Angelou's anti-Ebonics stance is that she has used it in, presumably, her own voice in some of her poetry. Nah, I don't mean at Clinton's inauguration in '97 (now you know the vernacular ain't good enough for national TV), but, according to Rickford and Rickford, it appears that Angelou did express herself in, to use their term, Spoken Soul in poems like "The Pusher" and "The Thirteens (Black)."[11] So, how come it's perfectly fine for Angelou to use Ebonics as a form of literary expression, but black kids and their teachers can't use it in inner-city public school districts like Oakland's? Seem to me like teachers—especially in such districts—ought to be exploring with their students the multiple functions (grammatically and rhetorically) of black varieties of speech in, let's say, Angelou's writing, instead of telling them that what the southern cotton picker spoke is *bad* English, and that they better not speak/write that way if they want to be *good* schoolchildren.

Last but not least at center stage is funnyman Bill Cosby. Ah, I remember back in the day when brotha Cosby (oops, I did it again, that should be broth-er Cosby) did the voices of many of those kids in the *Fat Albert* cartoon. Now, don't tell me that Mushmouth, Rudy, Russell, Fat Albert, and all dat motley group of black inner-city teens ain't speak a lick of Ebonics. What kind of urban ghetto was they in if they spoke standard English (in grammar, lexicon, and pronunciation) 100 percent of the time? We spoke Ebonics in my hood back then and none of us kids was ever so po' that we had to make musical instruments out of stuff we found in a junkyard. But now, writing in the ultra highbrow *Wall Street Journal,* Cosby tells the *Journal*'s readers (which, my guess is, doesn't include the Rudys and Fat Alberts of the world) that what the school board in Oakland was proposing to teach its teachers was not Ebonics but rather "Igno-Ebonics." Virtually calling Ebonics-speaking black folk out like that, Cosby suggests that the way we (some of us, anyway) talk is *ignant* and prone to racist caricature. I can understand the brotha dismissing some vulgar, misogynistic language in a rap song and his thinking any school board irresponsible for proposing that such language be adopted in the classroom (as was unthinkingly attempted in a Houston middle school a few years ago, according to email communication I received from a colleague in Texas).[12] But to call black vernacular speech in toto "igno," man, you might as well bust the *real* dirty dozens on our peops for continuing to use what we inherited from our mamas, grandmamas, and great granddaddies. I mean, it's like slappin' our linguistic forebears in the face, like undermining the vernacular tradition that keeps many of us grounded in this double-conscious society we live in.

But, yo, check this: After dissin' Igno-Ebonics speakers like that in the *Wall Street Journal,* sometime later the man turn around and on his then-sitcom (*Cosby*) was talkin' about "homes" this and "homes" that, like all of a sudden he down with Ebonics or the vernacular. (Apparently, according to Rickford and Rickford,[13] Cosby's been in a love/hate thang with vernacular speech since the '70s, even then imbuing characters such as family members with vernacular sensibilities in comic routines but disparaging vernacular speech in the public, political sphere.) That don't make no kinda sense to me. And what sense might it make to Ebonics-speaking kids when they hear their speech employed as comic relief on a mainstream TV sitcom but they themselves are vilified for using it in a venue that is specifically designed for learning about the effective uses of language?

All right, let me ease up off the harangue a bit, be fair, and cite some of Cosby's genuine concerns. Hinting early on at the utter absurdity of the OUSD Ebonics proposal, Cosby entitles his piece "Elements of Igno-Ebonics Style," presumably after William Strunk and E. B. White's standard-bearer for prose style, *The Elements of Style.* Cosby opens the content of the essay with a telling anecdote:

> I remember one day 15 years ago, a friend of mine told me a racist joke.
>
> *Question:* Do you know what Toys "R" Us is called in Harlem?
>
> *Answer:* We Be Toys.
>
> So, before the city of Oakland, Calif., starts to teach its teachers Ebonics, or what I call "Igno-Ebonics," I think the school board should study all the ramifications of endorsing an urbanized version of the English language.[14]

Although to me the difference between "We Be Toys" and the equally nonsensical expression "Toys 'R' [Are] Us" is ever so slight, Cosby considers the former to be egregious, a virtual racial epithet—so much so that, as I said, he calls all black vernacular speech "Igno-Ebonics." Let me see if I can get straight the logic here: If Ebonics is "igno," then those who speak it must be "igno" too—that is, Igno-Ebonics speakers, as I been sayin'. I'd hate to think that the brotha is dissin' a whole mess of rural and inner-city black folks (and, yes, some dear souls in the 'burbs too), but it sho sound like he callin' all these folks out they name—unless, of course, he considers the language alone as ignorant and not the people who speak it daily. But I know of few language theorists who view a person's or group's language as completely separate and detached from the individual and collective selves that produce it. As Gloria Anzaldua put it so cogently, "I am my language."[15]

What follows Cosby's opening remark is example after example of what he considers the "ramifications of endorsing" Ebonics. True to comedic form, he injects humor into each of the examples, such as his suggestion that a teenager who says to a patrol officer "Lemme ax you" might be misunderstood by the officer to mean that "he [the officer] is about to be hacked to death." By contrast, one of the more serious examples, one that will likely resonate with many *Wall Street Journal* readers, is the one having to do with applying for jobs. Cosby first lays out his general argument—albeit a non sequitur—in this way: If school boards start to recognize the legitimacy of Ebonics, a standard, universally understood language would then cease to exist and consequently the United States would regress into utter fragmentation and disarray (in effect, Babel revisited). With this extraordinarily catastrophic picture thus drawn, Cosby then shifts his focus to the practical matter of gainful employment—that is, the ever-so-solemn prospect that "Ebonics-speaking youths will not get jobs."

> If Ebonics is allowed to evolve without any national standard, the only language the next generation would have in common would be body language. At the moment—if there are any current rules to Ebonics—one of them seems to be that any consonant at the end of a word must be dropped, particularly the letter G. This allows certain words to be strung together into one larger word. Ergo, the Ebonically posed question "Where was you workinlas?" translates into English as "Where were you working last?"
>
> Of course, this query is most likely to be found on a job application, which means that Ebonics-speaking youths will not get a job unless they are aware that "working" and "last" are two words instead of one. Therefore, companies interested in recruiting Ebonics-speaking workers would need to hire Ebonics-speaking assistants to provide translations. That would open up employment opportunity by creating the new job of "Ebonics specialist." But even a staff of Ebonics specialists could cause chaos.
>
> Suppose an Ebonics-speaking nurse hands a patient some eye drops and says, "Put 'em in an ear fur near." (Translation: "an hour from now.") A non-Ebonics-speaking patient might fill his ear with Visine.[16]

Where Cosby got the pronunciation *ear* for "hour" and *near* for "now" is an utter mystery to me. It don't sound like nothin' (oops, I *shouldn't* be droppin' these "*g*'s," so says my trusty Strunk and White) I hear people say, even in Texas, an' ya'll knoow an' ya'll knoow how funny our talk sound to the non-TEXsun eaar, riight? This whole angle about people getting or not getting jobs because of Ebonics is pretty specious to me, because what black middle school or high school student with half a brain is going to stroll into a prospective employer's office and say, "Yo, dawg, can you like hook a brotha up? . . . 'Cause, you know, I gots to get paid!" Most young people, I would argue, are far more aware of language differences than we adults give them credit for. Why else would they expend so much time and energy trying not to sound like us—parents, teachers, public figures whose speech is often pompous and dull and way out of touch with their reality?

But Cosby's denigration of Ebonics on these grounds is but the surface of his at times caustic criticism. His rather implicit association of Ebonics with racism cuts far deeper. He first links the two in his opening anecdote about a racist joke ("We Be Toys") a so-called friend of his told him fifteen years ago. The personal account sets us up for the argument that a consequence of public sanction of Ebonics would be racism—presumably in addition to the racism African Americans already encounter (and of course who wants that?). Later, toward the end of the article, Cosby links racism and Ebonics a second time in his example of the "cultural impact" the widespread acceptance of Ebonics might have. In a strategically placed quip, he suggests that in an Ebonics-friendly environment Hollywood execs would feel at liberty to revisit racist spectacles like *Amos & Andy*. In his own words, his reasoning unfolds as follows:

> Another factor inherent in the widespread acceptance of Ebonics would be its cultural impact. In Hollywood, for instance, film studios would be delighted to have two categories instead of one in which to group African-American actors. While there always would be parts for "non-Ebonics black people," casting agents also would be asking: "Can you act Ebonics?" Naturally there would have to be English subtitles for Ebonics movies. (Maybe Ebonics is actually a conspiracy to resurrect the old "Amos & Andy" show.)[17]

Hmm, a conspiracy? Sounds serious. And if so, then there must be a conspirator, and just who might that be? Could it be some white racist Hollywood executive eager to capitalize on the Ebonics frenzy with a revival of minstrelsy; or is it instead black folks themselves (a radical few, perhaps) too "igno" to realize that by legitimizing Ebonics they settin' the whole race up for white folks to make us look bad? (And we sho wouldn't wanna look bad in front of them, now would we?) Either way, the results of this conspiracy are projected to be pretty dire: If we allow Ebonics a respectable place in mainstream American society, we become a target for racist caricature, the butt of our erstwhile friends' cruel and insensitive jokes. In a monolingual, ethnocentric, and xenophobic society like ours, I don't doubt that widespread acceptance of Ebonics might invite allusions to old-time minstrelsy, but Ebonics ain't got nothin' to do with that or any grand racist conspiracy. I mean, apart from its pidgin and creole origins (according to one linguistic hypothesis, anyway) in the racist hotbed of African slavery in America, Ebonics has little to do with the racism often encountered by its speakers.

Now, if Cosby really want to talk racist conspiracies (though I don't go much for conspiracy theories), then I'd offer this anti-Ebonics campaign as one—that is, as another in a long series of calculated efforts by the dominant culture to censure language and cultural differences and promote its own superiority. Mind you, I'm not saying that so-called standard English is inherently "white" or that every white American speaks it. That would completely ignore the critical influence of social class on varieties of speech, whatever an individual's race or ethnicity. In the realm of public perception, however, standard English (of whatever regional variation, except perhaps white southern dialects) is and always has been white people's speech. When I was a kid, my kinfolks oftentimes referred to it as *talkin' proper,* but even as a young'un I knew that it was another way of sayin' white people's speech, like the way this middle-aged white lady spoke when she would bring all her husband's work shirts over for Big Mama to iron and starch. Whether white Americans realize it or not, they (at least those who don't sound like hillbillies or so-called white trash) have accrued untold privilege and power based on the perceived association of whiteness with "good" or "proper" English. Why, even the young Angelou knew this when she purposely shunned "a Southern accent" and the "common slang" to be the blonde, light-blue-eyed girl of her dreams.[18]

Still, some folks will, no doubt, scoff at my charge, arguing as Rachel Jones did in *Newsweek* during the Ebonics debacle that they talk "right," not "white."[19] But see, therein lies the problem, this willful myopia: The very presumption that standard English is absolutely and essentially "right" (which is a false linguistic concept anyway)—that it is somehow independent or separate from the race, culture, and class of its primary speakers—indirectly reinforces the perception of whites as a raceless, colorless normative against which all other racial and cultural groups are judged deviant. It's like that color blindness nonsense we hear from anti–affirmative action advocates; it's easy to be color blind when you don't see yourself as having any color to be blind to, when you don't see yourself as anything but an authentic American existing perpetually in a state of natural entitlement, when you own *the* American language or voice that is, of course, naturally good, naturally right. For me, this is the bottom line: Like any other language or dialect, standard English ain't no neutral medium of communication, however "right" its adherents may think or feel it is. It's politically, ideologically charged, as all language and symbol systems are. That's what *rhetoric* teaches us about the function of language or discourse in society. European cats like Nietzsche, Mikhail Bakhtin, and Michel Foucault (to name a few) dropped knowledge on that decades, even centuries ago. I thought you knew.

So, I find it really strange (yet not unpredictable) that black folks like Jones—a national correspondent for Knight-Ridder newspapers who has been permitted the privilege to pen her thoughts on black dialect twice in *Newsweek* (once in '82 and then later in '97, yet they didn't publish my response to her '97 article, or anyone else's contrary opinion)—are clueless as to why some black kids rag on their peers for "talking white." They are so convinced of the absolute moral authority of their speech, of standard, middle-class speech, that they can't fathom anyone questioning its social relevance or seeing it as a threat to self and community. This, I imagine, was the mindset of the people who appeared on a June 7, 1999, ABC *20/20* program called "Acting White: Hurtful Accusation among Black Students." Hosted by *Good Morning America*'s Charles Gibson, the segment featured several "typical" Americans, black and white, who all shared the opinion that it was rather senseless for African American youths to criticize their peers simply because they spoke "good" English and earned good grades in school. While the harsh, at times violent, reactions young Ebonics speakers might have to their more socially and culturally mainstreamed peers are clearly misguided, I believe critics are themselves senseless (or insensitive) when it comes to grasping the social and cultural significance of the vernacular to these youths and to many adults in spite of the constant pressure to appropriate the standard dialect. Because most folks don't see the standard dialect as constitutive of white hegemonic values and worldviews (like I said befo, if you was up on yo rhetoric . . .) as bearing the ideologies of socially and racially privileged groups in America, they fail to take into account the psychological cost for these youths to assimilate voices, nay, selves that are so closely identified with white middle-class culture. Surprise, surprise, this issue never came up on the ABC program.

What troubles me, then, about this eagerness on the part of Ebonics critics to berate vernacular speech and extol the virtues of standard English is this nagging sense that their reactionary impulse derives not from some genuine concern for (let alone knowledge of) the language skills of black inner-city schoolchildren but from an all-too-willing capitulation to the assimilationist cultural model I've been alluding to. Or, worst still is my sense that this impulse is based on an educated, literate bias that essentially casts lower-class black speech and speech behavior as negligible at best and at worst, well, downright *niggerish*. After all, why can't African American (Ebonics-speaking) children be encouraged to use and value both; why cain't they be, in other words, bidialectal? I'll tell you why—because the American mainstream is so much on its own jock that it can't rationalize as human anyone that doesn't talk like it, look like it, and think and feel like it. But denigrating Ebonics or eradicating black vernacular speech is not the way to give Ebonics-speaking youths the English-language education they need to succeed in school or in life, at least not if it's important to us (and I really hope it is) to maintain a healthy respect for our integrity as a diverse and democratic nation. Fortunately, today's rappers recognize this instinctively, for they embody the African American vernacular and ain't 'bout to make apologies for it. Of all those who have weighed in on this Ebonics issue to date, rap artists, with their growing mainstream popularity and influence in America and abroad, will have the last word.

RECLAIMING THE VERNACULAR VOICE:
FROM WE REAL COOL TO WE BE CLUBBIN'

Nearly forty years separate Gwendolyn Brooks's "We Real Cool" (1960) from Ice Cube's "We Be Clubbin'" (1998), the lead song on *The Players Club* soundtrack, but what links them is their mutual attention to the nuances of black dialect, to the vernacular voice in poetry. In Brooks's case, we see an example of what linguists call the *zero copula,* meaning the absence of the verb *to be* after, in this case, the subject pronoun *we.* With Cube, however, the copula is present but in an *invariant* or *constant* form, which means that the *to be* verb isn't conjugated, doesn't vary in tense or number in accord with, again in this case, the subject pronoun *we.* Both vernacular forms have a long history in African American English usage in general and in African American literary usage in particular, even before Brooks wrote her illmatic "We Real Cool." That rap artists today consciously use such vernacular forms in their lyrics speaks to, on the one hand, the longevity of the vernacular tradition and, on the other hand, the attitude of the youth toward the black vernacular voice. Probably not since the black nationalism of the '60s have black youths en masse expressed themselves in a voice mainstream society so ardently detests. That's not to suggest that a new radicalism is afoot in the Hip hop community, for Hip hoppas ain't about being radical, just about

being real. And the ghetto, including its sense of linguistic style, is about
the realest thing they got goin'.

Anyway, back to what I was sayin' about Brooks's "We Real Cool."
Now, say the words aloud: *we real cool*. Again, but like you feeling it: *we
real cool*. Check the vibe, the sound, the attitude. Then try "correcting"
it by saying *we* are *real cool* and mark the difference in sound and
sensation, in sensibility and soul. Same deal with *we be clubbin'*; utter *we*
are *clubbing* (enunciate that "ing") and you have an altogether different
feel, even a different meaning since "be" here indicates constancy and
not tense.

Long before Ebonics became a hot media topic, though, the Hip hop
community had made it quite clear where it stood on the matter of the
black vernacular. On one of his earlier albums (1991's *Death Certificate*),
Ice Cube (O'Shea Jackson) aptly expressed the Hip hop attitude on black
vernacular speech when he snapped on those African Americans whom
he perceived as having turned their backs on their ghetto roots.[20] More
recently, the highly touted 1998 single "Ebonics" from now-deceased
Harlem rapper Big L (Lamont Coleman), though less adversarial than
Cube's joint, similarly expresses this sentiment when he declares: "I
know you like the way I'm freakin it, I talk with slang, and I'ma never
stop speakin' it."[21] While Cosby, Angelou, Mfume, and other celebs may
denounce the vernacular (including its fairly recent offspring, Hip hop
slang), because of the public stances taken by influential rappers such as
Cube and Big L, I don't think that Ebonics will die anytime soon. The
Hip hop artists who are putting the street vibe down on wax ain't about
to start changing their speech to suit the tastes of the dominant culture or
non-Ebonics-speaking consumers. Not even squeaky-clean rapper Will
Smith dares to crossover that much. Rap demands accommodation by
the mainstream, not the other way around. For this reason, as far as
language is concerned, I would say that rap artists straight up keep it real,
for by adhering to traditional black vernacular expressive modes and
at the same time reinventing or remixing them, they are preserving and
enriching the African American oral tradition for Generation Next.

At the Timberland outlet store in Waterloo, New York, I overhear a young white sister tell another about some Tims her baby daddy like

One of my first encounters with Hip hop's reinventing the black oral
tradition occurred when I was first exposed to hardcore rap back around
'90 or '91. A hot summer day (but, hey, what day ain't hot in Texas)
while I was visiting my sister just outside of Houston, I heard sounding
out from the car radio the chorus of this song about somebody's mama
being on crack rock. And I'm like thinking to myself, Yo mama's on

what? No, those little girls didn't say that. Man, I'm tellin' you I just about flipped when I heard those seven- to ten-year-old black girls singing that. Sis, who was in the midst of jawin' with me about somethin' at the time, probably thought her baby bruh must have been hittin' them damn books too long cuz I was making all this fuss over a rap song. But since I was just beginning my study of black signifying practices at grad school, I couldn't believe I was hearing a contemporary rap song with black children *signifying* and *playing the dozens.* I mean it was like being thrown back to the day when my sister and our cousins (all girls) would do jump-rope rhymes; or like when dudes in South Park would brag and talk about somebody's mama—but of course sans crack rock. Clearly, this wasn't back in the day, and it wasn't no ordinary jump-rope rhyme. It was a contemporary rap song on the local radio, a dude rappin' 'bout a female crack addict, the mother of one of the aforementioned little girls. "Your Mama's on Crack Rock" was originally published as a single in 1991 by a Miami bass-heavy rap group called the Dogs, featuring Disco Rick; more recently (in 2000), the song has been published on a compilation CD titled *Down South DJs.*

Rap's renditions of such black vernacular forms is what first got me seriously into the music, not so much the beats or rhymes. Though rap is unquestionably a musical art form, it's based on many of the vernacular discursive practices (rapping, capping, the dozens, signifying, loud talking, call/response, and so on) that constitute the African American oral tradition. But, of course, what most people recognize about rap is the obscure vocabulary, the ever-increasing catalog of Hip hop slang. In "Ebonics," for example, Big L offers a brief glossary of some common (especially for the East Coast or New York) Hip hop expressions.

> Yo, yo, a burglary is a jook, a woof's a crook
> Mobb Deep already explained the meanin' of shook
> If you caught a felony, you caught a F
> If you got killed, you got left
> If you got the dragon, you got bad breath
> If you seven-thirty, that mean you crazy
> Hit me on the hip means page me
> Angel dust is sherm, if you got AIDS, you got the germ
> If a chick gave you a disease, then you got burned
> Max mean to relax, guns and pistols is Gats
> Condoms is hats, critters is cracks
> The food you eat is your grub
> A victim's a mark
> A sweatbox is a small club, your ticker is your heart . . .[22]

As an Old Schooler, hey, I ain't shame to say that when I was teaching my writing-about-rap class not long ago I had to peep *The Source* magazine's January 1998 Hip hop glossary to make sure I understood the *slanguage* rappers use. I mean, being technically outside of the Hip hop community, how was I supposed to know that *flossin'* ain't got nutin' to do with dental hygiene, knowwhatI'msayin'? A few years ago, a brotha named Alonzo Westbrook compiled a dictionary of Hip hop slang, but he'll have to produce yearly editions of that baby to keep up with the Hip hop community's rabid lexical inventiveness.

Of course, nowadays, trying to be hip like we was back in the '60s and '70s, some baby boomers will at times pepper their speech with a few Hip hop expressions like *chill, homies, diss,* and *girlfriend.* Could this kind of appropriation of Hip hop slang portend growing acceptance of the vernacular as a whole? Maybe *Source* writer Carlito Rodriguez's spoof about the white mainstream—albeit the 1940ish, *Leave-It-to-Beaver* type, judging from the photos—appropriating Hip hop speech ain't all fantasy. In one of the shots to which he attributes such speech, pops is rapping to his old lady and his seed (his daughter and son) as they all happily browse the Sunday paper: "Boo, these sales at the Swap Shop are blazing. I can finally afford to cop Lucy those kicks she's been fiendin' for, and Junior, I'm gonna bless you with the phattest gear that none of your peops in school will be sportin'."[23] Though that would be a highly unlikely linguistic turn of events in middle America, clearly the Hip hop community is generating for itself and for the nation (at least a fair percentage of the nation's white suburban youth) a new lexicon, one that reflects Hip hop's many local and regional variations. That's evident in the various synonyms for even the most common terms like *chillin'* (which can also be *lampin', loungin', kickin' it,* or *maxin'*); *def* (alternatively *dope, slammin', blazin', smokin',* or, a largely East Coast expression, *john blaze*); and *papes* or *paper* (with probably the most synonyms: *scrilla, cheese/cheddar, ends, benjamins, dead presidents, lucci, dividends,* and *chips,* among others).[24]

So, for keepin' the vernacular tradition vibrant and strong like it s'pposed to be, I gotta give mad props to the young'uns holding it down in the rap game. Especially at a time when there's increasing pressure from some educated, upwardly mobile blacks to—as one progressive white professor of mine once put it—*bleach yo speech,* it feels good to see some of us reject that prevailing impulse to assimilate ourselves into color blindness. About five or six years ago I stumbled upon this book that tries to persuade black folk to get schooled on what the author calls the "better English." A young brotha by the name of Garrard McClendon, an English teacher in, I believe, Chicago, wrote the book, and in it he compiles a list of vernacular faux pas—from A to Z—things to avoid in what he considers formal, standard-English-speaking-only situations (job interviews, classrooms, and conversations with non-Ebonics speakers, for example). Although the brotha endeavors to show some sensitivity to the cultural significance of black vernacular speech, he is at times unwittingly condescending toward it (and its speakers) and yet is guilty of some ungrammatical (and I don't mean vernacular) writing of his own. More important, I find it a rather curious, status-quo tactic for him to associate standard English with everything good (or "better") and something like rap with the "many . . . evils in this industry's warping of the English language."[25] Like it or not, rap artists don't share the cultural elite's concern for the state of the English language. Rap wouldn't be rap and the black oral tradition wouldn't be the black oral tradition if black folk adhered to that limited linguistic worldview. Though rappers often do compromise certain values (like respect for black women and unity within and across black communities) in the process, rappers create and produce their art largely on their own terms, and linguistically that has made all the difference. Anyway, to wrap up this opening piece properly, I wanna recognize a few artists who I believe have been especially innovative at preserving what I've been calling the black vernacular voice.

First and foremost, I gotta give mad props to heads in the East who kicked this Hip hop thang off back in the day. Much love for staying true to our vernacular roots and representin' our peoples in unimaginable ways—in graffiti art, in break dancing, in deejaying, and in rapping. And to top that off some fifteen years into the game when we thought y'all fell off, you blew up the spot with the incomparable Notorious B.I.G. (Christopher Wallace), the one and only Big Poppa (may he rest in peace), who could spit the most natural vernacular sound with the simplest expression like the opening line in "Warning" (you gotta check out the CD, *Ready to Die* to hear the sample). And now, after Biggie has passed, y'all done graced us with an even rawer native son, the enigmatic DMX (Earl Simmons), whose association with the vernacular was nothing less than emphatic in the intro to his debut album *It's Dark and Hell Is Hot.* Then, three albums deep, the dark man hits us with "Who We Be"— the title of a song on *The Great Depression* (2001)—reminding us that "they" still don't know who "we" be in this democracy called America. Even Jigga (Shawn Carter) has stepped up his linguistic game with now-ubiquitous expressions like *foshezel my nizzel.* For the great unwashed, what those words mean is anybody's guess because in the rap game, denotations come second to creativity and origination. And finally, as I have already mentioned, before his passing not long ago, Big L also kept the listening public in check with his glosses on the Hip hop lexicon.

Big ups to my people, West side! Brothas on the left coast be funking us up with jiggety beats and keeping us on point with their unique variations on established Hip hop terminology. Chief among these avant-garde slang spitters is Yay (or Bay) area rap innovator E-40 (Earl Stevens), a.k.a. Fonzarelli, a.k.a. 40-Watter, a.k.a. whatever-he-wanna-call-hisself-next—Ya smell me? That's Forty's variation on the now common expression "Ya feel me?" Other 40-Watter turns of phrase include "What's bubbling?" "Hey pimpin'!" and "Fo' sheezy."[26] In a word, the brotha is practically inventing his own language, and Westbrook is gon have to break out with several more dictionary entries befo E-40's career is over and done—fo' sheezy![27] Down South—South Cali, that is—Snoop Dogg (especially before he hooked up with Master P's No Limit label in the late '90s) patented his own little tongue twisters such as *hizouse* (for "house") and *Drezay* (for his then–Death Row patna in rhyme Dr. Dre). And though Too Short (Todd Shaw) may have actually preceded him, Snoop (Calvin Broadus), for better or worse (most likely worse), popularized the West Coast pronunciation of that scandalous "B" word, coming off sounding sumpn' like *beotch*.

Now as for the real down South—the dirty, dirty—what can a native son say but, hey, it's all gravy, or, better yet, bab-e-que sauce (Texas-style, of course). From Miami to Atlanta on over to Memphis, Jackson, New Orleans, and finally to Houston, southern rappers be cookin' up some hella countrified funk, taking us back to the roots—that is, *ruts*. Much love and respect first of all to ATL's Goodie Mob for putting some of that good ol' fashioned soul food into Hip hop with pronunciations like *gul* (girl) and *huh* (her) and homey expressions like those Gipp makes in "Soul Food." And if that wan't enough to make yo mouf water, the Mob done spiced up their dishes with the soulful sangin' of, in particular, Cee-Lo Green in tracks like "Free." Man, I'm telling you, listening to those brothas on that debut CD is just about like being in a Sunday afternoon revival meetin' and the good eatin' that follows.

Anyway, while Goodie Mob be cookin' up fried chicken, collard greens, hush puppies, and macroni and chesse in the kitchen of Hip hop, with his signature "Ugh!" Nawlins (New Orleans to those who don't know) rapper and No Limit label CEO Master P (Percy Miller) be heatin' up that other soul food: hog maws and chitlins—in other words, some of that gut-wrenching, James Brown–esque kind of funk that, every now and then, is good for the soul. In addition, he and another Nawlins rapper going by the name of Juvenile have spiced up their raps with localisms/regionalisms such as for P *'bout it 'bout it* and for Juve *ha*, which he uses to punctuate each line of the song "Ha" on *400 Degreez* (1998).

But these vernacular innovations are relatively minor compared to what former No Limit soulja Mystikal (Michael Tyler) does on his CD *Let's Get Ready*. Talk about a voice of the Deep South. On the heavily rotated single "Shake Ya Ass" (or "Shake It Fast," the radio-friendly version), Myst sound like one of them dirty old men who hang out on the corner or at the local beer joint preying (albeit playfully) on women who pass by. I can't figure out how the brotha makes his voice sound nearly three times his age, but I can't help but think of an inebriated uncle or two he reminds me of on that track. In addition to the rather deep, raspy voice, Myst's use of the southern vernacular would have you thinking you was listening to pops out on a porch somewhere in Louisiana, Mississippi, or Alabama. And when he employs a call–response technique in the chorus, it's almost like being in the congregation of a traditional black church. Now, I ain't saying Myst be gettin' all sanctified in his rhymes, just that he makes a classic (be it sacred or secular) *response* to his companion's *call* (her rump-shaking performance, that is). Then again, the brotha does get a little "happy" by the end of the song. So whether out on the porch, around the corner, or in the church house, Mystikal is representin' for southern folk—even down to the sista he trying to bone, perfectly mimicking her response to a question some might ask her (you gotta listen to the song to see what I'm talking about).

Now, swanging over to . . . wait, hold up! We got a couple of new southerners come on the scene. Two 'Bama boys who go by the name Dirty is puttin' they own sonic spin on the East Coast's *you heard*: "Yean Heard," the title of one track on *The Pimp & Da Gangsta*. Southern rappers like Dirty, Three Six Mafia, and a local group in Austin, Texas, also speak of *that wood*, a reference to herb, or marijuana. Check also Dirty's grammar in another song off the album called "Hit the Floe." Atlanta native Ludacris is the other somewhat new southern language innovator, not so much for his use of slang but his emphatic black southern pronunciation of words like roof (*ruf*), library (*libary*), and others in songs like "What's Your Fantasy" (on *Back for the First Time*) and "Area Codes" (on *Word of Mouf*). Now, let's see we was swanging over to, ugh, the Sunshine State, to post–2 Live Crew/Luke-era Miami. Props to Trick Daddy and Trina, who not only put Miami back on the Hip hop map but also introduced the nation's youth to the vernacular negative (as in standard English "none" or "not any") in their raunchy but popular '98 hit song "Nann Nigga." Easing back northwest to the state of Tennessee, you got those *crunked out* playaz Eightball and MJG and up-and-coming rappers Three Six Mafia, who be *sippin' on syrup* and rockin' they own Grand Ole Opry.

Finally, though I rarely give my hometown credit for much of anything, I cain't neglect to give major props to my homies from the Bayou City who have added some twang to the Hip hop lexicon. Much love to Fifth Ward's Geto Boys, one of the first groups from the South to gain a national rep. Them Boys deserve a lexical entry all they own, especially Willie D, with his country colloquialisms in songs like "Clean

Up Man." Now what black man or woman in the Wards (South Park and Sunnyside too) don't know 'bout greasin' on some neck bones? But the example that stands out the most in my mind is D's pronunciation of jewelry in "Let a Ho Be a Ho" off the Geto Boys' 1990 self-titled album. Not unlike any of a number of cocky adult males who might say such things about or to their women in Houston, Willie D makes sure you know he ain't no henpecked man by tellin' huh what he ain't gon buy. While Willie D's accent and tone reflect a somewhat older generation, what I tend to think of as a kind of Texas bluesman's voice, relative newcomers like rappers Lil' Keke and Lil' Troy represent straight-up Now School slang but with a distinct local twist. A good example of this would be some of the verses from Lil' Keke's "Southside."

Terms like *butta* (though not usually used as slang for "car"), *Sace* (for "Versace"), and *blades* are now fairly common in the Hip hop lexicon. But other expressions appear to be strictly local derivations. Perhaps more important than these lexical variations, though, is the accent, and here I don't mean a Texas drawl like the speech of, say, former Texas senator Phil Gramm (heaven forbid that ever gets put on a rap record!). Though it's hard to pinpoint exactly, these brothas (as well as most blacks in Houston that I know) don't really fit that infamous Texas stereotype. I mean, sure there's some amount of drawl in their speech, but the Texas black vernacular in general and the H-town Hip hop idiom in particular are so much more than that—knowwhatI'msayin', Main? Oh yeah, that's often how the street vernacular in Texas and Louisiana (maybe elsewhere in the South as well) renders "man." You can hear it in some of the Geto Boys' early recordings, the Hot Boys' various CDs, and the debut CD by Lil' Troy. I think a good example of the kind of H-town accent or flavor I'm alluding to here would be that of Yungstar (Pat Lemmon) on Lil' Troy's "Wanna Be a Baller." His voice, though not all that appealing rhetorically, resonates with the odd but not unlikely mixture of a callow youth and a streetwise thug.

And what about the Midwest and female emcees, you might ask. Well, you know, this wan't s'pposed to be no exhaustive list, but with Nelly's "Country Grammar" having blazed the charts when it debuted, I guess I should say a word or two about the St. Louis native. Actually, I don't know that there's a whole lot midwestern about Nelly's speech in that song. Except for some local slang like *mon* (for "man," I believe), and, according to a *Source* article,[28] *hur* or *herre* (the pronunciation for "here"), and *fa' sho'*, the language differs little from that of, say, rappers down South. But for representin' "The Lou" and proudly proclaiming that his grammar be Ebonics, big ups to Nelly, his posse, the St. Lunatics, and all the Hip hop heads in the heartland of America.

As for sista emcees, to be honest, I can't think of one whose rockin' slanguage is anything like her male counterparts. Don't get me wrong; Eve, Foxy Brown, and Lil' Kim in NYC, Virginia native Missy Elliot, Chi Town's Da Brat, Trina and Mia X in Miami and New Orleans respectively, and producer Irv Gotti's latest gold mine Chuck Baltimore and Vita all got mad game, but I don't see them setting any real trends in the language department. Again, that's not to say that they ain't spittin' in true Hip hop style or that they don't have distinctive regional accents, but after listening to a number of recent CDs by these rappers (and others), I'm not very impressed by their use of the vernacular or any unique variations on Hip hop slang.

Some years ago, I thought that the West Coast (and then–Death Row label) rapper Lady of Rage would make a difference in this regard when she appeared on Snoop's debut CD, *Doggystyle,* but she hasn't been on the scene for a long minute now. And Mia X definitely adds a unique kind of home (as opposed to street) flavor to rap, at least on her first CD, *Good Girl Gone Bad.* And one of my personal favorites, Queen Pen, has this earthy, Millie Jackson kind of feel to her that seems straight-up New Yawk and street. Now, this ain't all that relevant to the African American vernacular, but I'll also throw in here what I presume to be Foxy's Trinidadian dialect in several songs on her latest CD, *Broken Silence.* The Caribbean sound is always infectious, but what Foxy does with it in terms of voice and verbal expression is crazy (me guess dem island roots is still alive in the half black–half Filipino sista). Still, as talented as they are, it's a rare female rapper who is as potent with the vernacular as, say, the voice of the animated host Cita of BET's onetime video program *Cita's World.* Like a radio deejay, Cita definitely keeps the ordinarily dull moments between songs (in her case, videos) hyped. The girl will introduce a video and the next minute she breakin' down politics or relationships or whatever else is on her mind. Some critics (and apparently a few of my students) think she's too ghetto or that she stereotypes black women, but personally I'm glad she doin' her thang. If it's not a front for mere sensationalism (but what comic routine or entertainment isn't?), then she should represent it unabashedly. Maybe with her help and with the help of Hip hop artists like the those I have mentioned, Ebonics detractors will come to accept what so many of us have been taught to despise or hate about ourselves. After all, whether we show it love or hate on it, ban or endorse it in public schools, the black vernacular is our mama tongue, America's mother tongue. It's central to that democratizing process Ralph Ellison raps about in "Going to the Territory" (in the collection titled *Going to the Territory*). What? Yean heard?

If today the griot is reduced to turning his musical art to account or even to working with his hands in order to live, it was not always so in ancient Africa. Formerly "griots" were the counsellors of kings, they conserved the constitutions of kingdoms by memory work alone; each princely family had its griot appointed to preserve tradition; it was from among the griots that kings used to choose the tutors for young princes. In the very hierarchical society of Africa before colonization, where everyone found his place, the griot appears as one of the most important of this society, because it is he who, for want of archives, records the customs, traditions and governmental principles of kings. The social upheavals due to the conquest oblige the griots to live otherwise today; thus they turn to account what had been, until then, their fief, viz. the art of eloquence and music.

D. T. Niane, Preface, *Sundiata: An Epic of Old Mali*

Another important aspect of African music was the use of folk tales in song lyrics, riddles, proverbs, etc., which, even when not accompanied by music, were the African's chief method of education, the way the wisdom of the elders was passed down to the young. The use of these folk stories and legends in the songs of the American Negro was quite common, although it was not as common as the proportion of "Americanized" or American material grew. There are however, definite survivals not only in the animal tales which have become part of this country's tradition (the Uncle Remus/Br'er Rabbit tales, for example) but in the lyrics of work songs and even later blues forms.

Leroi Jones (Amiri Baraka), *Blues People*

But then there's something else about that, about Watts and rap. Watts has always been [a] very, very vocal community. Maxine Waters is a rapper. People that come from out there talk good. I don't know why, those people have always been very, very vocal, and it's always been a rapping thing.

Anthony Hamilton of the Watts Prophets,
in Brian Cross, *It's Not About a Salary*

Rap has always been here for many years. When God talked to Moses and any other prophets, he was rappin' with them. If you look at the 30s and the 20s with Cab Calloway—Hi-De-, Hi-De-Ho, the bebop—they was also having they style of rap. If you look at the dozens where you talk about yo mama or yo papa, that was dealing with rap.

Afrika Bambaattaa, in *The Show*

Representin' Rhetoric in the Vernacular: Professing the Power of the Rap

Representin'. That's what the Hip hop community calls it when someone, especially a Hip hop artist (be it graffiti writer, break boy/girl, deejay, or emcee), gives "authentic" voice to the attitude, style, and collective identity of his or her hood and peoples. For instance, West Coast rap group South Central Cartel (the S.C.C.) might say "We representin' South Central, LA"; Bronx rapper Fat Joe might declare "I represent that Latin flavor of Bronx Hip hop"; or, as rapper and No Limit Records CEO Master P put it down after recently receiving an American music award, "New Orleans, Third Ward representin', you heard?" A problematic concept perhaps for its essentializing impulse (as if any community or people could be singularly represented), the term nonetheless is an excellent example of the unpredictable way in which the Hip hop community appropriates the language of the American mainstream and invests it with its own unique vibe. That's why the word is *representin'* and not *representing* or *representation*, though the differences between each form are slight.

Though I'm no rapper (not in rhymes anyway), in this chapter I want to do a little representin' of my own. Naw, I don't mean representin' South Park in Houston, Texas, where I spent a critical part of my childhood; and besides, Ganksta N-I-P, South Park Mexican, Lil' Keke, and them got that part of H-town pretty much sewed up. Since I call myself a rhetorician—one who conceptualizes and critiques discourses like rap— here I want to represent rhetoric—represent, that is, the verbal art of *rappin'* as definitive of rhetoric in the African American vernacular. Not that black vernacular rhetoric ain't already been represented, for some years ago African American literary critic Henry Louis Gates, Jr., posited "signifyin(g)" as the rhetorical principle in African American vernacular discourse. Excerpting Gates's chapter on the rhetoric of "signifyin(g)" in their groundbreaking anthology *The Rhetorical Tradition: Readings from Classical Times to the Present,* rhetoricians Patricia Bizzell and Bruce Herzberg clearly endorse Gates's conceptualization of African American rhetoric. I give Bizzell and Herzberg mad props for being the first to recognize, in a formal way, black vernacular discursive practices as part of the Western rhetorical tradition. Most anthologies, canons, and histories of Western or American rhetoric scarcely even mention the long tradition of African American formal oratory (speeches by Henry Highland Garnet, Mary Church Terrell, and Richard Allen, to name a few) let alone African American vernacular discourses (such as signifying, storytelling, toasts, or the dozens). Theirs is a model of the work that rhetoricians have yet to do—that is, to reconceptualize or reconstruct Western rhetoric so that it more accurately reflects historical reality.

But in spite of the authors' pioneering effort to inscribe African American discourses into the rhetorical history books, I am concerned about how they *represent* the black vernacular rhetorical tradition. Specifically, I wonder about their selection of a single text[1] that posits the African American trickster figure as the sum total of black vernacular rhetoric or, as Henry Louis Gates puts it, as the *homo rhetoricus Africanus,* man of African rhetoric. Of course, Gates is right to suggest that the West African trickster, Esu-Elegbara, or rather his African American cousin, the Signifying Monkey, is one of our most prominent discursive forbears; but is the monkey or the mythic trickster figure worthy of the designation *homo rhetoricus Africanus*? If so, then that ascribes a whole lotta *rhetorical* weight to one little mischievous simian and makes signifying the sine qua non of black vernacular discourse. And yet, how can that be if one of Gates's primary sources in support of his proposition doesn't deem it so? Surprisingly, Gates fails to acknowledge H. Rap Brown's proviso that "before you can signify you got to be able to rap."[2] The verbal art of *rap* or *rapping* (usually pronounced *rappin'*) is absent from Gates's conceptualization of African American vernacular rhetoric.

Not unlike Gates's "signifyin(g)," rappin' can be linked to African oral traditions, particularly the West African discursive tradition of the griot. Ultimately, like the griots of old, African American rappers preserve tradition—preserve, that is, the African American vernacular tradition through the art of eloquence and music. Or as Geneva Smitherman puts it in an essay on communicative practices in the Hip hop Nation, "The rap music of the Hip-Hop Nation simultaneously reflects the cultural evolution of the Black Oral Tradition and the construction of a contemporary resistance rhetoric."[3] In this chapter, then, I look at *rappin'* as key to understanding rhetoric in the African American vernacular. By drawing connections between the oratory of West African griots, the discursive practice of rappin' among African American street talkers, the Spoken Word poetry of the '60s and '70s, and contemporary rap poetry/music, I propose to show that African American vernacular rhetoric is best represented by what one might call the *power of the rap*.

Traces of Signifying from South Africa to Mali to Afro-America

Ironically, this line of critical inquiry came to me rather serendipitously while I was engaged in presenting a paper on signifying discourse at the First African Symposium on Rhetoric in Cape Town, South Africa, in the summer of 1994. Based on a tip about a book on South African history I received from Albie Sachs, an African National Congress party leader at the time and a keynote speaker at the symposium, I stumbled upon a brief reference to a certain black South African (pre-Apartheid) discursive practice that seemed strangely familiar to me. The book is titled *The Mind of South Africa: The Story of the Rise and Fall of Apartheid*, and in it the author, Allister Sparks, describes a certain war ritual among the Nguni, one of two black African language groups that settled in southern Africa perhaps as early as AD 300–800 but most definitely, Sparks assures, before the first Dutch settlement in 1652.[4] Apparently, at times of war (which were not often major skirmishes) the Nguni code required a formal declaration of war consisting of taunting and dancing before battle. Sparks states that "the armies would line up to *giya*, as it is called in the Nguni languages, which meant to prance before one another and exchange taunts and gestures of bravado. Women and children would turn out to cheer on their men."[5]

What amazed me about this Nguni ritual is that it appears to be consistent with the traditions of Africans relatively far removed (in space and time) from the Nguni. Specifically, it occurred to me that there is an account of just such a ritual in *Sundiata*, the epic of thirteenth-century Mali. The exchange of taunts and gestures of bravado between the epic's two main characters were so vivid to me as I read Sparks's account. But not wishing to fall prey to the essentialist trap, I was prompted to query how a war ritual in southern Africa could also be a common practice in West Africa. Since the term *giya* (or an equivalent of Sparks's translation of the term) doesn't appear in *Sundiata*, it's unlikely that the ritual is practiced by Africans universally. Historical accounts reveal, though, that migrations in sub-Saharan Africa were fairly common from the fourth century on. Most notably, the Bantu-speaking peoples migrated from West Africa to Central Africa, gradually expanding to southern Africa.[6] Still, this doesn't entirely explain the link between the Nguni and the inhabitants of Mali, as Mali, even during the vast empire of the thirteenth century, sits well north and west of the Cameroon-Nigerian seaboard boundaries of the Bantu language family.

In any case, the South Africa–Mali discursive connection appears at least partially accurate, and it suggests, I believe, something about discursive or rhetorical practices in Africa. Here, for example, is the ritual exchange—the formal declaration of war—between Sundiata, the would-be king of Mali, and Soumaoro, the Sosso king who usurped the throne from Sundiata's elder brother. Notice the exaggerated boasting and elaborate use of metaphor beginning with Soumaoro's second statement below.

> "Stop, young man. Henceforth I am the king of Mali. If you want peace, return to where you came from," said Soumaoro.
>
> "I am coming back, Soumaoro, to recapture my kingdom. If you want peace you will make amends to my allies and return to Sosso where you are king."
>
> "I am king of Mali by force of arms. My rights have been established by conquest."
>
> "Then I will take Mali from you by force of arms and chase you from my kingdom."
>
> "Know, then, that I am the wild yam of the rocks; nothing will make me leave Mali."
>
> "Know, also that I have in my camp seven master smiths who will shatter the rocks. Then, yam, I will eat you."
>
> "I am the poisonous mushroom that makes the fearless vomit."
>
> "As for me, I am the ravenous cock, the poison does not matter to me."
>
> "Behave yourself, little boy, or you will burn your foot, for I am the red-hot cinder."
>
> "But me, I am the rain that extinguishes the cinder; I am the boisterous torrent that will carry you off."
>
> "I am the mighty silk-cotton tree that looks from on high on the tops of other trees."
>
> "And I, I am the strangling creeper that climbs to the top of the forest giant."
>
> "Enough of this argument. You shall not have Mali."[7]

Unfortunately, Sparks's account of the *giya* doesn't include a similar example from the South African Nguni. Yet, he points out that the Nguni practiced the *giya* war ritual even up to the early nineteenth century. In fact, were it not for the renowned Zulu militarist Shaka Zulu, who despised these "paltry" ritualistic displays, it might have remained so well into the twentieth century.[8] In the case of Mali, however, the formal declaration of war was clearly a common ancient practice, for according to Mamadou Kouyate—the griot of the 1960 version of *Sundiata* (originally translated from Mandingo to French)—"just as a sorcerer ought not to attack someone without taking him to task for some evil deed, so a king should not wage war without saying why he is taking up arms."[9] The striking thing for me about the *giya,* though, is not so much the sociopolitical circumstances that gave rise to it (or its downfall, in the case of the South African Zulus) but the peculiar banter between the combatants, this penchant for battle with words before (and at times in lieu of) arms.

Though some seven-hundred-plus years later and a whole continent apart, those familiar with contemporary African American folk culture will easily recognize this kind of combative exchange. Generally, it's what we call in the United States *the dozens* (if yo mama or other relatives are the target) or *signifying* (if the comic insult is hurled at you), though today's Hip hop generation is likely more accustomed to the term *snaps* or *snapping*. Three books and corresponding audiotapes on snaps appeared in the mid-'90s, some featuring recognized Hip hop artists. Back in the day (the late '70s), though, Geneva Smitherman had already dropped some knowledge about snaps (signifying exchanges) on the urban and rural street corners of Black America.[10] Here's an example she gives of two bloods playfully snapping on each other in the '70s:

> "If you don't quit messin wif me, uhma jump down your throat, tap dance on your liver, and make you wish you never been born."
>
> "Yeah, you and how many armies? Nigger, don't you know uhm so bad I can step on a wad of gum and tell you what flavor it is."[11]

However, an even better example of this kind of boastful snapping or signifying can be found in the very lines that Gates cites from H. Rap Brown's autobiography, *Die Nigger Die!* In those lines, Brown (now Jamil Abdullah Al-Amin) describes how a signifying session typically began and then how he, being *Rap* Brown, would respond. Now, it is street talk, the province of machismo, so the rhymes tend to be sexually explicit, sexist, and full of ego—just so you know.

A session would start maybe by a brother saying, "Man, before you mess with me you'd rather run rabbits, eat shit and bark at the moon." Then, if he was talking to me, I'd tell him:

Man, you must don't know who I am.
I'm sweet peeter jeeter the womb beater
The baby maker the cradle shaker
The deerslayer the buckbinder the women finder
Known from the Gold Coast to the rocky shores of Maine
Rap is my name and love is my game.
I'm the bed tucker the cock plucker the motherfucker
The milkshaker the record breaker the population maker
The gun-slinger the baby bringer
The hum-dinger the pussy ringer
The man with the terrible middle finger.
The hard hitter the bullshitter the poly-nussy getter
The beast from the East the Judge the sludge
The women's pet the men's fret and the punk's pin-up boy.
They call me Rap the dicker the ass kicker
The cherry picker the city slicker the titty licker
And I ain't giving up nothing but bubble gum and hard times and I'm
    fresh out of bubble gum.
I'm giving up wooden nickels 'cause I know they won't spend
And I got a pocketful of splinter change.
I'm a member of the bathtub club: I'm seeing a whole lot of ass but
    I ain't taking no shit.[12]

Interestingly, the lines that follow closely resemble the nature meta-phors in the Sundiata–Soumaoro exchange:

I'm the man who walked the water and tied the whale's tail in a
    knot
Taught the little fishes how to swim
Crossed the burning sands and shook the devil's hand
Rode round the world on the back of a snail carrying a sack saying
    AIR MAIL.
Walked 49 miles of barbwire and used a Cobra snake for a necktie
And got a brand new house on the roadside made from a cracker's
    hide,
Got a brand new chimney setting on top made from the cracker's
    skull
Took a hammer and nail and built the world and calls it "The Bucket

of Blood."
Yes, I'm hemp the demp the women's pimp
Women fight for my delight.
I'm a bad motherfucker. Rap the rip-saw the devil's brother 'n
    law.
I roam the world I'm known to wander and this .45 is where I get
    my thunder.
I'm the only man in the world who knows why white milk makes
    yellow butter.
I know where the lights go when you cut the switch off
I might not be the best in the world, but I'm in the top two and my
    brother's getting old.
And ain't nothing bad 'bout you but your breath.[13]

Clearly, signifying ain't lost a beat on the bumpy ride from Africa to America. In fact, it seem like brothas been sigging since they stepped off the boat. But as revealing as the Sundiata–Soumaoro exchange is about early and modern African ritualized discourse (for example, forms of signifying) and the survival of this discourse in the contemporary United States, in itself the exchange represents a relatively small portion of *Sundiata*. For in its entirety, *Sundiata* is the griot's epic tale of old Mali. The "signifying" exchange in *Sundiata,* in other words, represents at best one of many discursive practices the griot reveals in the epic. In fact, in the case of the aforementioned exchange, it's not even the griot himself who signifies; rather as teller of this particular version of the *Sundiata* narrative, Mamadou Kouyate simply gives his auditors a rundown or report of the "signifying" session, or *giya,* that occurs between the epic's main characters, Maghan Sundiata and Soumaoro Kante, the day before battle. Thus, in the narrative, neither Kouyate or Balla Fasseke, who actually appears as Sundiata's griot in the epic, engages in signifying per se. What one finds in the speech of these griots is not signifying but rather a narrative form of oratory that in the African American vernacular one might call storytelling or, more loosely, *rapping.*

Now some may chide me for making what seems to be a gigantic leap here, but if we can accept Brown's assertion that one's ability to rap precedes his or her ability to signify, then, it seems to me, we can also concede that the griot's oratory precedes or supersedes the discourse of the Signifying Monkey. I am assuming here, of course, definite, verifiable links between West African griots (ancient and modern) and African American soul brothers like H. Rap Brown who have developed the black vernacular tradition of *rapping.* In what follows, I trace some of these links.

The Griot: Master of the Word

But before I do so let me first give some background on the griot, for even though the term has been often cited by Afrocentrists and rap music critics, the various griot types and functions in African societies aren't as often acknowledged or explored.

Though the precise origin of the term *griot* is unknown, Malian specialist in oral traditions A. Hampaté Ba explains that *griots* (a French term), or rather *dielis* (in Bambara and Mandingo), are a special caste of West African poets, musicians, singers, and magicians who bear responsibility for "entertaining the public and for enlivening the proceedings at official or private ceremonies."[14] Ba further points out that while some griots (probably those of low status) are said to have double tongues— that is, have the right as entertainers "to misrepresent the truth and invent lies"—others such as the royal griots (*dieli-faama*) are virtuous men who adhere devoutly to the truth.[15] He thus classifies griots into three broad categories: 1) musicians, singers, and composers; 2) ambassadors attached to royal courts or to individuals; and 3) genealogists, historians, and composers of oral texts.[16]

Thomas Hale, an American scholar of African literature, gives an even more complex account of the term *griot* and the various functions griots perform in society. In his excellent book *Scribe, Griot, and Novelist: Narrative Interpreters of the Songhay Empire,* Hale delineates the various terms for griot in West African societies. In addition to the Mande term *jeli* (alternatively *gawlo*), the term for "the lowest class of griots who insult people to obtain rewards," there is the Wolof term for praise singers, *gewel.*[17] Drawing on the work of Gordon Innes, Hale notes that the Gambian Mandinka use the term *jalo* for griot, but they qualify it to indicate certain special classes such as *danna jalo* for the hunter's griot, *mbo jalo* for the itinerant entertainer, and *fino jalo* for "griots whose perspective is more deeply rooted in Islamic studies."[18] The Soninke use the term *jesere* or *kusatage* for ordinary griot and *Jesere-dunka* for master griot.[19] "Among the Fulani in the Fouta Toro region," Hale reports, "the generic term for bard is *gawlo* or, less often, *mabo,* but *farba* designates master griot, while the *awlube* knows the genealogy and praises for a particular family and the *nyamakala* is simply a wandering singer and instrumentalist."[20] Farther east, other terms for the griot include *bendere* among the Mossi and *marok'a* among the Hausa.[21]

According to Hale's classifications, then, *djeli* or griot Mamadou Kouyate, the narrator of *Sundiata,* appears to be among the lowest class of griots—a *jeli* or *gawlo* in Mande-speaking societies. However, by his own account, Mamadou Kouyate professes himself a master griot—a *jesere dunka* (Soninke) or *farba* (Fulani) perhaps; he is a member of the

Kouyate family that has served as royal griots to the Keita princes since ancient Mali. Perhaps because of his royal status, then, he describes himself as no mere musician or historian but a "master in the art of eloquence."[22] In addition, he states that he and his forefathers are "vessels of speech," "repositories which harbor secrets many centuries old," for they are the "memory of mankind" and "by the spoken word [they] bring to life the deeds and exploits of kings for younger generations."[23]

By the end of the epic, Kouyate reveals how he acquired the knowledge of a griot. As a kind of itinerant pupil, he traveled from village to village throughout Mali to learn from the great masters in the art of speaking. The translator of Kouyate's epic tale (into French from Mandingo), D. T. Niane, gives even keener insight into the griot's technical training. In a note on the text, Niane explains that

> Griot traditionists [sic] travel a great deal before being "Belen-Tigui"—Master of speech in Mandingo. This expression is formed from "belen" which is the name for the tree trunk planted in the middle of the public square and on which the orator rests when he is addressing the crowd. "Tigui" means "master of."[24]

Thus, from these statements we can see that at some level the griot (some of them at any rate) is a kind of orator, a master in the art of eloquence. But just what kind of eloquence is he master of? Is he a master of signifying, say, in the order of H. Rap Brown, or perhaps Sundiata and Soumaoro? Niane calls the griot's craft the art of historical oratory, but elsewhere he also refers to it as the art of circumlocution because the griot "speaks in archaic formulas, or else he turns facts into amusing legends for the public, which legends have, however, a second sense which the vulgar little suspect."[25] In a sense, then, especially if we accept Gates's claim that circumlocution and indirection are essential components of signifying (that is, the metaphoric variety described by Claudia Mitchell-Kernan in *Language Behavior in a Black Urban Community*), the griot is perhaps a master in the art of signification. However, because signifying plays a relatively minor role in *Sundiata,* I'm apprehensive about this assertion. Again, signifying (or something quite like it) may constitute part of the griot's eloquence, but it's not the sum total of his art.

A sample of the griot's actual oratory, in fact, comes just a few lines after the Sundiata–Soumaoro "signifying" exchange. I quote the entirety of the griot's speech here to illustrate the structural and substantive components of griot oratory. To incite Sundiata for battle the next day, his personal griot, Balla Fasseke, reminds him of Mali's history:

Now I address myself to you Maghan Sundiata, I speak to you king of Mali, to whom dethroned monarchs flock. The time foretold to you by the jinn is now coming. Sundiata, kingdoms and empires are in the likeness of man; like him they are born, they grow and disappear. Each sovereign embodies one moment of that life. Formerly, the kings of Ghana extended their kingdom over all the lands inhabited by the black man, but the circle has closed and the Cisses of Wagadou are nothing more than petty princes in a desolate land. Today, another kingdom looms up, powerful, the kingdom of Sosso. Humbled kings have borne their tribute to Sosso, Soumaoro's arrogance knows no bounds and his cruelty is equal to his ambition. But will Soumaoro dominate the world?

Are we, the griots of Mali, condemned to pass on to future generations the humiliations which the king of Sosso cares to inflict on our country? No, you may be glad, children of the "Bright Country," for the kingship of Sosso is but the growth of yesterday, whereas that of Mali dates from the time of Bilali. Each kingdom has its childhood, but Soumaoro wants to force the pace, and so Sosso will collapse under him like a horse worn out beneath its rider.

You, Maghan, you are Mali. It has had a long and difficult childhood like you. Sixteen kings have preceded you on the throne of Niani, sixteen kings have reigned with varying fortunes, but from being village chiefs the Keitas have become tribal chiefs and then kings. Sixteen generations have consolidated their power. You are the outgrowth of Mali just as the silk-cotton tree is the growth of the earth, born of deep and mighty roots. To face the tempest the tree must have long roots and gnarled branches. Maghan Sundiata, has not the tree grown?

I would have you know, son of Sogolon, that there is not room for two kings around the same calabash of rice. When a new cock comes to the poultry run the old cock picks a quarrel with him and the docile hens wait to see if the new arrival asserts himself or yields. You have come to Mali. Very well, then, assert yourself. Strength makes a law of its own self and power allows no division.

But listen to what your ancestors did, so that you will know what you have to do.

Bilali, the second of the name, conquered old Mali. Latal Kalabi conquered the country between the Niger and the Sankarani. By going to Mecca, Lahibatoul Kalabi, of illustrious memory, brought divine blessing upon Mali. Mamadi Kani made warriors out of hunters and bestowed armed strength upon Mali. His son Bamari Tagnokelin, the vindictive king, terrorized Mali with this army, but Maghan Kon Fatta, also called Nare Maghan, to whom you owe your being, made peace prevail and happy mothers yielded Mali a populous youth.

You are the son of Nare Maghan, but you are also the son of your mother Sogolon, the buffalo-woman, before whom powerless sorcerers shrank in fear. You have the strength and majesty of the lion, you have the might of the buffalo.

I have told you what future generations will learn about your ancestors, but what will we be able to relate to our sons so that your memory will stay alive, what will we have to teach our sons about you? What unprecedented exploits, what unheard-of feats? By what distinguished actions will our sons be brought to regret not having lived in the time of Sundiata?

Griots are men of the spoken word, and by the spoken word we give life to the gestures of kings. But words are nothing but words; power lies in deeds. Be a man of action; do not answer me any more with your mouth, but tomorrow, on the plain of Krina, show me what you would have me recount to coming generations. Tomorrow allow me to sing the "Song of the Vultures" over the bodies of the thousands of Sossos whom your sword will have laid low before evening.[26]

In spite of a few indirect references (for instance, metaphoric expressions like the old and new cocks), the griot here doesn't appear to engage in any particular aspect of signifying. Instead, griot Balla Fasseke is direct, even hortative in his appeal to the young warrior. According to Hale, such exhortations or inciting of listeners to action is "one of the least known functions of the griot," though evidence of it dates as far back as the fourteenth century.[27] In one of the first written accounts about griots, medieval Islamic travel writer Ibn Battuta reports that the griots in the royal court of Mali would "stand before the sultan . . . and recite their poetry," which they considered to be "a kind of preaching."[28] Hale concludes from this and the preceding Balla-Fasseke example that the griot is, above all else, "a master of the spoken word"—a word that is in fact "endowed with an occult power, known as *nyama* among the Mande-speaking people."[29]

So if the griot isn't here signifying and yet he's considered to be a master of the spoken word, then how could one best describe his eloquence in terms of the African American vernacular? Some folklorists and linguists assume, perhaps rightly, that griot historical narratives like *Sundiata* closely resemble the African American toast in that they share conventions of the traditional epic poem. Roger Abrahams, Bruce Jackson, and William Labov have each noted the epic qualities of toasts like "The Signifying Monkey and the Lion," "Shine and the Titanic," and "Stag-O-Lee." British and American researchers Viv Edwards and Thomas Sienkewicz have even drawn explicit parallels between epic poets in Eastern Europe, West African griots (*jeli*), and African American "toasters." In *Oral Cultures Past and Present: Rappin' and Homer,* the authors write:

> In a similar vein, Lord (1960: 21–6) talks of the varying levels of performance in Yugoslav singers of heroic epics; and Johnson (1986: 24) notes that in West Africa only some jeli achieve the status of master singer and then only after many years of apprenticeship. Abrahams (1970b: 93) estimates that within any Afro-American neighbourhood there will be perhaps half a dozen accomplished "toasters" or performers of epic verse.[30]

From these statements, it would appear that the griot's eloquence is none other than the black vernacular toast, the rhyming folk poem that presumably originated in the 1940s or '50s as a later development of the African American folk song and ballad.[31] But Edwards and Sienkewicz's work ultimately goes a step further. In fact, the central premise of the book is that because of their highly developed oral skill, audience/speaker dynamics, and communal role, the Greek rhapsode (singer of epic tales) is analogous to the contemporary rap artist.[32]

> It is interesting to speculate further on possible links between the classical rhapsode and the contemporary rapper. In the absence of any documentation on the origins of the term "rap," we might do a great deal worse than falling back on to folk etymologies (Hardwidge, personal communication). To sustain the imagery of the sub-title of this book, it could be argued that Homer was, in fact, a rhapper![33]

The authors somehow seem to have missed Clarence Major's denotation of *rap* in *Juba to Jive: A Dictionary of African-American Slang* (which I will discuss), but even so they clearly see a link between epic poets, griots, and modern-day rappers. Such associations lead me to propose that the griot be considered a *master of rapping*—that is, as I see it, a master of African American vernacular speech (which may include—or at least enable one to engage in—signifying, toasting, the dozens, loud talking, the whole nine). But what specifically connects contemporary rap to ancient griot oratory? Or put another way, how do we get from Belen-Tigui, master of speech in Mandingo, to master of the power of the rap?

FROM BELEN-TIGUI TO THE POWER OF THE RAP

To answer this question, we first gotta get schooled on the history of rapping, 'cause some of y'all probably think the term was invented by the Sugarhill Gang when they released "Rapper's Delight" in 1979. Yes, rap *music* started about that time—well, actually earlier, when Kool DJ Herc started mixing records and some vocals around 1973–74—but see, we was *rappin'* when I was a kid back in the '60s and even befo that. As far as I can tell at this point, Clarence Major seems to offer the best historical account of the term *rap* or *rapping*.[34] In *Juba to Jive: A Dictionary of African-American Slang*, he points out that the term *rap* has long-standing origins in African and European cultures that may have converged among African American speakers in the 1940s. For instance, as a verb, *rap* has been used in Sierra Leone since the 1730s to mean "to con, fool, flirt, tease, or taunt."[35] On the other hand, as a noun in European usage it has come to mean any number of things, such as a false oath,[36] the theft of a purse,[37] or a cant since the seventeenth century.[38] Interestingly, Major notes that the term has meant "to talk or converse" since the 1870s, well before it was ever adopted by African American speakers. African Americans picked up the term, Major purports, in the late 1940s when *rap* came to mean "to hold a conversation; a long, impressive, lyrical social or political monologue; rapid, clever talk; rhyming monologue; conversation as a highly self-conscious art form."[39] Major's definition is, therefore, broad enough that it could perhaps easily support my assertion about a direct, rhetorical link between rap and the griot's unique oratory, especially his point about rap being a "lyrical social," "political," and "rhyming" monologue.

In her own lexicon titled *Black Talk: Words and Phrases from the Hood to the Amen Corner,* Smitherman likewise associates rap with talk—that is, "any kind of strong, aggressive, highly fluent, powerful talk."[40] However, she contends that rap became "talk" only after it crossed over from its original meaning: "[R]omantic conversation from

a man to a woman to win her affection and sexual favors."[41] Thomas
Kochman had earlier[42] noted this romantic aspect of rapping, but, unlike
Smitherman, he doesn't suggest that this meaning has any priority over
rapping as casual conversation. In fact, for Kochman rapping is primarily
talk, only not mere "ordinary conversation" but rather "a fluent and a
lively way of talking, always characterized by a high degree of personal
style."[43] Because one characteristically raps *to* rather than *with* someone,
Kochman further claims that "rapping is to be regarded more as a performance than verbal exchange"; that is, "rapping projects the personality,
physical appearance and style of the performer."[44] Now keep in mind this
notion of rapping/conversing as performance because it'll come up again
in the section on rap poetry and music.

Based on his ethnographic work in Chicago, Kochman identifies
three distinct kinds of rapping: rapping or narrating *to your peeps* about
something in the past, rapping (sweet talking) *to a honey* when you're
on the make, and rapping or throwing down some con *to a lame outside
the hood* when you're hustling for money or some other material good.
Put in Kochman's own words: 1) "To one's own group, rapping may
be descriptive of an interesting narration, a colorful rundown of some
past event"; 2) "Rapping to a woman is a colorful way of 'asking for
some pussy'"; and 3) "When 'whupping the game' on a 'trick' or a 'lame'
(trying to get goods or services from someone who looks like he can be
swindled), rapping is often descriptive of the highly stylized verbal part
of the maneuver."[45]

Kochman gives some helpful examples of each of these types of rapping, but since the first type most closely resembles the griot's oratory
(though some West Africans like Manthia Diawara might propose instead a resemblance to the third type of rap, that is, contemporary griot
speech as "whupping the game" on a gullible public),[46] I'll only cite the
example of that variety. (I should also mention, though, as Kochman
himself points out, the best example of rapping, especially as a kind of
persuasive discourse, can be found in the romantic variety as it's expressed
in the person of the sweet-talking pimp. We'll check him out later when
we peep chapter 4, "The Player's (Book) Club.") In the rap-as-narrative
example below, a Chicago gang member relays to a youth worker how
his gang was organized.

> Now I'm goin tell you how the jive really started. I'm goin
> to tell you how the club got this big. 'Bout 1956 there used
> to be a time when the Jackson Park show was open and
> the Stony show was open. Sixty-six street, Jeff, Gene, all of
> 'em, little bitty dudes, little bitty . . . Gene wasn't with 'em

then. Gene was cribbin (living) over here. Jeff, all of 'em, real little bitty dudes, you dig? All of us were little.

Sixty-six (the gang on sixty-sixth street), they wouldn't allow us in the Jackson Park show. That was when the parky (?) was headin it. Everybody say, If we want to go to the show, we go! One day, who was it? Carl Robinson. He went up to the show . . . and Jeff fired on him. He came back and all this was swelled up 'bout yay big, you know. He come back over to the hood (neighborhood). He told (name unclear) and them dudes went up there. That was when mostly all the main sixty-six boys was over here like Bett Riley. All of 'em was over here. People that quit gang-bangin (fighting, especially as a group), Marvell Gates, people like that.

They went up there, John, Roy and Skeeter went in there. And they start humbuggin (fighting) in there. That's how it all started. Sixty-Six found out they couldn't beat us, at *that* time. They couldn't *whup* seven-o. Am I right Leroy? You was cribbin over here then. Am I right? We were dynamite! Used to be a time, you ain't have a pass-port, Man, you couldn't walk through here. And if didn't nobody know you it was worse than that."[47]

Not exactly a precise rendition of Balla Fasseke's speech, I admit, but the point is that with rapping, ordinary conversation becomes a performance, one no less central to the maintenance of African American social life than the griot performances were and still are to West African societies. Besides, my sense from H. Rap Brown's concept of rapping is that the term is synonymous with the clever use of words—that is, with the ability of the speaker to use language effectively rather than with a particular discourse genre or form. In this respect, then, Bizzell and Herzberg actually got it right when they defined rapping as a "general ability to use rhetorical devices."[48] Like the griot, one could say, the rapper is a master of the culture's many rhetorical devices. But judging from Roger Abrahams's treatment of *rapping* in "Black Talking on the Streets," the term can claim no such universal application. In fact, unlike other discourse forms such as *signifying* and *sounding, rapping* doesn't even appear in his taxonomy of black street speech. In a glossary of terms at the end of the article, Abrahams reasons

With many informants in the last ten years there has been the feeling that the term *rapping* was the appropriate one

for this public (street) talking—a perspective seemingly
shared by Kochman when he noted that "Rapping [is] used
. . . to mean ordinary conversation." . . . But when asked
whether terms like *sounding* or *shucking* were a kind of
rapping, informants' responses are usually an initial giggle
and then an "I guess so." I think that the reason my informants laughed when I asked them whether such terms are
kinds of *rapping* was that while on the one hand rapping
means "just talking," on the other hand in its most common uses it refers to interactions somewhat less public than
the larger *playing* contest activities. That is, *rapping* in its
more pointed uses is something generally carried on in per-
son-to-person exchanges, ones in which the participants
don't know each other well; it is often therefore a kind of
out of the house talking which is primarily manipulative.[49]

Abrahams may have a point about this distinction between public/
private uses of the term *rapping,* but I don't think that it necessarily ne-
gates Kochman's, Smitherman's, or Major's definitions of the term and its
function in African American vernacular culture. Clearly, as a descriptive
term used in many urban communities, *rapping* can have a variety of
meanings, broad and narrow. For my own purposes, I opt for the broad
version because, as I've stated, rapping appears to be the most direct
link between griot oratory and African American vernacular discourses
in toto. Smitherman, in fact, infers such a link when in *Talkin and Testifyin* she relates what she calls the "power of the rap" to the traditional
African concept of *Nommo,* "the magic power of the Word."[50] After she
cites the Sundiata–Soumaoro exchange as an example of the workings of
Nommo in traditional African culture, she explains how *Nommo* manifests itself among African American speakers.

Even though blacks have embraced English as their native tongue, still the African cultural set persists, that is,
a predisposition to imbue the English word with the same
sense of value and commitment—"propers," as we would
say—accorded to Nommo in African culture. Hence Afro-
America's emphasis on *orality* and belief in *the power of
the rap* which has produced a style and idiom totally unlike that of whites, while paradoxically employing White
English words.[51]

As Smitherman breaks down what this means in practice, notice how she
identifies each of the various verbal performances as kinds of rap.

We're talking, then, about a tradition in the black experience in which verbal performance becomes both a way of establishing "yo rep" as well as a teaching and socializing force. This performance is exhibited in the narration of myths, folk stories, and the semiserious tradition of "lying" in general; in black sermons; in the telling of jokes; in proverbs and folk sayings; in street corner, barbershop, beauty shop, and *other casual rap scenes;* in "signifying," "capping," "testifying," "toasting," and other verbal arts. Through *these raps of various kinds,* black folk are acculturated—initiated—into the black value system. . . . *Black raps* ain bout talkin loud and sayin nothin, for the speaker must be up on the subject of his rap, and his oral contribution must be presented in a dazzling, entertaining manner. Black speakers are flamboyant, flashy, and exaggerative; *black raps* are stylized, dramatic, and spectacular; *speakers and raps* become symbols of how to git ovuh.[52]

"Orality and belief in the power of the rap" have, from this perspective, created the black vernacular style of speech, a distinctively Afrocentric style of English verbal performance exhibited in various types of rap, from signifying to toasting to testifying. Whether Smitherman means by this that *rap* is to be considered the architectonic term for African American vernacular rhetoric, as Gates proposes with "signifyin(g)," is not entirely clear. But construed as, in effect, the African American equivalent of *Nommo,* the power of the word, *the rap* or *rappin'* evidently represents a fundamental rhetorical principle in African American vernacular speech. And yet this is only half of the story, for the griot's oratory is best expressed through poetry and music. Thus, in what follows, I consider how rapping, *the power of the rap,* has spawned Spoken Word poetry and music.

FROM THE POWER OF THE RAP TO THE SPOKEN WORD

In a now out-of-print book on Los Angeles Hip hop titled *It's Not about a Salary: Rap, Race, and Resistance in Los Angeles,* Brian Cross gives a rather detailed account of the history of black Spoken Word poetry on vinyl. His account centers primarily on the period just after the Watts Rebellion of 1965, when, among other cultural developments like the café culture of South Central, a Hollywood philanthropist by the name of Bud Schulberg set up the Watts Writer's Workshop.[53] According to Cross, the Workshop showcased many African American poets, including the Watts Prophets (whom I discuss later), and established two distinct forms of grassroots poetry: "one that was concerned with expanding the tradition of the toast, and another mainly concerned with finding verbal analogies for the instrumental experiments of John Coltrane, Archie Shepp, Ornette Coleman, Horace Tapscott, and Eric Dolphy."[54] Thus as a result of the Workshop, the Spoken Word poetry developed in LA at the time was either toast oriented or what an analogous group of poets in New York, the Last Poets, later dubbed *jazzoetry*. Though somewhat subtle, this distinction is important because it explains why, on the one hand, toast master Rudy Ray Moore is considered by some the godfather of rap and, on the other hand, groups like the Last Poets (who recorded around the same time as Moore) are regarded by others as the first rappers. However, Cross doesn't elaborate on the distinction. Fact is, he don't even mention Moore or any of the Workshop poets who might have put their toast-oriented poetry on wax. I suspect that a few of these recordings might exist because in 1972 one of the Last Poets, Jalal Nuriddin (as Lightnin' Rod), did a toast album called *Hustlers Convention* and in, I believe, 1976 author and ex-pimp Iceberg Slim (Robert Beck) recorded some toasts on his *Reflections* LP. Like Moore's, their toasts were set to music, some sort of jazz or blues rhythms, and reflected various aspects of black ghetto hustling culture. Of course, long before these dudes, even Moore, blues musicians and jazz artists sang toast ballads like "Stag-O-Lee" and the "Signifying Monkey" on record.

But Rudy Ray Moore may be solely responsible for the popularity of the toast, taking it from the street corners to records and even to the big screen. This may explain why biographers David L. Shabazz and Julian Shabazz consider Moore, among other things (such as folkorist, comedian, rapper, singer, and overall entertainer), "a modern griot," because Moore is "a walking history book in our midst full of Black literature and culture."[55] Moore refers to himself simply as the "King of the Party Records" and, as I said, the "Godfather of Rapp."[56] Moore was (and still is) an adept teller of toasts. Although his first records were straight-up comedy routines—*Below the Belt* and *Let's All Come Together* in 1961 and *Beatnik Scene* sometime later—around 1965 he began doing toasts in his club acts. As Moore tells the story, some ol' wino name Rico inspired him to do toasts: "A wino named Rico used to come to the store. I guess Rico was 65 or 70 years old, and he'd recite old Black folklore toasts. He'd come in and tell these tales and the people would fall out from laughter. So I said to myself if Rico can do that and people are laughing at him and he's not professional, what will they do if I do it professionally and put it on a record?"[57] Eventually, Moore did put these routines, or what he calls his "raw-soul poetry,"[58] on wax, and voila, *rapping* on records was born! Dolemite, I mean Rudy Ray Moore, sets straight the history in the lines that follow.

So far as the recording edge of it, I probably am the beginning of rap today because it wasn't on record before me. Now the late Louis Jordan did a few things some years ago like "Brother Beware." He did a rap in the 40's and then Dusty Fletcher did a thing called "Open the Door, Richard."

"Richard, why don't you open that door?
The Landlady done locked me out. She
said I owe her some back rent, want to know
when am I gon' pay her?" He said
"She did good to get some front rent!"

Stuff like that was done by Dusty Fletcher in the 1940's.[59]

According to Moore, then, the history of "rap" records began in the 1940s with jazzmen like Louis Jordan and Dusty Fletcher and was picked up by him in the late '60s. Moore conveniently skips over a whole lot of history and recording artists between the '40s and the '60s (some of whom I will discuss) to dub himself the originator of rap records, but, hey, I ain't mad at him. His toast performances on wax and on film clearly had some influence on rappers in the late '70s and the '80s (even now in the new millennium). Moore's first so-called rap album, *Eat Out More Often,* didn't actually appear until 1970, a year after the Last Poet's debut and the H. Rap Brown autobiography I cited earlier. The album includes well-recognized toasts—"Dolemite," "Great Titanic" (that is, "Shine" or "Shine and the Titanic"), and "Pimpin' Sam"—and some jokes, set to some jazzy rhythms but a far cry from the jazz-oriented poetry that began to proliferate at this time.

This form of Spoken Word poetry, it seems, has a long history, even before the writers workshops in Watts and Harlem came along. Though the records of many of these early performance poets are little known today, there probably wouldn't have been a Spoken Word movement in the late '60s and early '70s were it not for their influence. Cross lists a few of the artists who made "spoken word" (or rap, depending on your definition) records from the 1930s to the early '60s: literary greats like Langston Hughes (who actually began public readings of his jazz-oriented poems with jazz accompaniment in the late 1920s and recorded his 1920s *Weary Blues* poems to music in 1958), James Baldwin, and Leroi Jones (Amiri Baraka) (*Black & Beautiful. . . . Soul and Madness, Sonny's Time Now,* and whose poems, even today, often include onomatopoetic jazz expressions); jazz legends Archie Shepp (the song "Malcolm, Malcolm-Semper Malcolm" on *Fire Music* and his *Live in San Francisco* album), Charles Mingus (his album *Symposium on Jazz*), Oscar Brown, Jr. (particularly "But I Was Cool" on his 1960 album *Sin and Soul*), and Slim Gaillard in the '30s and '40s; and other artists like Babs Gonzalez, Scatman Cruthers, Jon Hendricks, Eddie Jefferson, and, just like Rudy Ray Moore said, Louis Jordon.[60] Except for the work of jazz artists like Shepp, Mingus, Brown, and Jordan, these early Spoken Word recordings are difficult to find and, thus, to classify. The Smithsonian Institution's Center for Folklife Programs and Cultural Studies houses a vast collection of Spoken Word recordings by Langston Hughes and other poets and has released them on its Smithsonian/Folkways Recordings label. Still, one can generally assume that this early stuff is a mixed bag of poetry (from the writers), scats (from Gaillard and Cruthers), and jazz/talk compositions (from the jazz artists), all in one way or another ushering in the watershed period of Spoken Word poetry in the late '60s.

In the late '60s and early '70s, riding high on the revolutionary tide of the post–Malcolm/King era, in what is dubbed the Black Power and Black Arts Movements, young African Americans began taking up the cause through poetry. From Harlem, New York, to Watts, California, writing workshops sprang up to channel the immense energy and talent in America's inner cities. Cross's account covers a good number of the artists who put out Spoken Word poetry on wax. These include the Last Poets, the Original Last Poets, Gil Scott-Heron, Brer Soul (a.k.a. Melvin Van Peebles), Nikki Giovanni, Stanley Crouch, and the Watts Prophets.[61] Since I've yet to find the rare recordings of Van Peebles (*Brer Soul* and *As Serious as a Heart Attack*) and Crouch (*Ain't No Ambulance for Niggers Tonight*), I can't say exactly what kind of Spoken Word poetry these artists recorded relative to the others I will describe. I suspect, though, that the work of Crouch (as a writer) may resemble that of Nikki Giovanni, except that she uses black gospel music in many songs (see *Like a Ripple on a Pond* or *Truth Is on Its Way*) and an upbeat party sound for "Ego Tripping" (*Truth Is on Its Way*). Since the '60s, Jayne Cortez has also performed poetry backed by a blues sound provided by a live band. One of her earliest collections is, I believe, *Celebrations and Solitudes* (1974), but I haven't seen any available copies of it. However, a recent recording of hers with the Firespitter Band (1996) called "Endangered Species List Blues" appears on the compilation *Our Souls Have Grown Deep Like the Rivers*. Poet and professor Dudley Randall provides a discography of these poets and more in an anthology called *The Black Poets*, though it's not clear whether each of the classic recordings he lists includes percussion, jazz, or blues rhythms to accompany the poetry. One poet not included in his discography but whose record *Black Ivory* clearly falls under the rubric of Spoken Word is Wanda Robinson. The music she recites her romantic soliloquies to is a mellow jazz sound that is reminiscent of other '70s recordings, though the copy of the CD I recently found at a Cambridge, Massachusetts, record store isn't dated. More recently, many of the poets of the Black Arts Movement (Baraka, Haki Madhubuti, who formerly as Don L. Lee has a record called *Rappin' & Readin'*, Wanda Coleman, and Sonia Sanchez) are featured on a CD recorded live at the 1989 National Black Arts Festival.[62] This unique contemporary recording of Black Arts poetry is called *A Nation of Poets* and was released in 1990, but it's about as easy to find as *Brer Soul*.

Speaking of Brer Soul, that is, Melvin Van Peebles, his *Brer Soul* album is described by blaxploitation film critic Darius James as follows: "Backed by minimalist Mingus-like music, it is 'spoken-word' performance at its raw best."[63] James's reference to "Mingus-like music," of course, implies Van Peebles's use of a jazz sound, but what he means by "raw best" performance of Spoken Word is anyone's guess. Perhaps the album sounds a bit like the soundtrack Van Peebles later did in 1971 for his movie *Sweet Sweetback's Badasssss Song*. The movie's theme song is titled "Sweetback Getting It Uptight and Preaching It So Hard the Bourgeois Reggin Angels in Heaven Turn Around." The constant verbal exchanges between Sweetback and the chorus of black angels in the song, however, makes it sound less like a Spoken Word poem than a call-and-response session in Reb'en So-and-So's church. Interestingly, though, the call-and-response format mixed with alternating hymn singing and jazz rhythms seems to foreshadow the practice of sampling in rap. His 1972 (or possibly 1973) recording *What the . . . You Mean I Can't Sing?!* may more closely approximate the raw Spoken Word performance of *Brer Soul*, except that it substitutes the Mingus-like sound for an alternative musicality appropriate for singing. In an unexpected re-release of that rare album in the summer of 2003, Van Peebles relates how songs like "A Birth Certificate Ain't Nothing But a Death Warrant Anyway" could be "straight rap" were it not for the song's more musical orientation.[64] If this song and others off the album like "Save the Watergate 500" resemble his earlier recordings, then Van Peebles's style of rap is raw all right—the raw, improvisational conversation among brothas on the block.

The most widely acclaimed of the Spoken Word poets is, undoubtedly, the Last Poets, originally a collective of seven poets who took part in The East Wind, a black writers workshop in Harlem, New York, in 1968 that included Abiodun Oyewole (who left the group for a while after the first album to serve time in jail for robbery), Sulieman El-Hadj (who first appeared on the third album as Oyewole's replacement), Alafia Pudim (who later changed his name to Jalaluddin Mansur Nuriddin), Omar Ben Hassen (who left the group after the first two albums), David Nelson, Gylan Kain, and Felipe Luciano.[65] Due to some creative differences and/or other such dissension, Nelson, Kain, and Luciano left the group and performed separately under a similar name but with a slight variation, calling themselves the Original Last Poets. I'm aware of only one major record they released as a group[66]—that is, the soundtrack to a documentary film on the Last Poets (presumably on just the three of them) called *Right On!* The poetry on this album is quite similar to that of the other Last Poets, except Luciano gives this "original" bunch some nice Latin flavor in songs like "Un Rifle/Oracion-Rifle Player" and "Puerto Rican Rhythms." But David Nelson's "Die Nigger!!!" is probably the most famous piece on the Original Last Poets' album, especially since a few lines from it were sampled in 1991 by a then quite popular (and intact except for Ice Cube) N.W.A. (Niggaz Wit Attitude) on a track called "Real Niggaz Don't Die." According to an interview Nelson did in S. H. Fernando, Jr.'s book *The New Beats: Exploring the Music, Culture, and Attitudes of Hip-hop*, he wasn't too happy with N.W.A.'s perverted use of his words. But as I wrote in an essay on the song a few years ago,[67] N.W.A. simply exploited the various connotations of the term that some black folk use with great frequency. Yes, the brothers' use of the term reinforces some negative stereotypes about black folks, but in doing so they also take a few swipes at white racism and black elitism. Nuff said on that, though, lest somebody accuse me of calling them out they name.

In 1985 (though likely not the first time), journalist Sean O'Hagan dubbed the Last Poets the "first rappers," "the voice of ghetto anger and fiery jazzoetry."[68] That was probably a bit of media hype, since over the years so many artists have been credited with having originated what has come to be known as rap music. Nevertheless, the Poets themselves apparently see their craft as rooted in the rapping tradition I've been describing, specifically "the jail toasts and street raps."[69] Perhaps the strongest evidence of this influence is Nuriddin's 1972 solo joint, *Hustlers Convention,* in which he—as his street alias Lightnin' Rod—performs a rather personal toast about his days as a street hustler (see the next joint for a fuller description).

In any case, the Last Poets are best known for their scathing criticism of black apathy and white racism. Their self-titled debut album in 1969, for instance, presents a rich mix of socially conscious raps with brash titles like "Run, Nigger," "Niggers Are Scared of Revolution," "Black Thighs," "Wake Up, Niggers," "Jones Comin' Down," and "When the Revolution Comes." As an example of their brand of poetry, I often play for my rap class one of the Poets' most memorable poems, "Niggers Are Scared of Revolution" (led by Omar Ben Hassen). Much like Nelson's sentiment in "Die Nigger!!!" Hassen considers "niggers" to be lames when it comes to revolution. Hassen's closing verse manifests some compassion and empathy for these "niggers," but still the zealot's critical ire. Some readers may recognize from the piece a few lines sampled on a

N.W.A. song called "Niggaz 4 Life." Most of my students haven't heard of the Poets (just as I hadn't until a white colleague from Chicago hipped me to them when we were in Italy about ten years ago; funny, I've had to learn a lot about black creative production that way, serendipitously in unimaginable places and from unpredictable sources), and so they have no idea that stuff like this was around long before, say, Kurtis Blow and Run-D.M.C. Anyway, I want to cite some lines from one of the Poets' early poems to give you a sense of their style. Obviously, you won't be able to hear the percussion—the conga drums—in the background and Jalal Nuriddin's flow, but I think you'll quickly see why O'Hagan considers them rappers. The poem is titled "Wake up Niggers," and it appears in the Last Poets' print collection *Vibes from the Scribes*. The following are the opening lines of the piece.

> Night descends
> As the sun's light ends
> And black comes to blend again
> And with the death of the sun
> Night and blackness become one
> Blackness being you
> Peeping through the red the white and the blue
> Dreaming of boss black civilizations
> That once flourished and grew
> Hey! Wake up niggers! Or y'all through!
> Drowning in a puddle of the white man's spit
> As you pause for some draws in a mist of shit
> And you ain't got nothin' to save your funky ass with
> You cool fool
> Sipping on a menthol cigarette 'round midnight
> Rapping about how the Big Apple is outa sight
> You ain't never had a bite[70]

Clearly, these are some triflin' "niggers," or rather some black folk who are in a mighty stupor. In this sense, the Poets are like the biblical prophets who speak in order to incite (what they perceive to be) a *crooked* and *perverse* generation.

By the early '70s such poetic expression had become commonplace for the Poets, releasing some three albums between 1971 and 1974. Their style changed somewhat on their third album, *Chastisement* (released in '71 or '73, according to the contradicting sources I have), adding more jazz instrumentation and coining the phrase "jazzoetry," which denotes a fusion of the black oral poetry tradition and freeform jazz.[71] Interestingly, on this third release, the Poets, mainly Nuriddin, do a song that closely resembles the rap music that emerged a few years later in the mid-'70s. Called "E Pluribus Unum," the song is more fast-paced than most other Last Poet songs; that is, Nuriddin's lyrics are more in sync with the rhythms of the conga drum beats. Whether this was an aberration (experimentation?) or a new trend, I can't say, but at least one other Spoken Word poet that I'm aware of recorded a song in a similar style. The poet: Gil Scott-Heron; the song: "No Knock," off of his 1972 album *Free Will*. The song is a perfect example of what rap music was to become, only with a totally different kind of musical arrangement (for example, no punch phasing, scratching, or sampling, as became customary in rap music).

Heralded on his debut album cover as a "New Black Poet," Scott-Heron burst onto the music scene in 1970 with an album (and a book of poetry) called *Small Talk at 125th and Lenox*. Reportedly, Scott-Heron was inspired by a Last Poets' performance he witnessed in Ohio,[72] but he doesn't specifically acknowledge their influence in any of the statements Nat Hentoff quotes on the liner notes of the album. But his poetry definitely has much in common with the Last Poets, varying only perhaps in his use of the piano and his singing on certain tracks. In a collection of his poetry published in the United Kingdom by Payback Press in 2000, Scott-Heron makes clear that the contribution he made to the rap genre was largely musical: "that there was music in certain poems of mine, with complete progressions and repeating 'hooks,' which made them more like songs than recitations with percussion."[73] Somewhat like the Original Last Poets, Scott-Heron's first album has a strong performative quality to it as he introduces each poem or song to a live audience. Though "No Knock" (on *Free Will*) sounds more like rap—albeit Old School—within the Hip hop community Scott-Heron is best known for the classic line from his poem "The Revolution Will Not Be Televised" (on *Small Talk*). Chicago-based rapper Common (Lonnie Lynn) is one of many artists who has appropriated and revised Scott-Heron's famous line (see "The 6th Sense"). In the Scott-Heron original excerpted below, note the series of negations, first of '60s cultural icons and then of American commercial or consumer culture. In their many skits, excerpts from TV and movies, and references to material culture, rappers similarly offer critical reflection on American commercialism in their raps. Accompanied by conga drums, the last two stanzas of this poem read:

There will be no highlights on the *Eleven O'clock News* . . . .

The revolution will not be right back after a
message about a white tornado, white lightning, or white people.
You will not have to worry about a dove in your bedroom,

the tiger in your tank or the giant in your toilet bowl.
The revolution will not go better with Coke
The revolution will not fight germs that may cause bad breath.
The revolution will put you in the driver's seat.
The revolution will not be televised
will not be televised
not be televised
be televised
The revolution will be no re-run, brothers.
The revolution will be LIVE.[74]

Finally, I now turn to a group of Spoken Word poets who made their connection to the rappin' tradition crystal clear. Rising from the ashes of the Watts riots, like I said befo, the Watts Prophets debuted in 1971 with an album titled *Rappin' Black in a White World*. The four members of this group—Dee Dee McNeil, Otis Smith, Anthony Hamilton, and Richard Dedeaux—obviously recognized the connection between the emerging Spoken Word poetry and street-corner rappin'. Yet it's difficult to gauge precisely the degree of their influence on the recording scene since they were only able to produce one album before, Cross reveals, the FBI COINTELPRO (counterintelligence program) infiltrated the group and ended their promising career.[75] Consequently, Hip hop fans aren't too familiar with the Prophets. Folks who don't know the Last Poets surely don't know the Watts Prophets. Their album—which is all that and a bag of chips—isn't as widely available as the Last Poets' or Gil Scott-Heron's records. In fact, I was fortunate to stumble on one at a local record show not long ago. It cost me a nice sum of money, but even though I didn't own a turntable I just had to cop that album. It's a classic, baby, a gen-u-wine classic.[76]

The Prophets crafted a form of performance poetry rather different from that of Scott-Heron and the Last Poets, their sound tending perhaps more toward the dramatic than the musical. Heavy on call and response and at times even conversational in tone ("What It Is, Sisters"), listening to the Prophets is sort of like witnessing a three-act play (or eavesdropping on some bloods conversating 'round the way). Add to this the fact that roughly a third of the songs on the album have no musical accompaniment whatsoever. And those that are accompanied by musical instruments consist of a string bass and/or piano, instead of the usual conga drums or other percussion instrument.

The Prophets' songs also differ structurally from New York Spoken Word poetry. Several of the songs are designed as either a series of related short poems or as a single long poem with different subtitles performed by each member of the group. For instance, the album opens with a brief introduction of the group's name and album title. The Prophets then begin chanting "rappin' black, rappin' black" while McNeil raps the first title, "Sell Your Soul"; Smith follows with the second, "Take It"; Hamilton then presents the third, "Instructions"; and Dedeaux closes with the fourth, "Amerikkka" (a title that, perhaps not coincidentally, foreshadows rapper Ice Cube's solo debut, *Amerikkka's Most Wanted*). This kind of format is repeated in another selection called "What Is a Man." This time, though, McNeil literally sings the chorus while Smith raps on "A Pimp"; Dedeaux on "Tenements"; and Hamilton on "The Master"—the three titles listed after "What Is a Man" on the album cover. Perhaps, at least in the case of this last example, the idea is for each of the Prophets to give his response to or perspective on the ontological question.

As for the content or subject matter of the Prophets' poetry, it covers much the same material as other Spoken Word poets—politics, war, poverty, racism, self-hatred, to name a few. However, the Prophets seem to address these matters less like the polemicist or fiery orator and more like the wise seer or dialectician, often opting for example and narrative over direct accusation and ridicule. The lyrics to Hamilton's "Pain," I believe, work to some extent this way. The excerpt below is a subtle reflection on the irony of American capitalism and progress. Again the indented lines represent responses given by other members of the group.

> Pain!
>   Pain!
> Of people going to the moon
> While little brothers in Watts hustle hard all night trying to eat
> Hand me down hats, hand me down shoes, everything used
> And then you sick peckerwoods wanna know why we don't follow
>   rules
>   Pain!
> There are two little brothers that I know
> Who would someday like to go to a show
> Yeah! Just a plain old fifty-cent show
> How much did you say that last moon shot cost?

Some of the best Prophets poems, I think, are those that diss not so much white folks but blacks themselves, especially uppity, middle-class blacks. Hamilton does this quite humorously with a punctuated refrain in "What It Is, Sisters." Dee Dee McNeil also does it in "There's a Difference between a Black Man and a Nigger," only she specifically gets on the case of middle-class black men. I'm not sure how the Prophets reconciled this poem with Smith's rather misogynist "Pimp" rap on the A side, but Ms. McNeil is kickin' some mad feminist (or perhaps womanist) vibes in this poem. I suspect that it's because they see pimping in the broader context of the game America has run on black people since the slave ships, which I discuss in the fourth chapter of the book. Anyway, check out McNeil's flow in the opening and closing lines.

Honey, what's this Black world coming to?
This matter-of-fact-middle-class-Black-bourgeosie-ass-wish-I-was-
        rich-class-nigger man
    Nigger man
Honey, there's a difference between a Black man and a nigger
    Sho is
Nigger he look at me with hungry eyes
Tries to take me by surprise
With his fancy title, conservative dress
Whitey's man is at their best
Oh, how he lays it on
Opens the door, takes my arm, shows me off with the maximum
        charm
Haircut close against his head
Thinks he's alive when he's really dead
Fooled into believing white lies instead of the black truth . . .

Black Men preaching that they care
Sitting there proud to be Black with their natural hair
Rappin' Black!
And they say: Ain't it a fact that Black women today are
        overdemanding, selfish, and spoiled
Misled into using the pill and the coil
Complaining that Blackness means hard work and pain
Not knowing their place
Too much crap on their face
Dress is too short, too tight
Rap on!
In fact, nothing about this proud Black woman seems right
To hear them tell it
Teach
Well, I'd rather sell it
Than give it away
What you say?
Any day to somebody whose always got something to say
Like you ain't nothing no way, bitch
Bitch

Oooh we, that's hot! And that's just a small sample of it. Of course, reading the lines don't compare to hearing McNeil rap it, nuances of inflection and all. That is why I say that the Prophets' poetry is dramatic, like brothers and sisters rappin' outside the house on the porch ("garret," Big Mama used to say) or out on the co'na. So, I would argue that their poetry is an extension of the toast tradition and the closest link between Spoken Word and rap.

I have covered many Spoken Word artists (some in detail) and their contributions to a poetic movement that clearly presages rap poetry and music. Needless to say, though, my account isn't exhaustive; depending on how one defines "rap" or even "spoken word," there's a great deal more recorded and unrecorded material worth mentioning. Case in point, recently when I listened to Marvin Gaye's 1971 album *What's Going On*, I discovered that on the song "Save the Children" he raps or talks with his own vocals and music in the background. Then there was Isaac Hayes's "By the Time I Get to Phoenix" on *Hot Buttered Soul*, as well as Parliament's now-classic and heavily sampled jams "P Funk (Wants to Get Funked Up)" and "Chocolate City" (1975). In 1979, Isaac Hayes performed a duet with Millie Jackson on the album *Royal Rappin's* and just about every black person who lived through the '70s know how Ms. Jackson can rap. But the best early examples of the beats and rhymes of rap are the Last Poets' "E Pluribus Unum," Scott-Heron's "No Knock," and Clarence Reid's (a.k.a. Blowfly) "Blowfly's Rapp," a funky scatological brand of rapping that must have been the inspiration for Too Short, 2 Live Crew, and Akinyele. And as any good student of rap will readily admit, homage must also be paid to the American radio deejays who introduced R&B and their deejay skills to Jamaican listeners, and to the Jamaican deejays (such as U Roy) of the '60s and '70s who, in turn, developed toasting (*chanting 'pon the mike*) as a form of deejaying.[77] They, perhaps, are largely responsible for Spoken Word poetry entering into the phase of *pastiche*—artistic innovation through imitation and collage.

From Poetry to Pastiche

With such socially conscious lyrics and powerful messages as the preceding, it's easy to see how Spoken Word artists could be the contemporary African American equivalent of the West African griot, entertaining and inciting the black urban poor with their righteous rhetoric. But how could anybody in his right mind equate rap music artists, even the relatively clean-cut, Old School rappers, with griots? After all, rap music initially had little to do with inciting people to action or teaching folks about their history. In fact, back in the day when I was a freshman in college ('79–80) and we was jammin' to rap tunes like "Rapper's De-light" (Sugarhill Gang), "Freedom" (Grandmaster Flash and the Furious Five), "Funk You Up" (the Sequence), and "The Breaks" (Kurtis Blow), 'bout the only action we was incited to do was, you know, that rump shakin' kind. Ah man, we got down at our little frat parties and . . . uh, oh yeah, let me quit reminiscing. Anyway, rap (including deejaying) in those early days was all about gettin' everybody hyped to *par-tay*. This changed somewhat in '82 when Grandmaster Flash and the Furious Five came out with "The Message," a stark reality tale about coming of age in ghetto America.

Perhaps because of rap songs like "The Message," critics were quick to label rap artists the offspring of Spoken Word poets, the next genera-tion of griots to voice the frustration and anguish of America's urban ghettos. One of the first critics to anoint rappers in this way was British journalist and musician David Toop (first in *The Rap Attack* in 1984, and again in a revised edition, *Rap Attack 2: African Rap to Global Hip Hop*, in 1991). In *Rap Attack 2*, Toop traces rap's roots from disco and funk back to the griots of Nigeria and Gambia:

> Rap's forebears stretch back through disco, street funk, radio DJs, Bo Diddley, the bebop singers, Cab Calloway, Pigmeat Markham, the tap dancers and comics, the Last Poets, Gil Scott-Heron, Muhammad Ali, acappella and doo-wop groups, ring games, skip-rope rhymes, prison and army songs, toasts, signifying and the dozens, all the way to the griots of Nigeria and the Gambia.[78]

More recently, in *The New Beats*, S. H. Fernando, Jr., claims that rap and reggae "represent an extension of the African oral tradition of the griot, or storyteller, who recited the history of his tribal community—sometimes to the accompaniment of talking drums."[79] Not to front, but initially I balked at such seemingly glib assertions. As much as I had come to admire rappers and to receive inspiration from them, I found the connection between them and West African griots gratuitous and reduc-tive. But given griots' function as not only oral historians but also public entertainers—as those who bear the onus of delighting as well as instruct-ing an audience—I can see how, in spite of some contradictions in their messages and public personas, rappers have become, as Michael Eric Dy-son puts it, "urban griots dispensing social and cultural critique."[80] And besides, griots aren't (or weren't) always the godly messengers we often romanticize them to be. Hampté Ba says that "[some] griots have no particular responsibility towards the words they utter and are not even under any obligation to exercise discretion or to have absolute respect.

They can sometimes tell brazen lies without being held to account."[81] So whereas Toop seems to think that "hip-hop message and protest rappers" have their "ancestry in the savannah griots" and, on the other hand, "the Bronx braggers, boasters and verbal abusers" descend from the "black American word games known as signifying and the dozens,"[82] Ba's griots aren't limited strictly to rappers on the social or political tip. Among contemporary rap artists, then, a griot can be Dead Prez, KRS-One, or Too Short; Goodie Mob as well as UGK or the Liks; Lauryn Hill, Rah Digga, or even Hip hop's premier seductress, Lil' Kim. That's not to say that they all are equally gifted or inspiring on the mic; it simply says that just because they boast about sexual exploits, beat downs, or cream don't necessarily make them any less griots. They just ain't the kinda griots you associate with epics like *Sundiata* or the royal courts of ancient Mali. For griots of that ilk in Hip hop, Toop's message/protest rappers may be the best example: late '80s to early '90s era prophets of rage like Public Enemy, KRS-One, Kam, Brand Nubian, Paris, X-Clan, members of the Native Tongues posse (A Tribe Called Quest, Jungle Brothers, De La Soul), and others that critics like Tricia Rose (*Black Noise*), Nelson George (*Hip Hop America*), and S. H. Fernando, Jr. (*The New Beats*), have all (especially Rose) written deftly about.

One would, however, be hard-pressed to find the same kind of griot rapper in this new millennium, except for maybe Dead Prez, the Roots, and underground acts like Blackalicious. Generally absent the rage and straight-up political approach of that era, the message griots of this new generation from east to west are coming at us with some mad mystical, mathematical, metaphysical flows—as Rakim so eloquently puts it in "It's Been a Long Time" (*The 18th Letter*). Claiming to bring back the soul of Hip hop to rap music, Rakim, Pharoahe Monch, Common, Lauryn Hill, Black Star (Mos Def and Talib Kweli), Jurassic 5, and Black Eyed Peas (among others) are setting the standard for today's righteous griots. And as they do so, they are spawning a renaissance of the 1960s–70s era Spoken Word poetry. Why they've even inspired great intellectual minds like Cornel West to record a Spoken Word CD (*Sketches of my Culture*). As if to suggest that the mantle has been passed to this new breed of griots, the rapper Sonia Sanchez graces a cover of *Black Issues Book Review* (March–April 2000) with rapper extraordinaire Mos Def. And inside the issue, contributor Kalamu ya Salaam supplies an annotated discography of essential Spoken Word CDs, from Hughes's *Weary Blues* to Rakim's *The 18th Letter/The Book of Life* (that's the two-CD set). Among the ten listed are recent albums by old timers the Last Poets (*Holy Terror*) and Gil Scott-Heron (*Spirits*) and by contemporary Cortez-style poet Kamau Daaood (*Leimert Park*) and Jamaican dub poets Mutabaruka (*The Ultimate Collection*) and Linton Kwesi Johnson (*In*

Concert With the Dub Band). Finally, a compilation CD of New York Spoken Word artists (including some rappers, for example, Mos Def) called *Eargasms: Crucial Poetics Vol. 1* appears ninth on the list of Spoken Word recordings. Abiodun Oyewole of the Last Poets appears on the CD, providing the intro and outro. Not listed in the *Black Issues* article but another poetry record spawned from rap's influence is *Flippin' the Script: Rap Music Meets Poetry* (1996). The record comprises live club performances between 1993 and 1995—juxtaposing rappers (like Kool Kim of the UMC's, Seventeen, Essence Donn, Murder One) and poets (such as Bob Holman, Sonja Sohn, who performed with Saul Williams in the 1998 film *Slam,* and Sekou Sundiata) for what producer Bill Adler calls a collision of sensibilities, "the don't-give-a-fuck world of rap" and "the politically-correct world of poetry."[83]

The distinction between poetry (writing) and rap/spoken word, I should point out, is rather problematic—for as Tony Medina suggests in his introduction to *Bum Rush the Page,* serious poets who perform well on stage and write to effect social change shouldn't be ghettoized as merely urban, oral, street, and not as real writers.[84] The poems in the book could, in fact, easily work as both written text and oral performance. Though set to a beat, so could many of the tracks on *Eargasms,* such as Rha Goddess's "My Pen," Saul Williams's "Twice the First Time," and Jessica Care Moore's "My Caged Bird Don't Sing." In fact, Williams and Moore, in particular, have committed their poetry to paper just as much as they have done so to wax. Williams's *She* and Moore's *The Words Don't Fit in My Mouth* complement their work on records like *Eargasms* or *Amethyst Rock,* Williams's latest CD. Of course, any rapper worth his salt is as much a writer as he is an oral performer.

It's All Good

Although they don't mention griots specifically in their statements, the last word on this matter of roots or origins of rap should go to the undisputed innovators of Hip hop, Kool DJ Herc (Clive Campbell) and Afrika Bambaataa (given name publicly unknown). According to a statement quoted in Steve Hager's book, Herc's list of rap's roots or original influences extends to just two main sources: to James Brown and to Lightnin' Rod's *Hustlers Convention*—in other words, soul/funk music and the street toast. But in Michael Small's *Break It Down: The Inside Story from the New Leaders of Rap,* Bambaataa does just the opposite; he gives what may be the most comprehensive list of rap's origins to date. The portion of the list after bebop I find particularly interesting for the way that it suggests various subgenres of rap:

African call and response music
The Dozens: African-American call and response insults
Scat singing: Call and response, as in Cab Calloway's
  "Minnie the Moocher," 1930s to present
Bebop: Improvised nonsense syllables with jazz (Dizzy
  Gillespie), 1940s to present
James Brown: Soul rap, 1950s to present
Malcolm X, Louis Farrakhan: Knowledge rap, 1960s to
  present
The Last Poets: Political awareness rap, 1960s to present
Muhammad Ali: Boast rap, 1960s to 1970s
Nikki Giovanni and Sonia Sanchez: Poetry rap, 1960s to
  present
Jamaican toasters: Reggae rap, 1960s to present
Shirley Ellis: Wordplay rap, as in "The Name Game,"
  1965
Pigmeat Markham: Comedy rap, "Here Come the Judge,"
  1968
Issac Hayes: Love rap, 1960s to present
George Clinton: Funk rap, 1960s to present
Blowfly: Sex rap, 1960s to present
Barry White: Love rap, 1970s to present[85]

Now, I'm not about to challenge or question either of these august brothers on the way the history went down, but personally I prefer something in between these two extremes. Then again, Bambaataa's list sort of confirms my point about rap or rappin' being the rubric for African American vernacular rhetoric, as, for example, Muhammad Ali–style boasting (an important aspect of signifying) is just one variety of rap.

In this chapter, I have traced what I believe to be the main lines of descent from the ancient West African griot tradition to rapping (as talk) to Spoken Word poetry (including toasting) and finally to rap (as music). Though this trajectory has, in a way, been articulated before, few scholars make the claim, as I do here, that the verbal art of rappin' (not signifying or toasting per se) is likely the earliest African American antecedent of rap music and the strongest discursive link between medieval West African griot oratory and contemporary African American vernacular rhetoric. The field of African American Studies being what it is, virtually no African American Studies scholars, not even Gates, place rap at the center of an African American rhetorical tradition. For me, then, that makes the griot (not the Signifying Monkey or his great cousin, Esu Elegbara) the *homo rhetoricus Africanus*. The Monkey's signifying, in other words, is subsumed by the oratory or rappin' of the griot. Today, among youths worldwide (whether they are aware of this earlier oral tradition or not), rappin' clearly is the preferred rhetorical mode, bar none. Through rappin' (and of course Hip hop music and culture generally), youths from Armenia to New Zealand, Cuba to Korea, South Africa to Germany, Mexico to Senegal are learning how to use language, the vernacular, to represent self, community, and nation. So, it's all good, yo. Whether we rhetoricians get it straight or not, Hip hop is mad representin' black vernacular rhetoric.

I was a true hustler—uneducated, unskilled at anything honorable, and I considered myself nervy and cunning enough to live by my wits, exploiting any prey that presented itself.

Malcolm X, *The Autobiography of Malcolm X*

When he's down, he screams, he hollers, he scratches to get over. He splits before he lets the rest of the jungle know he's full of it. That's the monkey hustle. . . . [I'm] hustling to elude the monkey hustle.

Yaphet Koto's character in *Monkey Hustle*

'Cause it's all about money, ain't a damn thing funny
You got to have a con in this land of milk and honey.

Grandmaster Flash and the Furious Five, "The Message," in Lawrence Stanley and Jefferson Morley, *Rap: The Lyrics*

3

Can't Knock the Hustle?
The Gangsta Ethos from Stag-O-Lee
to Snoop D-o-double-g

Rewind. The time: the summer of '59. The scene: the renown player's venue Hamhock's Hall. Two young bloods, hustlers Sport and his "ace boon coon" Spoon are on the set, gettin' hipped to what's happenin' by a super clean, cool cat from the South side they call Hominy Grit:

> Diiiiig! I got some news you dudes could use that might help you get by.
> So I thought I'd nonchalantly mention the Hustler's Convention taking place at the end of July.
> It'll be at Hamhock's Hall, winner take all, and only the best can play.
> Cost you ten grand to get in, but you must continue to win or you won't be allowed to stay.
> There'll be money for the makin', bitches for the takin', and all you can shoot, snort, smoke, or drink.
> And a whole lotta lames'll fall victim to the games 'cause only true hustlers can think.
> Gon be hustlers galore, tryin' to score, travelin' by land, sea, and air.
> There'll be a —— plane New York and LA and other points distant and there.
> They'll start to arrive around 11:55, at number 66 Snake-eyes Square.

Won't be no cops on this beat, they been paid off real sweet, why
    even the mayor done copped him a share . . .[1]

Their heads reeling from Grit's rundown of the big event and the
sweet money they dream of making, Sport and Spoon remember, however, to keep the main hustler's rule: Don't blow your cool. In preparation
for the convention, the brothas cop them some of the finest vines: suits by
a Hong Kong tailor named Wang (Sport a "four botton rose" and Spoon
a spun "silk gold"), the sharpest kicks from Baby Blues, and "straw-
diamond blocks" from a hatter named Knocks. Smoking Panamanian
reds while cruisin' in their boss beige Caddy, these cats then hit the scene
ready to score. As they arrive at the spot,

> [they] could feel all the tension
> Building up at the convention
> As the hustlers began to arrive
> Must've been 9,000 or more that came through the door, the time
>   was 11:55
> There were pickpockets and dope peddlers, murderers and thieves
> Card-shark gamblers with aces up their sleeves
> Bank robbers, burglars, boosters, and pimps
> Prostitutes, call girls, and all kinds of nymphs
> Loan sharks, swindlers, counterfeiters, and fences
> Crooked politicians spending campaign expenses
> Hijackers, arsonists, bookies, and the mob,
> And anybody else who ever killed, cheated or robbed . . .

Now there "couldn't be no draw between [all these] masters of street-
ology," so, just as they had planned, Sport and Spoon hit it big—shooting
craps for 32 grand, hustling pool for another 30, and playing cards for
110. After all was said and done, they hustled 172 grand, but, would you
believe, Grit wouldn't let them leave without trying to take more than his
agreed upon share of 20 percent. So in order to flee with all the dough
that was rightfully theirs they had to cap two of Grit's men—the shots
ringing out and causing a hellacious riot until the cops showed up to give
chase to Spoon and Sport as they made their getaway. A fierce shoot-out
then went down; Sport got shot and beat down by the cops. Just barely
surviving the ordeal, he did a twelve-year bid on death row before he got
a new trial and was at long last let go.
    Fast forward. The time: Summer of nine-double-trey. The scene:
Brooklyn's Marcy Projects (or anywhere else in ghetto Black America).
Brothas in the streets still gettin' they hustle on, yet ballin' on a whole
'notha level. Like Chico, he can earn five grand if he makes a buy of two

keys from some Colombians; of course if he don't come back with the two keys, well, he knows the score: "Jay-Z's gonna stick your heads up your asses faster than a rat gets fucked," capiche? Enter Jigga, alias Roc-a-fella, a.k.a. Jay-Z. Big Willied out in his double-breasted, pinstriped Armani, silky white sash draped about the neck, fedora at a slight tilt, you know, gangsta mafia style. He's dipped in finest ice—rings, bracelet, watch—and dangling from his well-manicured fingers rests the finest Cuban stogie. The look in toto: classy, ah yes, but never flashy. Jigga's all that and then some with his "expensive clothes," "extensive hos," and "vintage flows." Cruising in the Lex Luger, profilin', stylin', while he's

makin' short term goals, when the weather fold
Just put away the leathers and put ice on the gold
Chilly with enough bail money to free a big Willy
High stakes, I got more at stake [steak?] than philly
Shoppin sprees, coppin three, deuce fever ah yeses
Fully loaded, ah yes
Bouncin' in the Lex Luger, tires smoke like Buddha
50gs to the crap shooter,
Niggas can't fade me
Chrome shocks beamin', through my peripheral I see ya schemin'
Stop dreamin', I leave ya body steamin'
Niggas is fien[d]in', what's the meanin'?
I'm leanin' on any nigga intervenin' with the sound of my money
    [machinin'?]
My cup runnin' over with hundreds
I'm one of the best niggas that done it
Six digits and runnin'
Y'all niggas don't want it
I got the godfather flow, the don juan Demarco . . .

Jay-Z's (Shawn Carter) "Can't Knock the Hustle" may be the '90s ode to the ghetto hustler much like Lightnin' Rod's (Jalal Nuriddin) *Hustlers Convention* was for the '70s. Backed by the soulful voice of Mary J. Blige (appearing in the hook "I'm just tryin' to get mine / I don't have the time / To knock the hustle for real") and the funky horns sampled from Kool and the Gang respectively, these odes vividly capture the ghetto street aesthetic: the vagaries of the ghetto soul hustling for cream to eat, to live, to be. In them we see dreams no longer deferred; we see the black hustler as master of his (or her) own destiny—thinking, acting, being—as he makes his way through the muck of this world only to find, having momentarily broken free of it, that the dream is illusory, is still deferred. That's how these songs about the ghetto hustler wind down—well, at least one of them does. Enlightened by the "whole truth" behind his jail experience, so the moral of the story goes, Sport declares, "It had cost me twelve years of my time to realize what a nickel and dime hustler I had really been, while the real hustlers were ripping off billions from the unsuspecting mens who are programmed to think they can win." As for the '90s ode, well, let's just say times done changed. In it there's no epiphany, no moral, no implicit injunction—only a bold but simple attestation: You can't knock the hustle. Nuff said, save perhaps to amplify per the ode's last lines:

> At my arraignment screamin'
> All these blacks got is sports and entertainment, until we even
> Thievin' as long as I'm breathin'
> Can't knock the way a nigga eatin'.

As a multimillion-dollar recording industry, rap may well be a hustle you can't knock. But along with the legit, big-time hustles for some lower-class blacks—entertainment and sports—there's also the illegit, what Jay-Z calls "thieving." Or did he perhaps mean that rap, figuratively speaking, is akin to "thieving"? It's a legit occupation, sure enough, but given all the controversy over its glamorization of violence (especially as it's creepin' on a come up in precious white middle-class neighborhoods), one might think of it as the metaphoric equivalent of gafflin' some fools for they paper. But, his Jigganess ain' just talkin' 'bout rap, for he has, or rather the persona he assumes has, you recall, extensive hos, 50Gs from crap shootin', and a sweet deal on some Colombian coke. That comes pretty close to what we call thieving, and for this hustler, unlike Sport, thieving is on "as long as I'm breathin'." And why shouldn't it be if, as Scoop Jackson alleges, "You can't knock the hustle" is the very law America was founded on.[2] And if not the law, perhaps the rhetorical principle that drives the *ethos* of the American dream(er). Why else would Flash and the Furious Five's ghetto child admire "all the number book-takers, thugs, pimps, and pushers and the big money makers" and "wanna grow up to be just like them"?[3]

All of this may sound like a ringing endorsement of the criminal behavior, violence, and misogyny often reflected in what many call gangsta rap, but I'm not proposing so much a defense of the music as much as I am attempting to explicate some of its arguably complex and contradictory contours. I'm especially interested here in the ways that rap artists construct the ethos of the ghetto hustler, specifically the gangsta or street thug. I believe that this *gangsta ethos* is constituted of not only contemporary adaptations of either the badman or trickster of traditional African American folklore, as some have argued, but is also a hybrid or a protean figure. That is, while badmen like Stag-O-Lee or tricksters like the Signifying Monkey each prefigure the O.G. (Original Gangsta) of gangsta/reality rap, rap artists draw on elements from both sources (as well as others like Dolomite) to create an image or myth for themselves that transcends the despair and hopelessness of ordinary ghetto life. Perhaps one could say that through the highly charged language of rap, these artists fashion themselves as, to use Cecil Brown's expression, "good Jiveass Nigger[s], because the character is based on the folk character of the black ethos."[4] Though often fraught with a depressingly sexist male attitude and myopic "do or die" worldview, the gangsta ethos models a kind of folk heroic action for many otherwise hapless ghetto youth. In what follows, I illustrate how this heroic action plays out in gangsta/reality rap of the last decade.

The Original O.G.'s: Stag and the Signifyin' Monkey

When my wife Artie had a baby boy, I said, "The nigger's name is Malik Nkrumah Stagolee Seale."

"I don't want him named that!" Artie said.

I had read all that book history about Stagolee, that black folkloric history, because I was hung up on that stuff at the time, so I said, "Malik Nkrumah Stagolee Seale!"

"Why Stagolee?" Artie asked.

"Because Stagolee was a bad nigger off the block and didn't take shit from nobody. All you had to do was organize him, like Malcolm X, make him politically conscious."

Bobby Seale, *Seize the Time*

Drawing on folklorist accounts of the African American tradition of oral poetry (for example, Bruce Jackson's "Get Your Ass in the Water and Swim Like Me"), writer and Hip hop aficionado S. H. Fernando, Jr., traces a direct line of descent from early prison toasts (that is, oral folk narrative poems) like "Stag-O-Lee" and "The Hustler" to gangsta/reality rap. In *The New Beats,* Fernando writes that

> These prison toasts, which tend to depict the criminal life-
> style of the hustler, are the parents of what is popularly
> known as "gangsta" rap, which paints vivid scenarios of
> the violent, often misogynistic culture of the streets.[5]

Fernando delineates two common types of hustlers who appear in prison toasts:

> the trickster, who lives by his wits, constantly scheming and
> manipulating others, and the "badman" who rules by force

and intimidation. Both victimize others in their ultimate quest to get paid, but on the streets, looking out for self is a necessary rule of the game.[6]

Not surprisingly, Fernando credits the badman hustler of African American folklore with the distinction of being the prototype of rap's O.G., that is, Original Gangster.[7] The O.G., he claims, is best represented in African American folk mythology by the badman hustler or "ruthless outlaw" Stag-O-Lee (alternately called Stagger Lee, Stackerlee, Stackalee, Stackolee, Stagalee, or just plain Stag).[8] Stag-O-Lee's legendary badness dates back to ballads of the 1890s,[9] though perhaps he was most popular in toasts of the 1960s, when a blood might step to you and say, "I ain got to brag, uhm like Stag."[10] Given Stag-O-Lee's unparalleled fearlessness and baaaaad rep (even with white folks!), it's easy to see how he might serve as a model for today's gangsta rapper. Indeed, the Stag-O-Lee toast reads much like any number of rap songs by the now-defunct rap group N.W.A. (Niggaz Wit Attitude). When N.W.A. came out with "Straight Outta Compton," "Boyz in the Hood," and "Gangsta Gangsta" (not to mention "F—— the Police"), these was like anthems for all the gangstas or gangsta wannabes in the inner cities during the late '80s—though Ice-T's 1987 rap song "6 'N the Mornin'" (on *Rhyme Pays*) was probably the initial catalyst on the West Coast, and on the East Coast, songs like KRS-One/Boogie Down Productions' "9mm Goes Bang" off the *Criminal Minded* LP. Carter Harris, a contributor to *The Vibe History of Hip Hop,* argues though that "before Eazy [E] gangstas were either pimps (Ice-T), conscious ghetto warriors (KRS-One), or small-time urban hoodlums (Schoolly D)."[11] He believes that "Eazy Muthafuckin' E defined a new archetype, the defiantly hedonistic hip hop thugsta who believed that keeping it real and seeking fame and fortune were one and the same."[12] Harris makes a valid point about Eazy E, who, though he often didn't write his own rhymes, made threats about smothering your mother or beatin' yo you-know-what seem the genuine premeditations of a cold-hearted killer.

Even though the badman or gangsta plays a major role in the African American folk tradition, none of these songs came about because brothas was literally sittin' around and reflecting on tales of Stag-O-Lee. Instead they arose largely due to the environment, to the drug dealing and gang banging that took place at the time in urban areas like New York and LA. In a *Spin* interview back in '88, KRS-One explains that

> This violence, it's everyday to the kid in the ghetto. No big deal. They could listen to that just as they listen to Madonna. The reason why we put things like that in there

is simply our philosophy on how to teach the kids about things that are negative in our society.

The concept is to be the first reality crew. . . . After you've partied and listened to everything, listen to our albums. We're not like the guys who come out and say, "Crack is wack, don't do that." The kids look at you like a goddamn idiot. Or the law: "Don't do it or you go to jail." Ain't nobody out here scared of jail. At least not the youth. So what I do is simply come out like their friend, like the guy they normally see on the street corner holding his pistol, holding his dick, with a car and a girl and a beeper.[13]

In spite of the fact that gang violence and the crack epidemic have tapered off somewhat since the late '90s (and that KRS-One might now recant some of what he said in that interview), many contemporary rappers (such as Spice 1, Beanie Sigel, and 50 Cent) represent pretty convincingly the gangsta ethos in their rhymes. Still I gotta say that, though they gon now—both brutally murdered in their prime—Tupac Shakur's and Christopher Wallace's gangsta personas are in many ways the realest of all. Anyway, gettin' back to the badman toast, peep this version of Stag-O-Lee printed in Roger Abrahams's *Deep Down in the Jungle.*

Back in '32 when times was hard
I had a sawed-off shotgun and a crooked deck of cards,
Pin-striped suit, fucked-up hat,
T-model Ford, didn't even have a payment on that.
Had a cute little broad, she throwed me out in the cold.
I asked her why, she said, "Our love is growing old."
So I packed all my little rags, took a walk down Rampail Street.
That's where all the bad motherfuckers went down to meet.
I walked through water and I waded through mud, Come a little
    hole-in-the-wall, they call the "Bucket of Blood."
I walked in and asked the bartender, "Dig, chief, can I get something
    to eat?"
He throwed me a stale glass of water and flung me a fucked-up piece
    of meat.
I said, "Raise, motherfucker, do you know who I am?"
He said, "Frankly, motherfucker, I just don't give a damn."
I knowed right then that chicken shit was dead.
I throwed a thirty-eight shell through his motherfucking head. . . .
She [the bartender's mother] said, "Who did this terrible crime, may
    I ask you please?"
I said, "Me, bitch, and my name is Stackolee."[14]

Stag may not be the ideal model for handling his bi'ness with women (he got "throwed . . . out in the cold" by his, after all) and he may not be much of a rapper, but he's got his gun (a shotgun and a .38, apparently) and deck of cards, and he know he the baddest O.G. out there in the streets. And in the rap world, none fit this prototype so well as the Notorious B.I.G. His gangsta persona in songs like "Gimme the Loot," as Armond White says, "made him hiphop's equivalent to a Hollywood blockbuster." "'Gimmie [sic] the Loot,'" he further claims, "is an extravaganza that is funnier, scarier, more complicated and more interesting than *Menace II Society, Boyz N the Hood, Straight Out of Brooklyn, Fresh* and most hiphop records put together."[15] Clearly, Biggie's gangsta bravado in this song closely mimics (in a way, outstrips) the legendary badness of Stag-O-Lee. Even still, I would argue that gangsta/reality rappers like Biggie Smalls at best only partially represent the badman à la Stag-O-Lee. Because of their dexterity with words—their virile boasts, I call them—they just as well might represent that other popular African American folk hero, the Signifying Monkey. In fact, some years ago (June '93) *The Source* ran a one-page article tracing rap's roots to the Signifying Monkey toast, what the writer called the "ultimate trash talking rhyme in the Black oral tradition."[16] For those of you who, like the Gen Y-ers I teach, still ain't hipped to these two black folk characters, let me drop a bit of science 'bout that. See, Stag-O-Lee is reputed to be a man of few words but unreserved action—a dude whose actions shonuff speak louder than his words.[17] The Signifying Monkey, on the other hand, is all talk; he'll signify and play the dozens on you (talk real bad about you, yo mama, daddy, grandma, great granddaddy, you know, all yo peoples), but because of his small size he ain't about to get up in yo grill. In fact, none of the versions of the tale I'm aware of have him resorting to physical force as Stag does. Like West African trickster figures—Ananse, Legba, Esu-Elegbara, and Ogo-Yurugu—the Monkey is the quintessential "braggart, yet his very braggadocio is humble."[18] You can witness his bragging in the classic toast "The Signifying Monkey and the Lion." Interestingly, in the version I cite below, the Monkey assumes the persona of the urban hustler or pimp, which further intimates his resemblance to rap's O.G. The excerpt is lengthy yet telling.

> Deep down in the jungle where the coconut grows
> Lives a pimp little monkey, you could tell by the clothes he wore.
> He had a camel-hair benny with belt in the back,
> Had a pair of nice shoes and a pair of blue slacks.
> Now his clothes were cute little things,
> Was wearing a Longine watch and a diamond ring.
> He says he thinks he'd take a stroll

Down by the water hole.
And guess who he met? Down there was Mr. Lion.
The monkey started into that signifying.
He said, "Mr. Lion, I got something to tell you today."
He said, "The way this motherfucker been talking 'bout you I
    know you'll sashay."
(He told the lion)
He said, "Mr. Lion, the way he talking 'bout your mother, down
    your cousins,
I know damn well you don't play the dozens.
He talking your uncle and your aunt's a damn shame.
Called your father and your mother a whole lot of names.
I would 'a fought the motherfucker but looked at him with a
    tear in my eye.
He's a big motherfucker, he's twice your size."
The lion looked down with a tear in his eye,
Said, "Where's this big motherfucker that's twice my size?"
That little monkey said, "I'll show you the way."
He went down and the elephant was standing by a tree,
And the lion said, "Hey, motherfucker, I hear you been looking for
    me."
Elephant looked at the lion and said,
"Go on chickenshit, pick on somebody your size."
The lion made a roar.
The elephant side-stepped and kicked his ass on the floor.
The lion looked up with a tear in his eyes.
Says, "I'm gonna beat you, motherfucker, though you're twice my
    size."
He looked back and squared off to fight.
The elephant kicked his ass clean out of sight.
Came back for ride or roar.
Elephant stomped his ass clean on the floor.
The elephant looked about, said, "What the fuck is this?"
The lion said, "You know you's a bad motherfucker, put up your
    fists."
They fought three days, and they fought three nights.
I don't see how in hell the lion got out of that fight. Coming back
    through the jungle more dead than alive,
Here goes the monkey in the tree with that same signifying.
He said, "Look at you, you goddamn chump.
Went down in the jungle fucking with that man
And got your ass blanshed and drug in the sand.
You call yourself a real down king,

But I found you ain't a goddamn thing.
Get from underneath this goddamn tree
'Cause I feel as though I've got to pee."
The lion looked up, said,
"That's all right, Mr. Monkey, if that's the way you want to play
The sun's gonna shine in your ugly ass some day."
Monkey looked down, said, "Long as the trees grow tall, the grass
    grows green,
You's the dumbest motherfucker the jungle's ever seen."[19]

There's a bit more to this brotha's telling of the tale, but that's enough to demonstrate how the Monkey relies on language (specifically taunts and boasts), not physical strength, to fashion himself a badman, a makeshift Stag-O-Lee. The Monkey is, in other words, a wicked (read: *bad,* as in good) signifier, preying on the hapless signified.

Now while gangsta/reality rappers do, like the Monkey, signify, I don't see them as pure imitations of this character type—for they rarely portray themselves as idle braggarts or averse to fighting, even if they've long left the streets or their gang-banging days. In his debut on Death Row, Snoop, a one-time Crip, reminds Death Row's adversaries that they won't hesitate to flex some muscle if challenged (see the intro to Dr. Dre's *The Chronic* CD). And yet one could argue, I suppose, that the Signifying Monkey's tree, his place of refuge from the inimitable Lion is, metaphorically speaking, for the gangsta rapper the recording studio—a sequestered space where he (or she, let me not forget self-professed gangstresses like Lil' Kim, Khia, Da Brat, Gangsta Boo, among others) boasts, taunts, and disses his enemies. But the growing list of rap artists who have participated in some form of real violence (such as Slick Rick, Snoop Dogg, and allegedly Sean "P. Diddy" Combs, Shyne, Jay-Z, Eminem, Beanie Sigel, C-Murder, Nas, and, man, about every other head from Beantown to the City of Angels) or have been a victim of it, many fatally (for example, Tupac Shakur, Biggie Smalls, Big L, Freaky Tah of the Lost Boyz, Jam-Master Jay, Soulja Slim, and, though not fatally, 50 Cent), greatly undermines that argument. I mean, gangsta/reality rappers rap about violence in the studio, but most, I'd venture to say, follow Bay-area rapper Ant Banks's prescription to stay strapped (in "Packin' a Gun," on the *Menace II Society* soundtrack).

So, I propose that the so-called gangsta rapper (particularly the most skilled of them) represents not one or the other, trickster or badman, but a continuously evolving hybrid of the two. Long befo G rap, in fact, Ulf Hannerz voiced opposition to seeing the trickster and badman as a dichotomy—a view supposedly held by Abrahams. Back in '69, Hannerz claimed that to separate the trickster and badman may be misleading, for smartness and toughness are only facets of a single if somewhat amorphous conception of ghetto specific masculinity which both Stackolee and the monkey serve. That is, most streetcorner men would be able to recognize both of them as cultural models for their own role, although they may personally emphasize one or the other.[20]

Likewise, in *The Life: The Lore and Folk Poetry of the Black Hustler,* Dennis Wepman, Ronald Newman, and Murray Binderman state that "the ideal role is a synthesis of the two [folk heroes], but favoring cleverness—a sort of tough trickster rather than a smart badman."[21] The authors consider Long-Shoe Sam, the narrator in "Mexicana Rose," as such an ideal hero because he can handle his bi'ness with a .44 but spends most of his time "recruiting and keeping whores."[22] Judging from the content of the toast, Long-Shoe Sam is definitely an exemplary blend of the trickster (or pimp) and gangsta. Sam proves his macking ability by coaxing Rose into his stable and demonstrates his flexing skills when Smitty Cocaine, his erstwhile partner, tried to put a cap in his you-know-what. However, if Rose hadn't taken the first bullet and if Smitty hadn't dropped his gun and ran after he shot her, Sam might not have even gotten the chance to go off on Smitty by shooting him "in the ass" and "in the teeth."[23] So while Long-Shoe Sam might be the ideal folk hero for the average street hustler, for gangsta rappers he ain't got enough game. In a typical G rapper's tale, shoot, our man Sam woulda saved Rose's life (not so much out of love but vested interest, she being his newly acquired bread and butter), smoked Smitty, and talked plenty of smack as he was doing it—knowwhatI'msaying?

Like Mike? Nah, Loc, If I Could Be Like Dolemite

> A real nigger always says that you can kill him, but you can never hurt his soul!
>
> Robert Deane Pharr, *The Soul Murder Case*

Perhaps a closer approximation to rap's O.G. is the folk character Dolemite, for, as Bruce Jackson points out, "Dolemite is the ultimate badass: he drinks, fights, fucks, and in between seems to brag about what he has just done or will do next. He suffers none of Stackolee's inarticulateness or the Pimp's [i.e., the Signifying Monkey's] limited perspective."[24] Hip hop heads might quickly give a nod of recognition here since Snoop D-o-double-g made Dolemite a household name when he alluded to the character's pimping and gangsterism as metaphoric of his own rapping

skills in "Nuthin' But a 'G' Thang." Note that I wrote "Dolomite," but
I probably shoulda written Dolemite because Snoop is most likely referring to comedian Rudy Ray Moore's character in the '70s blaxploitation
flick *Dolemite*. In fact, Moore's voice is featured on the very next cut off
of Dre's *The Chronic* CD, called "Deeez Nuuuts." And before his collaboration with Dre and Snoop, Moore had already dipped into the rap
game with a staged rap/signifying battle with Big Daddy Kane on Kane's
Taste of Chocolate album.

Now, as to the matter of the Dolomite toast, Jackson prints two versions in *Get Your Ass in the Water and Swim Like Me*, one of which is a
recorded performance by Moore in Buffalo, New York, in 1970. In that
same year, of course, Moore released his first album of toasts and jokes
called *Eat Out More Often*, which includes a version of the Dolomite
toast. The excerpts below are taken from Jackson's text, and they aptly
illustrate the extent of Dolomite's "badassness."

> Now Dolomite was from San Antone,
> a rambling skipfucker from the day he was born.
> Why, the day he was dropped from his mammy's ass,
> he slapped his pappy's face
> and said, "From now on, cocksucker, I'm running this place."

Already, even at such a tender age, one can see how bad Dolomite is.
He summarily puts his father in his place and, according to the passage
below, manhandles his infamous uncle, Sudden Death.

> At the age of one he was drinkin' whiskey and gin,
> at the age of two he was eatin' the bottles it came in.
> Now Dolomite had an uncle called Sudden Death,
> killed a dozen bad men from the smell of his breath.
> When his uncle heard how Dolomite was treatin' his ma and his pa,
> he said, "Let me go and check on this bad rascal before he go too
>   far."
> Now one cold dark December night,
> his uncle broke in on Dolomite.
> Now Dolomite wasn't no more'n three or four
> when his uncle come breakin' through the door.
> His uncle said, "Dolomite, I want you to straighten up and treat your
>   brother right,
> 'cause if you keep on with your dirty mistreatin',
> I'm gonna whup your ass till your heart stop beatin'."
> Dolomite's sittin' in the middle of the floor playin'.
> He said, "I see your lips quiver, Unc, but I don't hear a cocksucken

word you sayin'."
This made his uncle mad.
He led off with a right that made lightnin' flash,
but Dolomite tore his leg off, he was that damned fast.[25]

Up to this point we've only witnessed Dolomite's irreverent and violent behavior. But further along in the toast, as Dolomite gets older, we observe his keen wit and slick talk. Yeah, he can beat down the fearsome Sudden Death, but he can also boast and signify with the best of 'em, man or monkey. Perhaps not coincidentally—like any true pimp or player—Dolomite's eloquence is most evident when he raps to a woman about his sexual prowess. Kinda like the Sundiata–Soumaoro war with words before the action starts, Dolomite runs down his pedigree to Chi (Chicago) Mabel—who "of all the whores she was the boss":

"I swimmed across muddy rivers and never got wet,
mountains has fell on me and I ain't dead yet.
I fucked an elephant and [dared her to mutter],
I can look up a bull's ass and tell you the price of butter.
I fucked a mother elephant down to a coon,
even fucked the same damned cow that jumped over the motherfuckin
     moon."
Said, "I rode across the ocean on the head of my dick, and ate nine
     tons a catshit and ain't never got sick.
And you talk about wrappin' your good hot pussy all around my
     badass chin,
bitch: you ought to be blowin' up my ass trying to be my motherfucken
     friend."[26]

Of course, Dolomite is true to his boast—well the last part of it, at least. He rocks Chi Mabel's world—tragically, to the point of her death. But that's the ultramacho, misogynistic ethos on display in the toast and the one that, it seems to me, many G rappers try to effect in their rhymes.

Street-corner versions of the toast like this one may have contributed to the popularity of the Dolomite persona among G rappers, but more than likely, as I've suggested, the cinematic version Moore offers in the person of Dolemite, the "Human Tornado," has had the greatest impact on G rappers and the Hip hop community. The movie is, honestly speaking, a lame production (acting, general cinematography), but it brought before '70s audiences one particular black folk hero that previously had been heard of only in (some) black communities and in the occasional African American folklore collection. As Moore did in the '70s, now G rappers are bringing this black folk heroic tradition to the mainstream public through music and music videos. In *Dolemite*, Moore plays the lead character by that name, and D'Urville Martin, who earlier appeared in *Black Caesar* with Fred "The Hammer" Williamson, plays Willie Green, "the baddest motherfucker the world ever seen," according to the toast.[27] In the toast, though, Willie Green and his bad rep serve merely as a point of reference in a tale that focuses on one who is even badder—that is, "the little bad motherfucker called Dolomite."[28] To give the movie some kind of gripping plot, I suppose, makers of the film (Martin directed it) cast Green as Dolemite's archrival, who in the end gets capped by Dolemite, in a way like Billy Lion (Lyon) is done in by Stag-O-Lee.

However, unlike Stag, Moore's Dolemite smokes Willie Green more out of self-defense than mean-spiritedness or anger. Actually, Dolemite just wants to get his club back from Green. Oh, and there is the matter of a personal vendetta in the movie as well—for Willie Green was partly responsible for the murder of Dolemite's nephew. For the most part, though, the Dolemite represented by Moore in the film doesn't behave as viciously as the Dolemite of the toast. Though he engages in all of the folk character's accustomed fetishes—drinking (although I don't recall actually seeing him drink that much), fighting, screwing, and bragging—unlike him, Dolemite doesn't provoke gratuitous violence by bullying people or tearing you-know-what up just to show how bad he is. Dolemite simply reacts to the violence; he don't incite it. Still, he baaad—just not in the largely negative way the character in the toast is.

To use folklorist John Roberts's distinction, one could say that Dolomite resembles the "bad nigger" character in black communities during and after slavery and Dolemite parallels the "badman" or outlaw hero of black folklore. An especially subtle distinction perhaps for us laypeople, yet Roberts sees it as critical to a proper understanding of African American folk heroic creation.

> A consequence of ignoring the earlier manifestations of the badman tradition in black culture [in ballads] is evident in folkloristic discussions of the tradition, where there is a constant emphasis on the destructive and unproductive nature of badman heroes. In drawing this portrait of the badman, folklorists have basically relied on early fieldwork reports which suggested that a character-type known in black communities as the "bad nigger" served as the prototype of the badman of folklore. The uncritical acceptance of the "bad nigger," who most often acted as a neighborhood bully, as the real-life prototype for the badman of folklore not only has distorted the basis on which African Americans accept badmen as folk heroes, but has

also led to unproductive searches for the factors that have been most influential on folk heroic creation surrounding badmen in black culture.[29]

Having been paid by the town residents to "get [his] bad ass out of San Antone,"[30] Dolomite certainly sounds like a scourge to his community, the veritable "bad nigger" that Roberts describes. He was so bad, in fact, folks was celebrating when he passed away, overjoyed that they finally put that bad nigga to rest. Why even the preacher who presided over the services was relieved: "Ashes to ashes, dust to dust, I'm glad that this bad motherfucker called Dolomite is no longer here with us."[31]

Dolemite, on the other hand, appears to be subject to no such ill will from his community, even though as a sometime pimp he exploits the community's women for his own gain. Community residents are all pretty glad to see Dolemite get out of prison and get back on the streets. (By contrast, the townsfolk in the toast had locked up Dolomite for eight years before they finally paid him to leave town.) And once Dolemite is back on the streets, we can quickly see why folks welcomed him back: he entertains them with toasts (in the club and sometimes for free out on the corner), sympathizes with the most lowly of them (the drugged-out hamburger pimp, for instance), helps them economically by operating a popular place of leisure in the community, and even protects them from corrupt city government (including Willie Green, the mayor, members of the police department, all in collusion). Such qualities clearly distinguish Dolemite from Dolomite, intimating perhaps that the former personifies more the "badman" than the "bad nigger."

Concerning the concept of the badman in African American folklore of the late nineteenth century, Roberts states that "the relationship which developed between African Americans and the 'law,' personified in the white law enforcement officer, greatly facilitated the transformation of the black conception of the trickster to create the badman as an outlaw folk hero."[32] He further explains that in order to resolve the dilemma of condoning tricksterlike behaviors that victimized members of the community and to offer the community a model of heroic action that didn't threaten its values, African American singers and storytellers "combined their conception of the trickster with that of the conjurer to create the badman—a folk hero whose characteristic actions resembled those of a trickster but unfolded in the black community."[33] Given these probable developments in folk creation, Dolemite may well be molded after the image of the badman of early African American folklore. Yet since Roberts's analysis focuses less on toasts than on the earlier ballads and doesn't take into consideration toasts like "Dolomite," such an assertion is less than certain. Besides, if Roberts considers relatively nonverbal characters like

Stag (albeit the Stag of the folk ballads) as an example of a badman figure, then the badman profile hardly suits the more complex character of
Dolemite. Still, it's worth noting that Roberts views the badman tradition
as a transformation or progressive development of the trickster tradition,
which may also imply other, more recent developments such as Dolemite
as a transformation of the badman and the O.G. as a transformation or
progressive development of Dolemite.

Considering Moore's portrayal of Dolemite a bit further, it occurs
to me that if you take away his rather homely appearance (actually, take
that back, since looks ain't never been a prerequisite for one to call hisself
a pimp in the rap game), you have the perfect model for G rappers (some
of them anyway). Like the rap personas of Snoop, Ludacris, Cam'ron,
and many others, Moore's Dolemite controls the mic (raps or does toasts
in his nightclub routines), pimps or plays several women (or purports to),
knows how to hustle for mad chedda (Dolemite had him a stash tucked
away so that he could buy back his club in cold cash), and, when he has
to, flexes before playa haters (like Willie Green) and The Man (a.k.a. the
po-lice who framed him, sent him to jail, and, once he was out, tried to
do it to him all over again).

Thus, more than Dolemite, the Signifying Monkey, and Stag-O-Lee,
one might say that Rudy Ray Moore's Dolemite best models the gangsta
ethos of many contemporary rap artists. Actually, in a way both Dolemite and Dolomite prefigure the gangsta sensibilities of those notorious
Compton, Watts, Brooklyn, and Queens Gs—for some rappers come
across (at least in many of their songs) as straight-up "bad niggers" (following Roberts's definition). Now, I doubt that any of them is absolutely
one or the other, but I can see, for example, the South Central Cartel,
Spice 1, Compton's Most Wanted, Smif-N-Wessun (now Cocoa Brothaz),
Mac 10, the 5th Ward Boyz, Ganksta N-I-P, Cypress Hill, the L.O.X. (or
D Block), and a number of Now School folk like Beanie Sigel, Shyne,
M.O.P., and 50 Cent somewhat fittin' the profile. On the other hand, I
can imagine artists like Biggie Smalls, Ice Cube, Tupac, DMX, Scarface,
and Method Man to some extent reflecting the same "bad nigger" image
in their lyrics but also the more constructive qualities of Dolemite. Overall, though, I would argue, like Michael Eric Dyson does in *From God to
Gangsta Rap*, that one would be hard-pressed to pigeonhole any of these
artists, that gangsta/reality rappers in general are remarkably varied and
complex in their gangsta fantasies.[34] Sure, their bravado can be insensitive and inane at times, but, on the whole, it can hardly be reduced to a
simple dichotomy or even a few nuanced descriptors.

Perhaps the variety and complexity of gangsta/reality rap is dictated
not so much by the rappers themselves or any serious critical stance on
their part but by their preoccupation with self-construction, with affirm-

ing certain social and cultural aspects that mark their identity or sense of self and community. That is to say, in their attempt to craft an image of themselves that stays true to the ghetto hustler's creed, they by necessity touch on some complicated moral, social, and political issues facing black ghetto communities. Mind you, not that they be rappin' 'bout revolution or kickin' socially conscious rhymes as, say, Kam, Dead Prez, or the Roots. Rather, in representin' (or trying to and sometimes failing) what they perceive as their reality in the person of the ghetto hustler, these rappers broach, even if only superficially, social dilemmas much like Moore's Dolemite does. In this sense, perhaps one could say that G rappers continue the late-nineteenth-century folk practice of creating an outlaw folk hero that serves as a "model of emulative behavior," particularly for ghetto youth.[35] The question is, though, do G rappers do so without threatening the values of their communities?

Well, that's no easy question to answer, but let me try. Witness, as one example, how on Dr. Dre's *The Chronic,* Dre and Snoop deal with the dilemma of a young boy growing up in the ghetto. Flash and the Furious Five's "The Message" probably conveys the matter more effectively, but Dre's "Lil' Ghetto Boy" is more subtle and rendered more from the perspective of the young ghetto hustler than the slightly older ghetto participant-observer. The song opens with cacophony, the voices of a whole lotta black folk talkin' at (not *to*) one another. Then, the bass voice of one seemingly huge brotha rises resoundingly above the rest—resolute, as he sermonizes on behalf of the future of the little ones, even if need be unto his own death. The chorus of the song accentuates this sincere and desperate concern for the future of black youth, only it does so rather ambiguously. It consists of a sample from Donny Hathaway's 1971 song "Little Ghetto Boy," with a touching expression about the little ghetto boy's coming of age. Added to this are lines rendered in a feigned Jamaican accent, deftly conflating loyalty to the O.G.'s creed and the innocence of ghetto boyhood. Or, rather, innocence mixed with too-swiftly acquired adult experience, so that the little ghetto boy becomes the grown ghetto man . . . in the streets playin' . . . hustlin' . . . tryna get his. Snoop and Dre alternate turns on the mic—Snoop assuming the role of an eighteen-year-old con, resigned to doing his time and Dre the persona of a twenty-seven-year-old parolee who is out to hustle for the fast money yet again. Interesting for its oblique commentary on the generational change from fists to firearms, Dre's lines relate how the youths, the little ghetto boys of this new era, are strapped, as bewildering as that may seem to older ghetto hustlers.

Another intriguing twist to the song appears in the last few lines. Here Snoop flips the script on mainstream society's assumption that moral lessons should have been learned from time served (Snoop's character spent

four years in the county jail) and that the erstwhile hustler should have
forsaken his former ways. Apparently, life isn't quite that simple if you're
a little ghetto boy growing up on the ghetto streets; you out to survive,
even if survival inverts the moral order. This kinda G attitude ain't much
different in the East Coast world of reality rap, the rationale only more
direct. In "Can I Live," Jay-Z tells us straight up that "we hustle out of
a sense of hopelessness, sort of a desperation. Through that desperation,
we 'come addicted, sorta like the fiends we accustomed to servin.' But we
feel we have nothin' to lose, so we offer you—well—we offer our lives."
It may be a lame excuse perhaps for the socially destructive activities the
hustler engages in—drug dealing, gambling, pimping, and various other
crimes—however, as Julius Hudson concludes in his study of what he
calls the hustling ethic in inner-city Baltimore of the early '70s,

> one might well argue that the social system of the hustler
> represents a systematized form of deviant behavior, but in
> the final analysis this behavior could be appropriately clas-
> sified as adaptive behavior. In effect, the hustler's society
> represents the lower-class black's original and indigenous
> means of waging a "war on poverty." Members of this
> subculture, and numerous ghetto residents, feel that the
> hustler's anti-poverty effort is considerably more successful
> than the government's.[36]

    Roberts also reports that concerning societies at the turn of the cen-
tury and the folk heroic creation these societies inspired, such crimes
weren't categorically condemned by community residents. Viewing certain crimes largely as forms of entertainment and potential sources of
extra income, some turn-of-the-century communities tolerated a degree
of lawlessness.

> Some black communities had areas, sometimes known as
> "bottoms," in which a lack of social restraint against cer-
> tain types of illegal activities became well known. Brochert,
> for instance, suggests in his study of turn-of-century alley
> communities in Washington, D.C. that the attitudes of the
> residents in economically depressed neighborhoods allowed
> certain types of illegal activities to become widespread. He
> states, for example, that in alley communities "Many ac-
> tivities viewed as criminal by the larger community were
> not viewed as such by the residents. Many of these 'crimes'
> were in fact forms of recreation and enjoyment." He men-
> tions playing the numbers and craps, as well as bootlegging

and drug peddling, as illegal activities commonly tolerated in these communities.[37]

Roberts is quick to point out, however, that a community's tolerance for such activities was on occasion tested by the presence of professional gamblers, pimps, and bootleggers who "increased the risk of an unwanted encounter with the 'law' or being involved in a serious violent incident by pursuing illegal activities not simply as recreations but rather as professions."[38] For G rappers, on the contrary, the professional criminal—especially the pimp and the drug kingpin—has been something of a hero because of the large sums of money and mass appeal he possesses. So if in their raps they take on the personas of professional criminals, then one might deduce that their attempts to fashion a model of heroic action seriously undermines the community's values. Even so, if, on the other hand, they—like those earlier African American singers and storytellers—make clear the consequences of their heroes' actions, if they "incorporate a recognition that [their heroes'] brand of justice [is] not accepted by the society or even the black community as a whole," then the community's values could remain intact.[39] This clearly is exemplified in "Lil' Ghetto Boy."

Of course, not all gangsta/reality rappers address the consequences of their characters' actions. Caught up in the glamour and glitz of that G thang, some fail to acknowledge even what Sport learned, let alone what he left unresolved. But there are sufficient examples of, at the very least, the recognition of misunderstanding and, thus, conflict between the outlaw and the community in which he (or she) does his (or her) bidding. Biggie nicely illustrates this in a song off *Ready to Die.* In what seems to be a stirring autobiographical account, Biggie's "Everyday Struggle" relates how the community reacts unfavorably to his chosen profession (namely, drug dealing) but yet does not recognize the inauspicious circumstances that regrettably led him to it. Tupac presents a similar affectation in many of his recordings. One that often stands out for me is "Pain," a song that he recorded for the *Above the Rim* soundtrack. Like Biggie, here Pac recognizes society's hatred of the street thug, but he quickly counters the reproach with the charge that society fails to see the person of the thug. As if genuinely groping for answers, Pac heightens the pathos of the charge with a series of provocative rhetorical questions—questions that when entertained on rare occasions by America's politicians, social critics, and media pundits receive only pat responses or solutions (in other words, learn a trade or slave at some minimum-wage job and you too can achieve the American dream—never mind that their hard-working parents haven't done so after twenty-some-odd years of work).

Reflecting on the tragic lives of the urban poor in lyrics from songs like these, Biggie and Tupac often evoke empathy for the young brotha who resorts to crime to evade poverty, though they seem to realize that his doing so victimizes the community as a whole. At the end of "Everyday Struggle," Biggie sums up the situation rather fatalistically by pointing out that life is what it is in the struggle. It's hard to say exactly how much any rapper understands the scope of the urban deprivation they rap about, but I would have to say that throughout much of his short career Pac was probably the most adept at giving voice to the more tragic and conflicted ghetto sensibilities. Not that homes always got everything straight or righteously represented all of ghetto Black America. But Tupac Amaru Shakur had this extraordinary, almost instinctive ability to make the most wretched members of society, what he calls *thug niggaz,* seem real, palpable, human, and in this I see a special kind of folk heroic creation. I don't mean here a kind of sophism where Pac made the worst seem the better cause; rather I mean art that earnestly gives voice to the humanity of those who, in a sense, have been dehumanized, whether by the system and its hollow moral code or by their own misguided attempts to overcome the system. Perhaps *Poetic Justice* director John Singleton, who had his share of dealings with Tupac in the filming of the movie, has Pac pegged right when he muses, "Tupac spoke from a position that cannot be totally appreciated unless you understand the pathos of being a nigga, a displaced African soul, full of power, pain and passion, with no focus or direction for all that energy except his art."[40] One can't help but sense, for instance, in spite of the religious incongruity, the power and tragic pathos of this art in his now famous phrase about heaven having a ghetto for thug niggaz (see "If I Die 2Nite").

Considered by some critics as one of rap's most abrasive and abusive stars, however, Tupac hardly seems like a man prepared to be or to create in rhyme a heroic figure for destitute blacks, especially young black males, to emulate. In fact, at first glance, it's easy to see in him all the characteristics of that classic bad nigga Dolomite. His mythic autobiographical account in "Cradle to the Grave" sounds like a page right from the Dolomite toast (see the first few lines of the song on *Thug Life: Volume 1*). Add to this all of his criminal antics and his vitriolic attacks on record, especially his Makaveli album *The Don Killuminati: The 7 Day Theory,* and you just about got that "ultimate badass" Dolomite. Armond White's excellent biography on Tupac sorts through many of the negative as well as positive aspects of Pac and his music. White mentions, for instance, that Tupac's move to Death Row Records and his new Makaveli persona took him from originally only *reacting to* "the confusions of double-consciousness and the anxieties of modern wickedness" to *acting* instinctively on them.[41] As Makaveli, White believes that Tupac "represented a meaner version of going-through-hell hiphop youth, a harsher, even more conflicted Tupac than the Bay Area crew ever could have imagined."[42]

Even without any consideration of the Makaveli persona, though, by all counts Tupac was an enigmatic figure—not simply because of the awkward mix of gangsta sensibilities and Black Panther overtures in his music but because he tried to do, as White notes, what Paula Giddings says of the work of poet Don L. Lee: "to redefine herohood in the black community."[43] This, I believe, is what Thug Life was supposed to be about, especially the "Code of Thug Life" Tupac developed with his imprisoned stepfather Mutulu Shakur around the time of his debut album *2Pacalypse Now*.[44] Even in "Cradle to the Grave," Tupac hints at this bold mission of turning us suckers into thugs. By the time of his third solo album, *Me against the World*, and his own imprisonment on rape charges, Tupac would reveal the heavy burden of this mission in "So Many Tears." Tupac's ardent devotion to the ghetto thug and his ethical appeals to hustling suggest that in spite of his success as a multimillion-dollar rap star—or quite possibly because of it—he wanted to create out of the very stuff of ghetto depravity a model of heroic action.

But did Tupac succeed in redefining herohood or creating a model of heroic action for young brothas (and sistas) in the ghetto? Probably no more or no less than Rudy Ray Moore did as Dolemite. Audiences in the '70s, as I recall from Houston's black radio stations (KCOH and KYOK) and one of its main theaters in the Wards (the Majestic Metro), did see in Moore's Dolemite (among other blaxploitation characters, which I touch on in the next chapter) something heroic, something worth savoring for personal encouragement and psychic uplift in an integrated yet still very white hegemonic universe (especially Hollywood's version).

Of course, this wasn't the opinion of *all* blacks then, and not surprisingly it isn't the view of more mainstream (liberal and conservative) blacks today. Admiration for a Dolemite or a Tupac is a mere cop-out, these black folks say—an excuse for not trying hard enough to beat (or more politely, *compete with*) The Man in the "right" way. University of California–Berkley linguist John McWhorter appears to be the latest prophet of the "right" called to portend the wages of the sins of Black America's dark soul. Making his case recently in the conservative NYC publication *City Journal*, McWhorter, for instance, states: "By reinforcing the stereotypes that long hindered blacks, and by teaching young blacks that a thuggish adversarial stance is the properly 'authentic' response to a presumptively racist society, rap retards black success."[45] When did American society become "presumptively racist"? And since when have racial or ethnic stereotypes ever trumped their racist source in hindering black progress? McWhorter's article gets better—for a substantial part of the fault lies with America's long-beleaguered English teachers. (Johnny, or rather Jaekwon, can't read, in other words, because English teachers are teaching kids today to rap instead.)

> Many fans, rappers, producers, and intellectuals defend hip-hop's violence, both real and imagined, and its misogyny as a revolutionary cry of frustration from disempowered youth. . . . The National Council of Teachers of English, recommending the use of hip-hop lyrics in urban public school classrooms (as already happens in schools in Oakland, Los Angeles, and other cities), enthuses that "hip-hop can be used as a bridge linking the seemingly vast span between the streets and the world of academics."[46]

I can appreciate McWhorter's concern about misogyny in rap music (Lord knows brothas need to step up in defense of sistas' dignity and honor), but I wonder if this generosity extends to the so-called welfare queens conservatives often berate in their rants against what's often referred to as the *liberal rhetoric of victimization*. Probably not, since taking "undeserved" money from the government has to be a far greater offense than being the victim of sexism. Right? And as for his swipe at NCTE for seeing pedagogical value in Hip hop, it is a huge leap to assume from this that the organization endorses misogyny and violence in rap lyrics (the majority of its members are women after all). I have been a member of NCTE for fifteen years, and I don't know nobody in the group who would propose using bootylicious, bump-n-grind songs or videos as a bridge to teach English, K–12. I mean, it ain't like we be giving talks on Ludacris's "Area Codes" or Outkast's (Big Boi's) "The Way You Move" videos during conference sessions, urging fifth-grade English teachers to have their pupils sing along with the hooks and mimic the latest dance moves of the dozen or so half-naked women in them. NCTE is simply doing what any responsible educator should—that is, tapping into the cultural interests of students instead of, as is usually the case, putting school culture at complete odds with the popular culture they consume and identity with.

But, as McWhorter sees it, Hip hop isn't what The Dream was supposed to be about:

> But we're sorely lacking in imagination if in 2003—long after the civil rights revolution proved a success, at a time of vaulting opportunity for African Americans, when blacks find themselves at the top reaches of society and politics—we think that it signals progress when black kids

rattle off violent, sexist, nihilistic, lyrics, like Russians reciting Pushkin. Some defended blaxploitation pictures as revolutionary, too, but the passage of time has exposed the silliness of such a contention.[47]

Revolutionary? Who talkin' 'bout revolution? Resistance maybe—that is, an outright rejection of normative culture, what some seem to (mis)take for The Dream. How much imagination does it really take to pledge allegiance to that? Far less I would argue than it would to construct from the vagaries of double-consciousness an ethos or folk heroic figure whose power derives from an unromanticized view of the world. Lawrence Levine speaks to this mode of folk creation in his classic work *Black Culture and Black Consciousness: Afro-American Folk Thought from Slavery to Freedom*. Published before the first rap record, the book doesn't offer any insight into gangsta/reality rap, but it sheds light on key elements in African American bandit lore that are congruent with gangsta rap.

> Those who are satisfied with their lot, who possess a sense of power, who share a feeling of integration with their society are not generally those from whom the lore of banditry emanates. The prerequisite for the creation of such figures in white as well as black society has been a sense of frustration and powerlessness. The "sicknesses," the anxieties, the tensions, the profound feeling of social and cultural dislocation that are inherent in bandit lore are shared, to one extent or another, in the folklore of both whites and blacks. It must be reiterated that the crucial cultural difference in these folk figures is that whites have tended to sanitize and civilize them, to make them benefactors who dispense social justice to the entire group, while Negroes have refrained almost entirely from this form of ritual. If a sense of realism and perspective are signs of "health," then the usual interpretations of the meaning of black bad men should at least be balanced by the observation that black bandits, instead of being rendered more appealing by romantic sentimentality, were portrayed with the kind of unadorned realism generally lacking in white bandit lore.[48]

If we insist, therefore, on invoking the righteous rhetoric of civil rights as against the Hip hop imagination (particularly its most vile elements), shouldn't we as well dismiss much of what the black vernacular tradition has had to offer to the history of American folklore and music?

In fact, we could label it all minstrelsy as some folks, even a few rappers, have done with hardcore rap.[49] From the classic toasts to the dirty dozens to the early blues[50] and now to gangsta rap lyrics—why not consider it all just a bunch of niggers cooning for the white man's delight and dollars? Sounds simple enough, but according to W. T. Lhamon even something as perverse as minstrelsy can function variously.

> Indeed, this late in the cycle, it seems most important to notice how blackface performance can work also and simultaneously *against* racial stereotyping. The way minstrelsy saps racism from within has almost never been mentioned. Its anti-racist dimensions—occasionally abolitionist but usually supplemental to both abolitionist and anti-abolitionist doctrine—are remaining secrets among the phenomena of blackface performance.[51]

Thus the gangsta ethos represented by artists like Tupac does, I believe, serve as a model of heroic action for those who attempt to hustle their way through and, if lucky, out of the ghetto. As Michael Eric Dyson put it in a recent biography of Pac, "His art changed people's lives. His stirring raps made many people see suffering they had never before acknowledged. It helped many desperately unhappy young people reclaim a sense of hope and humanity."[52] Indeed, yet Pac's raps may not have a similar effect on young black females, unless "Shorty Wanna Be a Thug"—the title of a song on *All Eyez on Me*—is meant for little Tamika as well as little T, lil' Tremaine.

Judging from the subject of a recent documentary called *Gangstresses*, quite a few shorties, little Tamikas, are growing up to become thugz or gangstaz equal to their male counterparts. That's what they gotta do to survive, so says Mary J. Blige in one segment of the film. Yes, for the paper these women do the usual dirt—sell drugs, sell their bodies, shoplift, and operate porn businesses—but they also hustle and stay strapped to resist victimization from shiftless, no-good men. I mean, dudes be jackin' these women, muscling them out of they hustle (legit or otherwise), and women gettin' tired of it. Man, this one sista, she got beat so bad she nearly died at the hands of huh so-called man. Some do get killed. I mean straight-up domestic violence, not even because of some dude tryna squeeze a sista out of the drug business her man left her in charge of when he was sent to prison (as was dramatized in one episode of the film). Ruff Ryder First Lady, the self-proclaimed pit bull in a skirt, Eve did a touching song and video about this a few years ago called "Love Is Blind." There the sista did end up in the grave. Anyway, some crazy you-know-what like this force these women to go gangsta, to protect themselves and their families. Ain't no glamour in what they do, fo sheezy. Just hard livin' and a hard attitude to keep life from weighing too heavily on the heart. These are the musings I hear from the rhymes of Bonnie Clyde, Uneek, and Pri, three underground NYC rappers who represent those who often are the victims of gangsta bravado.

G Rap 2000 and Beyond

What will become of the gangsta ethos, rap's O.G., in the new millennium? Will he or she be shamed into submission by conservative critics like William Bennett, C. Delores Tucker, and Bill O'Reilly? Will he be increasingly overshadowed by the popularity of crossover acts like Will Smith? Media pundits have long predicted (called for?) the gangsta rapper's demise, especially after the violent, gang-style deaths of Shakur and Wallace. And the still-fresh-in-everybody's-head tragic shootings at Columbine High School in Colorado and elsewhere have bolstered their conviction. Violent rap lyrics desensitized these children to violence, they, including our then-president Bill Clinton, have said. From the rap artist's perspective, though, ain't nothing changed but the time of day. They still gangstaz, only instead of Snoop rappin' about 187s on undercover cops (on the *Deep Cover* soundtrack), he now spittin', along with Pac at the time, about a gangsta party (from Tupac and Snoop's "2 of Amerikaz Most Wanted" on *All Eyez on Me*). Look like Ice Cube was right: gangstaz don't dance but they do boogie. And they pray (Shyne's "Gangsta Prayer" on *Shyne*); cry (Bizzy Bone's "Thugz Cry" on *Heaven'z Movie*); be global, geographically and technologically (Ja Rule's "Worldwide Gangsta" on *Pain Is Love* and Trick Daddy's '98 CD *www.thug.com*); reflect more than a one-dimensional side of themselves (Styles' *A Gangster and a Gentleman*); and like no wanksta ever could, take a bullet (nine of them, actually) and live to tell many a gangsta tale (50 Cent's *Get Rich or Die Tryin'*).

So instead of falling off, G, seem like gangsta/reality rap is multiplying and stackin' mo' paper in the process. By 2-triple-0, it had made a curious yet foreseeable shift from the small-time gang banger on the streets to the big-time mafia don in the corporate boardroom. For a visual representation of this, check out the threads in the N.W.A. "Straight Outta Compton" or Snoop "What's My Name?" video compared to what you see Snoop wearing on the cover of his *Doggfather* CD or what Ice Cube sportin' as the self-proclaimed Don Mega in his "Pushin' Weight" video. Looking further over my limited collection of CDs and several *Source* and *Vibe* magazine ads just at the dawn of the new millennium, I can't help but notice the growing list of Italian mafia types: Master P on his *Da Last Don* CD; P's younger brother C-Murder (Corey Miller) on his solo

joint titled *Bossalinie;* Fat Joe dubbing himself the Puerto Rican Don of
the East on his CD *Don Cartagena;* the No Limit posse (P, C, and Silk),
who refer to themselves as Tru on a CD they entitle *Da Crime Family;*
a Tennessee group calling themselves Three 6 Mafia; and last but most
intriguing of all producer Irv Gotti's Murder Inc. label/collective, which
includes Ja Rule, R&B singer Ashanti, Vita, Charli Baltimore, Cadilac
Tah, among other heads, and the latest recruit, Nasir Jones, otherwise
known as Nasty Nas. The intrigue, well, that's due to the fact that the
name "Murder Inc." is a direct borrowing from the name of a band
of mobsters in the 1930s. I made the connection at some point when I
happened to catch a movie on cable that tells the story of these real-life
gangster hit men. And a recent (October '02) *Source* article on the Inc.
confirms their appropriation of the Albert Anastasia assassins. I guess
there's something to be said for gangster movies, at least those document-
ing history, however sordid. It clearly shows the influence of historical
fact on the gangsta ethos, the deliberate attempt to construct a collective
identity based in reality yet a pure product of the Hip hop imagination.

  In spite of these clear associations to the gangster mafia persona,
longtime Hip hop critic Nelson George denies all but a few records as
definitive of what many consider gangsta rap:

> Besides, what's gangsta rap anyway? Listen to any of
> N.W.A.'s albums, as well as Eazy-E's solo efforts, Dr. Dre's
> *The Chronic* and Snoop Doggy Dogg's *Doggystyle.* In their
> celebration of gatts, hoes, gleeful nihilism, and crack as
> the center of their economic universe, these albums darkly
> display everything people fear about gangsta rap. But
> outside of this collection of records—most of them with
> brilliantly modulated vocals supervised by Dr. Dre—I'd
> be hard-pressed to agree to label any other major rap
> star a gangsta rapper. For example, the work of Ice Cube
> (except for his insipid West Coast Connection project) and
> Scarface are way too diverse and eclectic to fit a simplistic
> mass media stereotype.[53]

George's point here is well taken. It underscores the diversity in so-called
gangsta rap. Inasmuch as G rap artists do rap about shooting, killing,
or maiming some person or group, they are surprisingly inconsistent at
conveying this message in their larger body of work. And yet I don't think
that even George would deny that reality rappers have a fetish for the
ethos of the gangsta. While one might attribute this to rappers' repeated
viewings of *The Godfather* movies and *Scarface,* I think that it's more ac-

curate to say that the communities some of these artists grew up in and, in a few cases, still live in provide ample creative material for their dark reality tales.

Ultimately, the future of G rap is going to be decided by the real-life thug life, by the day-to-day sluggin' and thuggin' in America's urban wastelands: New Orleans's Third Ward; H-Town's Fifth and Third Wards; inner-city Cleveland; Cali's Oak Town, LBC, and South Central, LA; NY's five boroughs; and the city of Washington, DC, the subject of a fairly recent HBO documentary called *Thug Life in DC*. The young bloods (many as young as fifteen or sixteen) who appear in this documentary are all doing time in prison for being real gangstaz (small time but nonetheless real and dangerous). For instance, one seventeen-year-old inmate who goes by "Bruno" is on lockdown for shootin' a policeman and murdering another teenager. When asked by the warden what makes him a thug, Bruno confidently responds: "I'm the definition of a thug. Ain't run no games. I don't go for nothin'. Ain't gon let nobody chump me if they big or small. Ain't goin' for nothin'. I'm gonna handle mine the best way I can. If I gotta stab somebody, kill somebody, take somebody's stuff . . . do what I can. . . . If I can't get any, I take it." Now sentenced to twenty-five years to life and nearly two years after said interview—the reality of his mistake thus having set in—Bruno sheds a bit of his earlier defiant air and bold proclamation of thug life. His is a sad story, no doubt, but the real tragedy is that so many boys (and increasingly, girls) like Bruno assume prison or death to be their lot in life, what Cornel West once called hopelessness[54] but what I prefer to call hope unfulfilled. That may be why devotion to thug life comes through so forcefully in the music; the art reflects the self and the self reflects its conditioning, a condition not of hope in grand ideals but in the ambiguity between real and ideal. As Bruno says in his response to the warden's next question about how he came to develop this attitude, he says rather uncertainly, "Don't know; guess it's in my blood." Blood? More likely, the paradigm—for so many brothas before him have blazed that dim, yet discrete trail.

So, unless DC and so many other urban wastelands (like New Orleans's Third Ward, billed as "One of the Deadliest Projects in America" in a *Murder Dog* ad for the DVD *Straight from the Projects: Rappers that Live the Lyrics*) soon become urban oases, how can we honestly knock G rappers' hustle? But, hey, go ahead knock what they be rappin' if you wanna, but if you ever happen to find yourself, say, in a place called Brownsville (home of Brooklyn rappers M.O.P.), you might not wanna question the reality of what they allude to in "Ante Up." Think gangsterism is Hip hop hype elsewhere in Bucktown? Well, not so according to this very *real* sign posted on the NYC Olympia bus lines:

Don't be Hustled!

Protect yourself and your belongings. If a hustler solicits you, refuse.

Hustlers will threaten you or will keep your belongings if you don't pay what they demand. Hustlers are not
licensed and do not have insurance.

Man, just think—if cities started issuing licenses for hustling and insurance companies started doling out policies, then brothas and sistas could
legitimize they hustlin', form unions for hustlers' rights. Seriously, though,
the young cats in *Thug Life in DC* are a sad testament to Common's line
in "The 6th Sense" about street dreams being deferred. If young brothas
like Bruno had any real dreams of escaping the ghetto through street
hustling, those dreams have clearly been deferred for them, for those who
love them, and for those in their community who at one time saw hope
for the future in the younger generation. And yet, these days quite a few
rappers still profess thug life, in much the same way as Bruno does. But
even there, whether it's the L.O.X. (D Block), G Unit, or Trick Daddy,
proclaiming oneself a thug (or gangsta) is more a sensibility, an ethos
than a profession. Though most of us wouldn't want our young'uns emu-
lating Trick Daddy's dining etiquette (or lack thereof) in his "I'm a Thug"
video, I gotta give it to him for using the medium to critique class preju-
dices and racial stereotypes and to represent the humanity of Hip hop's
thugz. After all, who can blame the man for preferring Wangs-n-Thangs
takeout over the overpriced fare at some upscale French restaurant?

"

I'm a Black man
A pimp
All the swinging, young hip brothers dig me
I'm their symbol; I'm real
With me they can relate and associate
You see, I came from those same shabby shacks
Wore those same funky rags on my back
But growing up in a world of dog eat dog I learned
That the dirtiest dog got the bone
Meaning not the dog with the loudest bark
But the dog with the coldest heart
I became the North Pole
Cold, cold, cold, cold
My blood is like ice water in my veins
Which the engine of my heart keep pushing through the deep
    freeze of my frame
I take hoe money and feel no pain
Like White men do, only White men pimp niggas and lames
That's where I got the idea for the game
Bunco, that's what it is
But not that lame shit like the white-boys play
Because once I start playing the game, I improved it right away
You see, I wear a hundred-dollar fronts and two-hundred-dol-
    lar slides
And a hog is the only thing in which I ride
And niggas can't get that dignified
I have two and three grands in my pocket everyday
Hoes doe [cold?] king is the name of the game I play
But you know folks tell me, that if I had applied my ability in
    another way
Ain't no telling where I would be today
Because I'm so damn [cute]
White girls melt like butter when they look into this pretty tan
    face of mine
Black girls, well, they know I'm fine
Keen and mean and don't give a damn
But I know the truth
If I had a Masters, I wouldn't be a damn bit fu[r]ther
I'd just be fooling myself and selling out my brother
I'd still be unhappy
Because I'm black! And I'm not free
I want freedom, freedom, freedom now!
So you better watch out for me
Cause I'm a Black man, a timebomb destined to explode
But you can't tell where I'm coming from
And the next time instead of buying a cadillac, I'm gonna buy
    myself a gun
        Otis Smith of the Watts Prophets, "A Pimp"

"

4

The Player's [Book] Club: Ghetto Realistic Fiction from "His Last Day" to "Pimpology"

Homegirl musta forgotten all about the "political part" Melvin Van Peebles spoke of in the excerpt I showed from the PBS documentary *I'll Make Me a World,* 'cause as soon as she saw the opening scene of *Sweet Sweetback's Baadasssss Song* with Van Peebles's very young son Mario acting out a sexually explicit scene with a woman—a prostitute—twice his age, she jetted. Naively, I had hoped that she left the room to get water or use the restroom, but in the back of my mind I knew she was disturbed by the scene and would not return to view the rest of the film. (The student did, however, remain in the course, but I promised her that I would let her know if similar scenes appeared in the other films we were scheduled to view.) Although at the time I thought that I had adequately prepped the class for our screening of *Sweet Sweetback's Baadasssss Song,* I don't blame her for opting not to view it since I clearly hadn't given enough forewarning about the contents of the film to soften the blow of that shocking first scene.

In class two days later when we discussed the film, that scene came up again. In fact, it colored many students' impressions and judgments of the entire film. These students simply couldn't rationalize the director's use of a child—a ten-, eleven-, or twelve-year-old boy—to play a role like that, even though midway through that brief scene the character of the young boy transforms into a full-grown man (played by Melvin Van Peebles himself). Several times I tried discussing other, more prominent aspects of the film, like why so much of it covered the main character

Sweetback (Van Peebles) literally running about the city, but some students kept bringing up that opening scene and a couple of other scenes that were similarly explicit. And yet all of the students seemed to recognize the basic plot: Sweetback is an orphan kid taken in by prostitutes at a whorehouse. They happily feed him, give him new clothes, and put him to work as a towel boy. Once he matures, he learns their lurid trade and becomes a main attraction at their freak show, a bizarre sex play that caters largely to blacks but also to some whites in what appears to be inner-city LA. Two white cops show up one night during a performance and coerce Beetle, the proprietor of the whorehouse and freak show, into loaning them one of his men to lock up for a night so that they can demonstrate to their superiors that they're doing their job. Reluctantly (largely due to the potential lost profit), Beetle tells Sweetback to go with the officers for the night. Now, while they was driving along in the squad car, the po-po receive a call on the radio 'bout a disturbance. See, another squad had busted up a meeting of black revolutionaries (some would-be Panther types). With Sweetback in tow, the officers arrive and arrest the young leader of the group, Mu-Mu (or Moo-Moo), and shortly thereafter begin goin' Rodney King on him right there, with Sweetback handcuffed to one of them. Well, Sweetback can't just stand there and watch the young brotha get violated like that for no apparent reason, so after a few minutes' hesitation he takes the handcuffs dangling from one of his wrists, wraps the loose end around his knuckles, and boo-ya! He goes ballistic on them crooked cops, beating them almost to death (later, I believe, they do die). After whupping up on them cops, you know Sweetback has to step. So the rest of the movie (roughly 75 to 80 percent) is about Sweetback running from the cops all over the city and later the desert on his way to Mexico, tryna get help from this or that person along the way and sometimes (at least with the women) having to use his sweet back, his stock and trade, to get it.

My students picked up on most of these aspects of the film, but that didn't really alter their view about what they considered the extremely poor taste of that opening scene. And, to be quite honest, it's hard to argue against their point. After all, why make the subtext of Sweetback's every action—even his very mark of identity, his name—signify sexual prowess? Why play on such a blatant stereotype of black masculinity? Unfortunately, I didn't have much of an answer for them. Certainly, Van Peebles could have made a potent enough political statement without Sweetback's signature *sweet back,* as some students suggested, but I couldn't altogether agree with them that the story as such would have been any more realistic or its message any more compelling. Sure, those explicit scenes do distort Van Peebles's political message to some degree, but such distortion is not uncommon in life as in art. In fact, it makes for a more complex representation of urban social conditions that Sweetback starts out prostituting himself for a living (he never seems to engage in any sexual activity for the sheer pleasure of it) and progressively becomes revolutionary rather than starting out that way, say, as the activist Mu-Mu does or even as the religiously devout reverend appears to do. Maybe I'm too influenced by our reading of Black Panther leader Huey P. Newton's political analysis of the film. In "He Won't Bleed Me: A Revolutionary Analysis of *Sweet Sweetback's Baadasssss Song*," Newton infers the social and political implications of Sweetback's occupation.

> They are in a house of prostitution not of their own will but because of the conditions the oppressor makes for us. They are there to survive and they sell their love to do so, therefore our love is distorted and corrupted with the sale. When you have nothing else left you give up your body, just as when you are starving you might eat your fingers; but it is the conditions which cause this, not the desire to taste your own blood; you have to survive. . . . .
>
> What happens is not a distorted act of prostitution even though it takes place in a house of prostitution. The place is profane because of the oppressive conditions, but so are our communities also oppressed. The Black community is often profane because of the dirtiness there, but this is not caused by the people because they are the victims of a very oppressive system.
>
> Yet within the heart of the community, just as in the film, the sacred rite of feeding and nourishing the youth goes on; they are brought to their manhood as liberators.[1]

None of us entirely bought Newton's interpretation, especially his patriarchal notion that Sweetback symbolizes the heroic liberator of the women who raised him (his sweet, sweet back notwithstanding). Still we were struck (well, some of us anyway) by his point that the prostitution in the film (and in real life) has more to do with illustrating systemic oppression and victimization than with exploiting the sexual mores of black men and women. Though often branded by conservatives as a liberal cop-out, the racial-victimization angle makes some sense when one considers how African Americans ended up in the ghettos of America's cities in the first place. But if Newton is right that through the character of Sweetback—however stereotypical he may appear to be to some of us—Van Peebles is "righteously signifying,"[2] then the message about victimization and redemption may be forever lost to many viewers.

The movie soundtrack Van Peebles recorded with '70s soul band
Earth Wind & Fire also reflects the revolutionary impulses of the film. In
particular, the "baadasssss song," titled "Sweetback Getting It Uptight
and Preaching It So Hard the Bourgeois Reggin' Angels in Heaven Turn
Around," underscores Newton's point about generations of black oppression and Sweetback's noble attempt to break the cycle. Witness the
exchange between Sweetback and the Bourgeois Reggin' (I read somewhere that this word is "nigger" spelled backward, and, based on my
knowledge of Van Peebles's work, I would say that it probably is) Angels
in the following lines. The excerpt is from Newton's essay; however, I
place in italics Sweetback's responses to the Angels' cynical remarks.

They bled your mama
They bled your papa
But he won't bleed me

Use your black ass from sun to sun
Niggers scared and pretend they don't see
Deep down dirty dog scared

Just like you Sweetback

Just like I used to be
Work your black behind to the gums
And you supposed to thomas tell [sic] *he done*

You got to thomas Sweetback
They bled your brother
They bled your sister
Yeah, but they won't bleed me

Progress Sweetback

That's what he wants you to believe

No progress Sweetback

He ain't stopped clubbing us for 400 years
And he don't intend to for a million

He sure treat us bad Sweetback
We can make him do us better

Chicken ain't nothing but a bird
White man ain't nothing but a turd
Nigger ain't shit

Get my hands on a trigger

You talkin' revolution Sweetback

I wanta get off these knees

You talkin' revolution Sweetback[3]

Resistance to racial oppression clearly pervades the song, but the song appears late in the film, long after "Sweetback Losing His Cherry"—the song that accompanies the opening scene my student jetted on. Van Peebles's indelicate mixture of sacred (the church choir singing of religious hymns "Wade in the Water" and "This Little Light of Mine") and secular (the in-yo-face visuals of the young, yet-to-be-named Sweetback losing his cherry) elements in the scene may have been tantamount to blasphemy for this black female student of middle-class, Christian upbringing, but for other students, especially the men (all white except for two), the scene simply made the politics of the film somewhat difficult to discern.

Given this confusion and controversy, you might ask, what was I thinking when I decided to show my class *Sweet Sweetback's Baadasssss Song*? Why would I wish to expose students to what some (then in the '70s when the movie first appeared and now nearly thirty years later as the Hip hop community rediscovers it) consider the more sensationalized and morally degrading aspects of African American culture? Well, as a rhetorical critic, I ain't inclined to dismiss cultural or pop-cultural material simply because it's deemed by some as morally reprehensible or because some black folk think it make us look bad. On the contrary, I think that we look just as bad (if not worse) if we (especially black critics and intellectuals who claim the right to speak for *us*) have absolutely no understanding of such material, for then we subject ourselves to the uninformed and biased views of others, liberal or conservative, who have little or no genuine interest in the welfare of America's urban ghettos (except of course when it profits them, as is often the case with record executives who rack up million-dollar record sales off the latest ghetto rap star signed to their label). And besides, as I told my students from day one, my idea for the course on black pulp fiction wasn't about perpetuating stereotypes or pathologies of black social behavior but about trying to understand *black ghetto hustling culture* (the term used by ethnographers Christina and Richard Milner in *Black Players: The Secret World of Black Pimps*) through critical engagement with its various forms of artistic representation. Not that I always agree with the author's, director's, or lyricist's representation, but I ain't mad at 'em for puttin' it down like they did on wax, on screen, and on paper, cuz—like it or not—The Life has been and still is an integral part of black ghetto culture and can't be denied artistic expression. But anyway, back to what I was sayin' 'bout *Sweetback*.

With its curious mixture of politics and pulp, Van Peebles's *Sweet Sweetback's Baadasssss Song* may be considered one of the earliest cinematic representations of ghetto realistic fiction, for after it came the "pure" pulp genre critics refer to as blaxploitation, which brought to life on the silver screen the lives of black ghetto pimps, prostitutes, drug pushers, gangsters, thieves, con artists, and the like earlier fiction writers described on the page and, to a lesser extent, on wax (e.g., in recorded street toasts). But what is *ghetto realistic fiction*? Is it another name for what the literati call *pulp fiction*? Not exactly, though at times I find it convenient to use the two expressions interchangeably. True, both are standard pulp—that is, rife with the usual lowbrow, sensational material (street crime, brutal violence, graphic sex, drug abuse, and vulgar language)—but *ghetto realistic fiction* has far more to do with the subculture of the black urban poor than mere pulp fiction. Quentin Tarantino's hit movie *Pulp Fiction*, for example, is definitely pulp, but it isn't what I'd call *ghetto realistic fiction* because, though clearly influenced by the blaxploitation movie genre, it doesn't really depict black ghetto hustling culture or contribute to the development of the expressive genre one critic calls *ghetto realism*.

In what follows, I make a case for viewing black pulp like Gordon Parks, Jr.'s *Super Fly,* Iceberg Slim's *Pimp,* and Too Short's "Pimpology" as varied expressions of *ghetto realism*. Actually, from street toasts about The Life to films, books, and music on ghetto hustling culture, one can see a long tradition of ghetto realistic fiction no less relevant to African American cultural identity and experience, I would argue, than the canonized works of African American literature. Stocked with volume after volume of ghetto realistic fiction, that is, the player's (book) club tells the story of the playa in us all.

BEEN KEEPIN' IT REAL: GHETTO REALISM FROM OLD SCHOOL TOAST TO HIP HOP BOAST

While not a few rap artists undeservedly justify their violent street tales with the now-hackneyed pronouncement that they're "keepin' it real," the phrase nonetheless might aptly apply not only to a subgenre of rap music called gangsta/reality rap but also to a (sub)genre of African American literature that one critic has dubbed *ghetto realism*. Reportedly, the term was coined by Greg Goode in a 1984 article in *MELUS*, the journal of the Society for the Study of the Multi-ethnic Literature of the United States, but one would be hard-pressed to find the term referred to there. Titled "From *Dopefiend* to *Kenyatta's Last Hit:* The Angry Black Crime Novels of Donald Goines," the article presents a nice overview of the pulp novels of Donald Goines (a.k.a. Al C. Clark) but, for whatever reason, only hints at the concept of *ghetto realism*. The passage where Goode appears to allude to the concept is the following: "Nevertheless the Goines corpus is important because it is perhaps the most sustained, realistic, multifaceted, widespread fictional picture ever created by one author of the lives, activities, and frustrations of poor urban Blacks."[4] Goines's publisher Holloway House has printed this very statement on the back cover of some of his books (e.g., *White Man's Justice, Black Man's Grief,* and *Death List*), yet with some modest but significant revision. Still attributed to critic Greg Goode, this modified version of the statement introduces the term *ghetto realism:*

> In his five-year literary career, Donald Goines provided perhaps the most sustained, multifaceted, realistic fiction picture ever created by one author of the lives, choices, and frustrations of underworld ghetto blacks. Almost single-handedly, Goines established the conventions and popular momentum for a new fiction genre, which could be called ghetto realism.[5]

With the exception of a few lexical changes in the first sentence, the addition of the second sentence clearly is the most recognizable change in Goode's statement about Goines's works. Apparently, Goode sees Goines's "realistic fiction picture" of the "lives, choices, and frustrations of underworld ghetto blacks" as constituting not just one writer's stylistic idiosyncrasies but an entire literary genre. That's a mighty bold assertion, considering how purist literary scholars tend to be about classifications of literature. Yet, considering the sixteen novels Donald Goines authored, the claim has some validity and may even be groundbreaking in literary criticism—if, that is, we can be sure what precisely Goode means by the term. As we've seen, Goode's definition of ghetto realism is rather inconclusive, more general observation than theoretical proposition. In the article I cited earlier (sans the cognomen *ghetto realism*), about the closest we come to a detailed explication of the term is, presumably, the following statement in which Goode characterizes Goines's various works.

Because Goines's ghettos are like zero-sum-game societies in which one man's gain must be another's loss, his characters cannot thrive or even survive without breaking the law. His books are automatically crime novels similar to the way in which *Caleb Williams* is a crime novel. The law broken is sometimes the white man's legal code, and sometimes the Ghetto Golden Rule:

What goes around comes around. Often, therefore, the sadistic pimp loses his best woman, the murderer dies, the hustler gets sent to jail, and a sort of automatic inner city justice is maintained. In other books, all the major characters die. In these books Goines seems to be expressing the hopelessness of life in the ghetto.[6]

"Zero-sum-game societies," "the Ghetto Golden Rule," and ghetto hopelessness appear from this passage to be the major characteristics of Goines's ghetto realism genre of black fiction. Apparently having access to some "other" version of Goode's *MELUS* essay, however, Goines biographer Eddie Stone introduces other characteristics of the genre. In the epilogue of *Donald Writes No More: A Biography of Donald Goines,* Stone quotes from the essay the general theme of Goines's fiction:

As Greg Goode has written: "The overall theme of the Goines corpus, however, seems to be that the ghetto life of the underprivileged black produces a frustrating, dangerous double-bind effect. One has only two choices, neither wholly desirable. One may settle for membership in the ghetto's depressed, poverty-stricken silent majority, or opt for dangerous ghetto stardom. Goines' characters do the latter; they become pimps, prostitutes, pushers, numbers operators, thieves, gangsters, and contract hit men. This choice extracts its price, for the characters, even those who have the reader's sympathy, lose their humanity as they gain success. Because 'what goes around comes around' and because even the novels' protagonists are forced to exploit, cheat and kill even loved ones in order to survive, it is not uncommon that most of Goines' major characters die violent, often horrible deaths."[7]

The Ghetto Golden Rule (What go around come around) is again mentioned here, but the notion of a "double-bind effect" differs from anything in the primary Goode text (i.e., the sans ghetto realism version)—unless, however, it is an alternative expression for "zero-sum-game societies." Quite possibly, the two concepts are closely linked, yet I'm inclined to see the "double-bind effect" as a distinct aspect of ghetto realism—as, in fact, definitive of the genre because it seems to be an underlying assumption of ghetto existence. You either get ovuh through hustlin' (pimping, hoing, thieving, slangin' cane, and the like) or you don't get ovuh at all; there's no "real" third option. As Goines himself puts it in the words of his young gangsta protagonist Prince, "There are two kinds of people in the world: the haves and the have-nots. If you were hungry, if you needed clothes, if your rent was overdue—take it. It was better to be a taker than one of those who got took!"[8]

Stone believes Goines to have been "just about the only writer who ever practiced" ghetto realism, but the way I see it brothas and sistas been creatin' ghetto realistic stories since the street toasts of the 1930s, if not earlier. To take just one example, a toast called "Sporting Life" succinctly captures the spirit of ghetto realism:

> You forget the quote that the Christians wrote
> About honesty and fair play,
> For you can't live sweet not knowing how to cheat;
> The Game don't play that way.[9]

Of course, I'm not suggesting here that toasts represent ghetto realism to the same degree that Goines's novels do. I simply submit that if there is such a genre called "ghetto realism," then one will find evidence of it first in the African American oral tradition and later in the literature of Donald Goines.

In fact, if my understanding of the concept is accurate, then ghetto realistic fiction may have preceded Goines not only in the oral tradition but in African American literature as well. That is to say, Goines may be just one of many writers between, say, the '30s and the '70s whose work has established the ghetto realism school of fiction. Since highbrow literary publisher W. W. Norton has done the unthinkable and reissued some long-neglected black ghetto crime novels in what Norton editors Marc Gerald and Samuel Blumenfeld have dubbed the Old School Books series,[10] the mainstream public has now been made aware of other black fiction writers who published their works a decade or more before Goines but, for whatever reasons, never received the ghetto acclaim that Goines did. Gerald claims to have discovered forty of these obscure writers,[11] though not all of them wrote about the ghetto underworld. While we needn't concern ourselves here with who, if not Goines, wrote the very first piece of ghetto realistic fiction, the pioneering work of these early writers is surely worth acknowledging as a critical part of a venerable black ghetto realistic oral and literate tradition.

Of those works reissued in the Old School Books series, chronologically, the following appeared before Goines's first novel, *Dopefiend*, in 1971. First, Chester Himes's prison novel titled *Yesterday Will Make You Cry*, which appeared in 1952 originally as *Cast the First Stone*, is an expurgated pure pulp version that Himes's editors imposed on him in place of *Yesterday*. (Likely unaware of this, ironically, Goines paid tribute to this latter version of the novel when he wrote his own prison story in 1973, called *White Man's Justice, Black Man's Grief*. I should also note here a short story Himes wrote well before *Cast the First Stone*. Written while Himes was serving time for robbery in the Ohio State Penitentiary, "His Last Day" was published in *Abbott's Monthly* in 1933 and is, thus, a very early example of ghetto realistic fiction, particularly the zero-sum-game philosophy of the main character Spats.)[12] Second, there is Herbert Simmons's 1957 novel *Corner Boy*, about a teenage drug dealer who meets with a tragic end. Third, you have Clarence Cooper, Jr.'s 1960 novel *The Scene*, which vividly depicts the ravages of inner-city drug addiction, a condition Cooper himself, like Goines, suffered from throughout much of his life. Fourth is Charles Perry's 1962 James Joyceian novel *Portrait of a Young Man Drowning*, though, like Himes's *Yesterday Will Make You Cry*, its main characters are underworld whites instead of blacks. And fifth, there are two additional works by Clarence Cooper—one a 1963 novella about the numbers racket called "Yet Princes Follow" (published in a collection titled *Black!*), and the other a 1967 novel called *The Farm* about a love story set in a federal drug rehabilitation center. Some other early pulp novels that weren't, to my knowledge, republished by Norton but have been recently printed by other presses include Clarence Cooper's *The Syndicate* (1960) and *Weed* (1961) by Payback Press (1998), and Robert Deane Pharr's *The Book of Numbers* (1969) by the University Press of Virginia (2001). In '73, Pharr's story about a couple of numbers runners in 1930s Richmond was also made into a film of the same name directed by Raymond St. Jacques.[13] Cooper's *The Syndicate* is an urban pulp tale not unlike Tarantino's *Pulp Fiction* or Goines's *Daddy Cool*, yet the protagonist, Andy Sorrell, a syndicate hit man, appears to be white, as do most of the characters in the novel. *Weed*, on the other hand, is peopled with the black working class and the variously delinquent (drug pushers and users, whorehouse proprietors, prostitutes and johns, pool hustlers, adulterers, murderers). In spite of (or perhaps in light of) the delinquency of most of the characters (including Cullen, the police detective who turns a blind eye to the whorehouse because of his love for one of its women), Cooper's work reveals the depth of their humanity, the intricate psychological underpinning of human relationships.

Like I said, all of that was before Donald Goines got hipped to the writin' game and dropped his first piece in '71. Goines wrote sixteen novels in the short span between 1971 and 1974, the year that he and his wife were gunned down at his apartment in Detroit. *Dopefiend* was published in '71; *Whoreson* (though written before *Dopefiend*) in '72, along with *Black Gangster* and *Street Players; White Man's Justice, Black Man's Grief,* and *Black Girl Lost* appeared in '73; *Eldorado Red, Swamp Man, Never Die Alone, Crime Partners, Death List, Daddy Cool, Cry Revenge!* and *Kenyatta's Escape* all came out in '74; and finally *Kenyatta's Last Hit* and *Inner City Hoodlum* were published posthumously in '75. Around the same time that Goines began writing fiction and years later, other writers apparently took up the ghetto-realistic-fiction mantle. Norton has reissued some of the works of these writers, such as Pharr's second novel, *S.R.O.,* a rather odd semi-autobiographical work about the assorted drunks, drug addicts, prostitutes, and pushers who populate a dilapidated Harlem hotel; Pharr's fifth novel, *Giveadamn Brown* (1978), a dark comedy about a young man's underworld rise through drug pushing and numbers running; Vern Smith's 1974 novel *The Jones Men,* on the lucrative but dangerous drug business; and finally Roland Jefferson's pulp/protest novel *The School on 103rd Street* (1976), concerning a mysterious murder that took place in riot-torn Watts of the early '70s. Around 1975, Pharr also published his third and forth novels, *The Welfare Bitch* and *The Soul Murder Case,* but both remain out of print.

Most of these ghetto crime novels, critics seem to agree, are better written than are Goines's novels. And in the Black Pulp Fiction course, my students found Clarence Cooper's *The Scene* a far more "literary" novel (read: more like the canonical fare in English lit courses) than the extremely pulpy Goines novels we read, *Whoreson* and *Black Gangster.* I tend to agree with them on that, which leads me to believe that perhaps Cooper's primary audience was really the literary establishment, not necessarily people who resemble the characters in his books—that is, the black ghettorati who relish a good story styled in street vernacular. In this sense, Stone may be right to argue that Goines's novels constitute a literary genre unto themselves. They often reflect the then-current idiom of The Life and, more important, the sophisticated street knowledge and experience that Goines, unlike other writers, acquired through years of having participated in The Life and having suffered some of its grisly consequences (e.g., living in perpetual fear of incarceration or death).

But even if the black authors I've mentioned didn't write their stories ostensibly for ghetto audiences—actually some of them probably did, but few of them, it seems, with the possible exception of Cooper, were really a part of the ghetto hustling subculture to the degree that Goines was—

Goines still wasn't the first ghetto-hustler-turned-writer to exhibit an intimate knowledge of The Life in novels directed to a primarily black ghetto audience. If no one else, certainly Iceberg Slim (a.k.a. Robert Beck)—who published at least three books before Goines, *Pimp: The Story of My Life* and *Trick Baby* in 1967, and *Mama Black Widow* in 1969—deserves that distinction. Though not quite as prolific as Goines, Iceberg Slim did, however, write a total of eight books (albeit not all novels) over a ten- or twelve-year period. After publishing the three novels (*Pimp,* his first, being the more autobiographical of the three), Iceberg went on to publish in 1971 a collection of essays called *The Naked Soul of Iceberg Slim;* he wrote and published several short stories between '76 and '79 that were collected in a volume titled *Airtight Willie & Me,* released in '79. *Long White Con* and *Death Wish* appeared in '77, and reportedly his last work, a novel called *Doom Fox,* was written in '78 but wasn't published before his death in 1992. The book was picked up by Grove Press and published in '98 with a forward by LA rapper and actor Ice-T.

Quite strangely, while Stone acknowledges Beck's influence on Goines in portions of *Donald Writes No More,* in the epilogue of the book he makes no mention of Beck's novels in connection with *ghetto realism.* Perhaps Stone sees his novels as markedly different from Goines's. Having covered more aspects of street life (from dope fiends to pimps, hit men, gangsters, numbers runners, and even the prison system) and in a somewhat more gritty, unrefined style than Berg, Goines is clearly no clone of the man he once strove to emulate. And yet, such characteristics of Goines's writing do not, I would argue, necessarily make him a more "ghetto realistic" prose writer than Berg. In fact, because of his careful attention to detail in his character sketches and dialogues, Iceberg Slim's fiction tends to exude "ghetto realism" on every page. This is especially true of Slim's depiction of the pimp's use of the language of deception, which I discuss later on.

Apart from the novels published in the '70s, the Spoken Word poetry of this period also reflects aspects of ghetto realism. Probably the best examples of this are the Watts Prophets' poem "A Pimp," which I cite in the epigraph, and Lightnin' Rod's *Hustlers Convention,* though the latter kind of dismisses The Life in the end. In spite of seemingly counterrevolutionary impulses in "A Pimp," the Prophets (Otis Smith in particular) make no compromises about the black man's alternatives, for true (social and political) freedom for the black man, so it goes, won't come through the earning of graduate degrees but by playing the same game (i.e., pimping) the white man has played on "niggers and lames"—only playing it better, or failing that, resorting to revolutionary action (i.e., arms).

An even more popular form of media that has contributed to the development of ghetto realistic fiction in the early to mid-'70s is the blaxploitation movie. Now I know civil rights groups like the NAACP de-monized such films when they first appeared (starting with *Shaft* in '71 and *Superfly* in '72) because of their concern about the films' negative depictions of black culture. Since Hollywood hadn't shown any serious interest in black cinema generally or in positive, consciousness-raising black images in particular prior to blaxploitation films (the Hollywood-pimping-the-hood school of cinema, you might say), it makes perfect sense for the NAACP to protest the making of these films. On the other hand, though, Hollywood's pimpin' of the ghetto[14] doesn't negate the ghetto realities it tried to depict. And it don't negate either the enormous popularity of the films then with the baby boomer generation and now among the Hip hop generation. That's not to say that the depictions are free of negative stereotyping—for often they're laden wit 'em—but that a stock element in many of the films appears to be the "double-bind effect" Goode considers the overall theme of Goines's ghetto realistic fiction. We saw a bit of this already in the pre-blaxploitation flick *Sweet Sweetback's Baadasssss Song*, though because of the film's sparse dialogue it's not so easy to discern. Even Goode claims a link between the criminal pro-tagonists in Goines's novels and outlaw blaxploitation heroes like "Sweet Sweetback, Slaughter, Trouble Man, The Mack, Willie Dynamite, Black Gunn, Black Caesar, the Black Godfather, Black Samson, and Blackbelt Jones."[15]

One of the best early examples of the "double-bind effect" in a blax-ploitation film is Gorden Parks, Jr.'s *Superfly*, released in 1972, the same year that Goines published his second, third, and fourth novels (*Whore-son: The Story of a Ghetto Pimp, Black Gangster,* and *Street Players*). In the film, the main character, a drug pusher named Youngblood Priest (Ron O'Neal), wants out of The Life and his plan is to make one last score so that he'll be set for life. But as Priest attempts to free himself from The Life, he engages in some interesting dialogue about the ghetto condition. In the first of such encounters, his partner, Eddie (Carl Lee), runs down the hustler's rationale for participating in The Life.

> Priest: I'm gettin' out Eddie.
> Eddie: Gettin' out of what?
> P: The cocaine business.
> E: Oh, Sweet Jesus, man those junkies must've knocked a hole in your head. You gon' give all this up? Eight track stereo, color TV in every room, and can snort half a piece of dope everyday. That's the American dream, nigga! Well, ain't it? Ain't it? You better come on in, man.
> P: How much money we got, Eddie?
> E: About $300,000. That's a hundred and fifty each. It's

about enough to keep your nose open for about a year. I
know it's a rotten game. It's the only one the Man left us to
play. And that's the stone cold truth.

The life that Priest now enjoys is the American dream, Eddie assures him, and it could only be so by the "rotten game" (drug dealing or
hustling in general) that the white man has left for brothas and sistas to
play. One might seriously question the veracity of Eddie's claim here, but
right or wrong it's a common perception held by persons in The Life and,
to some extent, in the ghetto at large. In a later conversation between
the two partners, after an impromptu meeting with some cops who are
on the take in the drug business, Eddie further points out the futility of
the ghetto hustler trying to earn a living in what they deem the *square*
world.

> Eddie: When I get out what I'm gonna do? I don't know
> nothing else but dope, baby. Taking it, selling it, bankrolling
> some other small-time pusher. Hell, you got this fantasy
> in yo head about gettin' out of The Life and settin' that
> other world on its ear. What the fuck are you gonna do
> except hustle? Besides pimping and you really ain't got the
> stomach for that. Now, man I ain't puttin' you down. If it
> wasn't for you I probably wouldn't be here. I'd be ODed
> some place. I'm just trying to make it[?] real, baby, like it
> is. I mean[?], maybe this is what you supposed to do, this
> is what you grow into.

Priest doesn't respond here to Eddie's criticism of his plan, but in another scene that takes place at Central Park with his main woman Georgia (played by the supersweet and sophisticated Shelia Frazier), Priest
gives his perspective on what awaits him in that "other world."

> Georgia: Look, maybe you should get out now before
> something really bad happens. I could be happy with a
> plain life, poor one even. . . .
> P: What would I do? With my record I can't even work
> civil service or join the damn army. If I quit now, then I
> took all this chance for nothin', and I go back to being
> nothin', workin' some jive job for chump change day after
> day. Look, if that's all I'm supposed to do, then they gon
> have to kill me cause that ain't nothin'.
> G: What will you do when you get out?
> P: I don't know. Not so much what we do, it's having a

choice, being able to decide what it is I want. Not just to
be forced into a thing because that's the way it is. Gon buy
me some time, baby—some time that isn't fucked up with
things we gotta do. Just to be free.
G: And will that make you happy?
P: I don't know. I don't know. I just know I can't be happy
the way it is now, and I never was.

Much like Eddie, Priest is determined to live his life comfortably,
only he wants to do so without the mental and physical strain of having to hustle for it. He wanna be free to choose what to do with his life,
instead of being obliged, say, to a low-paying job because, he supposes,
there ain't much else for a black man in square White America. Life has
to mean more than that for Priest; he can't be something while working
for nothing.

My man Huggy Bear, I mean Link (played by Antonio Fargas), expresses the same sentiment in director Jack Hill's *Foxy Brown* (1974).
Though the movie focuses more on Link's sister, Foxy Brown (the original Foxy, none other than the superfine Pam Grier)—that is, on how bad
and yet how sexy Foxy is—the two of them at one point engage in a striking conversation about the "double bind" that ghetto blacks, especially
black men like Link, find themselves in. And ironically, though she herself
is apparently secure with her life's work (the nature of which is never
actually revealed in the film), Foxy doesn't have a clue what her brother
should do for an honest living.

Link: Foxy, look, I'm a black man, and I don't know how
to sing and I don't know how to dance and I don't know
how to preach to no congregation. I'm too small to be a
football hero, and I'm too ugly to be elected mayor. When
I watch TV, and I see all them people and all them fine
homes they live in and all them nice cars they drive and I
get all full of ambition. You tell me what I'm supposed to
do with all this ambition I got.
Foxy: I don't know, Link. I just don't want to see you end
up in jail or shot down in the street somewhere.

Up to the time of this exchange with Foxy, Link has been dealing
drugs for a local crime organization but has promised her that he would
look for some kind of honest work (which was really just a ruse to get
her off his back). Actually, he believes that hustling is the only way he
can ever come close to having the luxuries that he sees lavishly displayed
on TV. He dismisses the customary paths of (limited) success for ghetto

men—entertainment, sports, preaching, and politics (which, I believe, was only an option in certain chocolate cities at the time like Detroit)— because he don't fit the profile. Thus, like Priest and Eddie in *Superfly,* Link lives an all-or-nothing kind of existence. He aims to be a rising star in the ghetto, but, having sold out Foxy's man, an undercover narcotics agent, to the mob to settle a debt, he in the end loses not only his integrity but also his life. He gets checked, in other words, by the Ghetto Golden Rule: What go around come around.

That's 'bout how it went down in the ghetto in the '70s, or so it would seem from the novels and films I've reviewed. Brothas and sistas (though in many blaxploitation films, for some reason, the sistas—except for the pimp's hos—seem to have legit jobs and generally be on the right side of the law) had to hustle hard to get them a slice of that American pie. (This aesthetic or rhetorical principle, I believe, is the driving force behind contemporary films like *New Jack City, Boyz N the Hood, Menace II Society, South Central,* and, director John Singleton's more recent hood-ography, *Baby Boy*—but, hey, that's a whole 'notha essay.) Perhaps to an unrealistic degree these books and films play up the "do or die" mentality of ghetto living. In most of these works, in fact, we scarcely hear from the "depressed, poverty-stricken silent majority" that constitutes, according to Stone, the other membership of the ghetto.[16] Were their voices more prominently featured in the aforementioned works, would then black pulp fiction more accurately represent ghetto life? Does the ghetto majority, in other words, suffer from the same deterministic or hopeless outlook on life as the ghetto hustler? And if they choose not to hustle their way out of impoverishment, are they then any less "real" than those who do? These are difficult questions to answer. Certainly, from a sociological perspective, the ghetto (nonhustler) community member is an integral part of the urban ghetto scene, without whom there could be no proper representation of the ghetto subculture. On the other hand, though, from a strictly aesthetic perspective, artistic expression isn't designed to represent every community member's lived experience or perception of reality. Artistic expression and representation of social reality are necessarily partial, selective, a kind of synecdoche, for there are times when for the sake of, say, authenticity an artist is compelled to paint a mere species of reality as though it were the whole.

In spite of its gleeful nihilism, gangsta/reality rap of the '80s and '90s may be just such a species posing as the essence of black cultural and social reality. If so, then, as I've already suggested, it's merely picking up where the ghetto realistic fiction writers of the '70s (and earlier) left off, spinning gritty tales of ghetto life largely from the perspective of those whose hope for economic survival and security rest on The Sporting Life. Their perspective on social reality isn't of course shared by blacks in the 'burbs and maybe not even by most black folk in the inner cities, but must it be for it to be considered a form of ghetto realism? Former *Politically Incorrect* talk show host Bill Maher had on numerous occasions pointed out that many of his African American friends (presumably middle and upper-middle class) are sick of the degrading images of blacks in gangsta rap because those images don't represent *them*. Funny, rappers be saying the same thang about the black bougie images reflected in, for example, *Family Matters* or *The Cosby Show*—that they don't represent the Wards in New Orleans and Houston, or the projects in Chicago or Baltimore (see HBO's *The Corner* for one representation of an inner-city reality). Essentialism cuts both ways, I suppose, when one's sense or estimation of self depends so heavily on a universal black association or disassociation with white mainstream America.

But if rappers (many but not all) do anything at all in their music, they endeavor to stay true to the source from which they sprang, to keep in tune with the ghetto (street) sensibilities that, in part, made them who they are in the first place. Does that mean then that they are, in effect, keepin' it real? Perhaps only insofar as the game they're compelled to play is real. Within the confines of game behavior, that is, these young men and women are as real as real can be. And though often blind to his own destructiveness, the pimp has peeped the science of the hustling game and become its major ghetto player.

Selling Da Game: Pimpin' Ghetto Realism for American Dreams

The real glue that holds any bitch to a pimp is the long scratch she's hip she's stuck for. A good pimp could cut his swipe off and still pimp his ass off. Pimping ain't no sex game. It's a skull game.

Iceberg Slim, *Pimp*

You got to sell her a dream, man. You got to let her know it's a much better way wit you.

The Bishop Don "Magic" Juan, in *Pimps Up, Hos Down*

Like *Superfly* and *Foxy Brown*, *The Mack* (1973, by Michael Campus) addresses the "double-bind effect" of ghetto living, only this time the lead character has chosen the very pinnacle of ghetto realistic enterprises— that is, to be the smooth, sweet-talking mack man or pimp. According to critic Darius James, *Willie Dynamite* (directed by Gilbert Moses III in 1974) is a better pimp movie than *The Mack*, but, having viewed the film recently, it doesn't sufficiently manifest aspects of ghetto realism like the "double bind." *The Mack* opens with the protagonist, Goldie (Max Julien), as a car thief who serves five years in prison, is released, and goes back to the streets, only this time he's going to pimp his way to the top. Meanwhile, during those five years, Goldie's younger brother Olinga (Roger Mosely) has taken to organizing a revolutionary group to create, in his words, "a black America within but without white America." The setting for the film is Oakland, California, a veritable hot spot for pimping at the time. (In fact, some real pimps, four of the Wards brothers, have minor roles in the film.) Some time after Goldie has gotten himself a sizable stable of female prostitutes, including a prized white one whose father, oddly enough, is a corporate lawyer, he and his brother meet in a park and discuss their different strategies for overcoming social conditions in their Oakland ghetto. For Goldie, pimping is not only his chance to escape ghetto poverty, but also it is his means of becoming somebody, of being a hero to neighborhood youth.

> Olinga: You really don't understand, do you? Hey, man, don't you realize that in order to make this thing work, man, we got to get rid of the pimps, and the pushers, and the prostitutes, and then start all over again clean.
> Goldie: Hey, look nobody's pushing me anywhere, okay? I mean not you, not the cops, nobody, man. I mean, you wanna get rid of the pushers, I'll help you, but don't send your people after me.
> O: Oh, come on John, can't you see that we can't get rid of one without gettin' rid of the other. We come down on both of 'em at the same time in order for this whole thing to work for the people.
> G: Nobody's closing me out of my business. . . .

Olinga responds to John's (that is, Goldie's) resistance here by appealing to the flesh-and-blood relationship between them, that because they're brothers he would deeply regret having to go up against him. However, Goldie doesn't see it that way. For him familial ties and community bonds have no bearing on what he does as an individual.

> G: Look, being brothers ain't got nothing to do with it, man. I mea———, I got a right to live my life the way I wanna live it. I mean, being rich and Black means something, man. Don't you know that? Being poor and Black don't mean shit. We're living in different times. When you and I were young kids, I mean there were no heroes. We got all sorts of heroes now. There's kids out there who look up to me, man.
> O: Man, can't you see that's just teaching black kids to

exploit their own kind? And that's sick!
G: Well, it's not sick. It's sick when you get a chance to get
out of a rat-infested ghetto and you don't.

Although here Goldie appears to be insensitive to his brother's concern about the bad example he's setting for ghetto children, it's interesting that in an earlier scene with these very youths Goldie strongly urges them to never say that they want to be like him. With a bribe of a little money for them and their families, Goldie instead charges them to stay in school and go on to become a lawyer, a doctor, or "anything you wanna be." Some of my students saw this gesture on the part of the pimp as hypocritical, and that it may be to an extent, but the reality of the situation is that a person in The Life, one who knows firsthand its many risks and consequences, may be the best person to deter kids from going the same way. In spite of his own incorrigibility, Goldie seems to be convinced that through his care there's hope for the ghetto youth to resist the "double bind" and make it in the white, square world. It's a comforting thought, but given the odds against them, including the ever-tempting, high-profile status of the ghetto pimp, it's not a very realistic one.

This high regard many ghetto youth (especially males) hold for the pimp derives from any number of things—his flamboyant dress, fancy cars, easy living, sex appeal—but above all they are enamored by his exceptional ability to rap or use language to manipulate others, especially women. To be a pimp is, in other words, to be a kind of trickster, one who by means of rhetoric can create from ghetto realities the illusion of ghetto grandeur. On the one hand, like the Signifying Monkey, the pimp signifies to get his victims to submit to his mischievous will; but, on the other hand, unlike the Monkey, he signifies not for sheer sport or psychological dominance over his adversaries but for ghetto glory and good old American green. In *Get Your Ass in the Water and Swim Like Me*, Bruce Jackson notes that the pimp is the most recent in a long line of African American folk characters who use "trickeration" to get ovah in the rural and urban American jungles.

> If the trickster o[f] early nineteenth-century American black
> folklore, the Rabbit, was doing his trickeration against
> larger animals who wanted to kill or control him, and if
> the trickster of late nineteenth-and early twentieth-century
> American black folklore, John, was doing his trickeration
> against the cruel master or boss who wanted to get more
> out of him than was reasonable to require, the Pimp trick-
> ster of the mid-twentieth-century period is working his
> trickeration against everybody: outsiders and insiders, his

own kind and others, men and women, whites and blacks. In the vicious world of the streets, he seems a brutal, but not unreasonable, revision of the American Dream, the Horatio Alger story.[17]

According to Thomas Kochman, this kind of "trickeration," this use of language to con, to coax, to dupe is what the pimp stakes his reputation on. The pimp was, in other words, a *rapper* long before emcees dreamed of pimpin' their hard-luck tales into a mic to clock *scratch* (a term pimps used for money back in Iceberg's day). In "Rappin' in the Black Ghetto," Kochman explains how the pimp works his trickeration, or game.

> Rapping then, is used at the beginning of a relationship to create a favorable impression and be persuasive at the same time. The man who has the reputation for excelling at this is the pimp, or mack man. Both terms describe a person of considerable status in the street hierarchy, who, by his *lively and persuasive rapping* ("macking" is also used in this context) has acquired a stable of girls to hustle for him and give him money. For most street men and many teenagers he is the model whom they try to emulate. Thus, within the community you have a pimp walk, pimp style boots and clothes, and perhaps most of all "pimp talk," is a colorful literary example of a telephone rap.[18]

I probably had me some of them pimp socks and kicks back in the day, cuz see the pimp style was so integrated with black culture (at least black urban lower-class culture) that you could be sportin' some pimp shades or a pimp shirt and not even know it. Pimps in the '70s just had that kind of influence on fashion, even the mainstream fashion world, according to some observers. I was only a teen at the time, but I knew how players were supposed to look and did my best to act the part. I'm getting a little nostalgic here, I know, but understand that I ain't saying the pimp lifestyle, even in the '70s, was morally, politically, socially legit. I'm hipped to the fact that of all the ghetto hustler types, except perhaps for gangster murderers or hit men, the pimp is the worst, indeed the most exploitative. After all, at the twilight of his pimping career, Iceberg himself even regarded pimping as an offshoot of the free market capitalism that gave rise to American slavery. My female students also never hesitated to remind me how they couldn't stomach the way pimps treated their women. Many of them felt that these men must suffer from a deep-seated hatred for their mothers and, by association, all women. I was somewhat skeptical of that Freudian angle at first, but after peeping the "gorilla" pimp antics of the young Iceberg Slim (then called Young Blood) and Goines's pimp character Whoreson with their pimp sticks (coat-hanger wires used to beat their women into submission), I was more than convinced that pimps can be utterly cruel, vicious, and hateful toward women, even they mamas.

Though violence is resorted to by not a few pimps, however, the heart and soul of pimping is actually the clever con. As Jackson so aptly puts it, the black pimp "makes his money by trickery: he tricks his whores; his whores 'turn tricks' and call their customers 'tricks.'"[19] Kochman nicely illustrates the pimp's trickery with an example of a "telephone rap" between a pimp and a prospective whore. The rap comes from Iceberg Slim's autobiographical novel *Pimp: The Story of My Life,* where, early in his pimping career, he tries to draw into his fold an ex-whore named Christine. After having gotten the rundown on her (which is a critical preliminary move for any bona fide pimp) from Silas, a resourceful employee of the hotel in which he resides, Iceberg calls her up and raps.

> "Now try to control yourself baby. I'm the tall stud with the dreamy bedroom eyes across the hall in four-twenty. I'm the guy with the pretty towel wrapped around his sexy hips. I got the same hips on now that you x-rayed. Remember that hump of sugar your peepers feasted on?"
>
> She said, "Maybe, but you shouldn't call me. I don't want an incident. What do you want? A lady doesn't accept phone calls from strangers."
>
> I said, "A million dollars and a trip to the moon with a bored, trapped, beautiful bitch, you dig? I'm no stranger. I've been popping the elastic on your panties ever since you saw me in the hall."[20]

Knowing that Christine was at that time bored with her life and trapped in a marriage to a man she didn't love, Iceberg shrewdly shifts his initial focus from the sexual attraction between them to his interest in rescuing her from a bad situation. Slim plays the same game when he cops his fourth girl, a waitress by the name of Jo Ann—only since she's a novice to The Life he exploits her apparent need for a glamorous lifestyle and emotional security.

> I said, "Jo Ann, I gotta congratulate you. You're not only lucky, you're smart. You knew when you saw me that I was going to be your man. I'm hip that you were just waiting to meet me.

"You have wanted since you were a little girl to live an
exciting, glamorous life. Well, Sugar, you're on 'Blood's'
magic carpet. I'm gonna make your life with me out-shine
your flashiest day dreams.

"I'm a pimp. You gotta be a whore. I don't have squares.
I'm gonna be your mother, your father, your brother, your
friend, and your lover. The most important thing I'm gonna
be to you is your man. The manager of the scratch you
make in the street. Now sweet bitch, have you followed
me so far?"[21]

Those reassuring lines should have been quite enough to sway Jo
Ann, at least they were so for Goldie's young white whore, whom he
turned out with similar promises of a loving relationship on multiple
levels (as father, brother, mother, as well as lover). Yet, Iceberg goes on to
tempt Jo Ann, sort of like Satan tested Jesus in the New Testament gospel
of Matthew, with all the worldly attractions that were within his power
to provide.

I reached down and took her hand. I took her to the win-
dow overlooking the city. I held her against me.

I said, "Look out there, baby angel. Out there is where
you work. Those streets are yours because you're my
woman. I've got five 'G's' in fall money. If you get busted
for anything, even murder, I can free you. 'Baby Bitch,' this
family is like a small army. We got rules and regulations we
never break.

"I am really two studs. One of them is sweet and kind
to his whores when they don't break the rules. The other
one comes out insane and dangerous when the rules are
broken. Little baby, I'm sure you'll never meet him.

"Never forget this family is as one against the cold, cruel
world. We are strong because we love each other. There's
no problem I can't solve. There's no question I can't answer
about this game."[22]

These two examples clearly demonstrate the pimp's shrewd use of
language to manipulate some women's defenseless psyches. A traditional
pimp origin myth even equates him with the biblical serpent whose persuasive speech deceived Eve and made Adam, as the myth goes, the first
trick.[23] As we discussed such passages in class, though, some of my students were quick to argue that a woman would have to be pretty malad-
justed to fall for the "lame" cons of these pimps. They figured that the

women were probably abused or otherwise mistreated in childhood or early adulthood. This was certainly the case for Christine, who had already been a whore once before Iceberg met her, but Jo Ann, on the other hand, didn't seem to have any such history of rape, childhood incest, or physical/emotional abuse. Unfortunately, none of the books or films we looked at spoke to this, at least not from the woman's perspective, save perhaps for Lu Lu (Carol Speed) in *The Mack*. When Goldie tells Lu Lu that as kids growing up together he imagined her as a being a "big time nurse or lawyer" instead of turning tricks, she responds: "Yeah man, you know, that would be righteously together if I was white; shit, I don't have to tell you how hard it is for a nigga to earn a decent livin'. Besides it's just a job that pays the bills, man." Like her fellow male characters, Lu Lu conveniently, though not unjustifiably, attributes her choice of The Life to white racism and economic self-sufficiency. The women interviewed in Brent Owens's other HBO documentary, *Hookers at the Point,* may broach this subject, but the program hasn't re-aired in recent months.

Although from a male perspective, Iceberg gives some insight on the matter in a few of his essays in *The Naked Soul of Iceberg Slim.* There he points out that, yes, many of the women who become whores were prior "kick-outs from broken homes"; but he states that they were also "students, waitresses, entertainers, barflies, middle-class kooks, and even daughters of preachers."[24] Their reasons for taking a man, a pimp, instead of whoring independently range from the pragmatic—protection from all kinds of dangers on the streets, advice on life's sundry complexities, and legal help to avoid jail time—to the deeply psychological—"she needs the pimp to drive her, to punish her, to make her suffer so that painful guilt for her bitch dog existence can be relieved."[25] According to Slim, these women also have a hunger for notoriety and punishment (psychic and/or physical) that the "phony glamour and cruelty of the pimp" satisfies.[26]

Whatever the psychological disposition of the women whom the pimp solicits into his "family," the pimp's game must be exceptionally tight if he is to acquire a large enough stable to attain the good life. Iceberg Slim used two strategies to stay at the top of his game: what pimps (old-time ones, at least) call the *overlay* and the *prat out.* Before his death in 1992, Slim had planned to publish a book called *The Game for Squares* that would have explained such principles of the pimping game to squares. Although he never completed the book (to the chagrin of many a gameless square, I imagine), in a 1990 interview with former MTV rap host Fab Five Freddy[27] he discusses two of the main points covered in the manuscript, the *overlay* and *prat out.* Iceberg describes the *overlay* as the act of talking at length to "cover a particular mistake or sin you might commit in a relationship."[28] Pimps have observed this tactic frequently employed by women on men, and thus they reverse the game on women and play them for tricks. To illustrate how the principle would work in typical heterosexual relationships outside of the pimping game, Iceberg gives an example of a brotha who is prone to gamble but doesn't want his lady to know: he "castigate[s] in her presence anybody that gambles and tears[s] them down, sayin', 'How stupid can this muthafucka be? F'Christ's sakes, do you know what that nigga did? First, th' nigga had fifteen thousand dollars in the bank. Would you believe this dumb muthafucka blew all that money in Vegas th'otha mornin'?'"[29]

The principle of the *prat out* Iceberg defines as "pretend[ing] indifference to enhance desire."[30] According to Slim, it's especially effective with the "prettiest bitches" because the cold or warm indifference titillates their desire so much that "their egos have to capture you for no other reason but to get revenge."[31] In *Pimp*, Iceberg gives an excellent example of his own use of the prat out and overlay with one of his prettiest women. At the crack of dawn one mornin', after a long, gainful night of trickin', one of Slim's whores, the "newest, prettiest girl," Kim, puts his game to the test when she publicly confronts him about spending time with her.

> Then in her crisp New England accent she said, "Are you coming back to my pad this morning? You haven't spent a night with me in a month. So come back okay?"
>
> A good pimp doesn't get paid for screwing. He gets his pay-off for always having the right thing to say to a whore right on lightning tap. I knew my four whores were flapping their ears to get my reaction to this beautiful bitch. A pimp with an overly-fine bitch in his stable has to keep his game tight. Whores constantly probe for weakness in a pimp.
>
> I fitted a scary mask on my face and said, in a low, deadly voice, "Bitch, are you insane? No bitch in this family calls any shots or muscles me to do anything. Now take your stinking yellow ass upstairs to a bath and some shut-eye. Get in the street at noon like I told you."
>
> . . . I knew the bitch was trying to booby-trap me when she spat out her invitation. "Come on, kick my ass. What the hell do I need with a man I only see when he comes to get his money? I am sick of it all. I don't dig stables and never will. I know I'm the new bitch who has to prove herself. Well Goddamnit, I am sick of this shit. I'm cutting out."[32]

After pausing for air and a smoke, Kim continues:

> "I have turned more tricks in the three months I have been
> with you than in the whole two years with Paul. My pussy
> stays sore and swollen. Do I get my ass kicked before I
> split? If so, kick it now because I'm going back to Provi-
> dence on the next thing smoking."
>
> She was young, fast with trick appeal galore. She was a
> pimp's dream and she knew it. She had tested me with her
> beef. She was laying back for a sucker response.
>
> I disappointed her with my cold overlay. I could see
> her wilt as I said in an icy voice. "Listen square-ass bitch, I
> have never had a whore I couldn't do without. I celebrate,
> Bitch, when a whore leaves me. It gives some worthy bitch
> a chance to take her place and be a star. You scurvy Bitch,
> if I shit in your face, you gotta love it and open your mouth
> wide."
>
> . . . I went on ruthlessly, "Bitch, you are nothing but a
> funky zero. Before me you had one chili chump with no
> rep. Nobody except his mother ever heard of the bastard.
> Yes, Bitch, I'll be back this morning to put your phony ass
> on the train."
>
> I rocketed away from the curb. In the rear-view mirror,
> I saw Kim walk slowly into the hotel. Her shoulders were
> slumped. Until I dropped the last whore off you could have
> heard a mosquito crapping on the moon. I had tested out
> for them, "solid ice."[33]

The prat out came hours later when, playing out her threat to leave
him, Iceberg picks her up and takes her to the train station. Once they
arrive at the station, however, Kim loses her cool and blurts out: "Daddy,
are you really going to let me split? Daddy, I love you."[34] The prat then
follows:

> I started the prat action to cinch her when I said, "Bitch, I
> don't want a whore with rabbit in her. I want a bitch who
> wants me for life. You have got to go. After that bullshit
> earlier this morning, you are not that bitch."
>
> That prat butchered her. She collapsed into my lap
> crying and begging to stay. I had a theory about splitting
> whores. They seldom split without a bankroll. So, I cracked

on her, "Give me that scratch you held out and maybe I'll give you another chance."[35]

The real key to these principles, or rather to *playing*, according to Iceberg, is to exercise *strength* and *willpower* over your emotions, to "prat 'em and keep your swipe outta 'em," as the master pimp "Sweet" Jones once taught the young Iceberg Slim. This means, more specifically, to not listen to your ego but instead to question "any move any woman makes," for in the pimp's view, "every female move is like a player" and a "player takes *nothing* for granted."[36]

So once you get pass the sex and money part of it, pimpin' is really about making calculated power moves, about understanding the psychology of women (and, of course, the men who lust after them) and knowing how best to appeal to their sensibilities at any given moment—not a far cry from Aristotle's idea of the orator taking stock of the personalities of audience members in order to persuade them.[37] This isn't to say that pimps, even one as ill as Iceberg Slim, have all or even most women figured out but that through years of practice they acquire a pretty keen sense about (some) women's pressure points and effectively use these to get from them what they want.

And yet according to the pimps interviewed in Christina and Richard Milner's 1972 ethnography, *Black Players,* the kind of moves or psychological games the pimp plays on women are not unlike those people play on each other every day, for in black ghetto hustling culture the verb *pimpin'* can also refer to "the broader activity of using human emotions to get money"—a pretty handy rhetorical aim if you ain't got a pot to piss in, knahmean?[38] In the book, the authors give the example that "a child who cajoles his mother out of extra allowance money is *pimpin* off his mother."[39] In less crass terms, one could say that the child is *playing* or *running a game* on his mama, which, as the authors point out, suggests, on the one hand, a "con game" and, on the other, "the conception of life as a series of games, the most basic of which is the *survival game.*"[40] The kid is, you might say, a born player in the survival or hustlin' game. And so like most players in this game, he views or will come to "view all of society as a network of those who game and those who are gamed on."[41] Put in the more vulgar argot of the pimp, everyone "in his time is both a trick and a pimp, but the trick is to feel like a pimp most of the time, at least within your own value system."[42] None of my students, I'm sure, would consider themselves pimps, but, man, they be doing some mighty hard pimpin' for A grades in my courses. But, hey, I ain't nobody's ho! Then again, if I'm straight on this pimp philosophy, I gotta admit that when the price is right (my pride, ego, or rep) I too get caught in a compromising position. This subtle characterization of human relations is superbly illustrated in what one pimp in the Milner study has described as a triangular exchange of wealth and psychological gratification between the pimp, ho, and trick:[43] "This is the only way we can get back at the Man, you know. You rob him of his love, you dig, yeah, and his money. And in turn you're going to do this or that, but in turn it goes right back to the Man in far-out clothes, fancy clothes, jewelry and cars, see? So it's like a triangular thing, you know, from the Man to the woman, back to the pimp, right back to the Man."[44]

Each of the three—pimp, whore, trick—have, it seems, certain psychological needs that they must pay another to gratify. The trick's need is obvious; it's his need for illicit sex that puts prostitutes and pimps in business in the first place. The whore needs the intangibles: "a strong man, a goal, a set way of life, and love or the allusion of love," and she buys all these with the money she earns and gives to the pimp.[45] Finally, the pimp, he needs to, well, look like a boss pimp. To look the part, the pimp needs the luxuries (see previous quotation) that, more often than not, he can only get from the trick (not, mind you, the very person who paid for the pimp's whore but any man, white, black, or brown who has the social standing and means to engage in the pimp's business).

Of course, we legit members of society, we ain't hipped to how the triangle applies to us, how we oftentimes play each other to gratify our selfish desires. Whether we know it or not, though, the way the pimp sees it, the pimpin' game cuts across the grain of American social life.

> Every American major institution, from the law courts and the business Establishment to the Armed Services, is viewed by the players as a pimping situation. They see society itself as a network of people gaming off each other for money, power, or some kind of ego-gratification. The preacher is a pimp gaming off his congregation, the politician is a pimp gaming off his constituents, the law-enforcement system pimps the lawbreakers, the wife is a ho gaming off her husband who is her trick, the employer games off his workers, the Whites pimp the Blacks, and the federal government pimps everybody![46]

Now that's real! What law-abiding American citizen hasn't at one time or another felt pimped by the gov'ment 'round tax time? And you know if the average American citizen feels that way, then folks in the ghetto gon feel like they ain't nothin' but hos and tricks to the system. As one member of Chicago rap group Do or Die put it in *The Source*, "The system is pimpin' us, so we gotta try to pimp the system."[47] And that's just what the pimp tries to do; he tries to flip the script on the sys-

tem that's gaming on him. Knowing, that is, that some privileged white
men like to venture on the dark side every now and then, he pimps black
women to turn his ghetto reality into his own version of the American
dream. In the process, though, sadly, sistas get caught in the middle, op-
pressed by The Man for being black and exploited by the black pimp for
being women. But then, those in the game would remind us, if you in The
Life, you know the score. The price for playing the game is the risk of
falling prey to it.

POSTMODERN PLAYAZ: PERPETRATIN' THE PIMP AS POETRY FOR PAPER, POWER, PROPS

Although the pimp has apparently lost an edge in the African American
sense of cultural style since his heyday in the '70s (alas, long gone are the
days of ads for superfly pimp socks and shades), he remains a significant
part of street culture and—due largely to reality rap—the Hip hop imagination. What else could explain the scene in Jay-Z's video "Who You
Wit II" (off his *In My Lifetime, Vol. 1* CD) where, looking like Goldie or
Pretty Tony, Jay-Z holds court at what appears to be the annual Player's
Ball and garners the prized accolade of Mack of the Year? Maybe rappers
today be trippin' off them old mack movies or be jockin' Iceberg Slim for
some playa prestige; yet, as some recent documentaries attest, pimpin'
is still a hustle of choice for some black (and white) men in America's
urban ghettos.

   According to one such documentary—Brent Owens's *Pimps Up, Hos
Down,* which aired on HBO during the fall of 1998 and the winter of
1999—the rise of drug dealing (especially crack cocaine) in the inner cities around the mid-'80s struck a considerable blow to the pimpin' game.
Matter fact, the game got so bad at one point that some pimps even
switched over to slangin' rocks, leaving a bunch of hos pimpless. Brothas
still made big money slangin' cane in the late '90s; however, pimps seem
to have reclaimed their once venerable position in The Life. In fact, according to film directors Albert and Allen Hughes (*Menace II Society,
Dead Presidents*), who have recently completed their own documentary
film called *American Pimp,* some pimps are currently "doing so much
money and so much business, they're living in Hawaii and they've got
ten girls and are pulling in $1,700 a night average for one girl, tax free
money."[48] And apparently these '90s pimps be mad flossin' at the annual
(or semi-annual) International Player's Ball (as featured in *Pimps Up,
Hos Down*). Not, of course, in the kind of rags that Goldie sported in
The Mack—except one cat, Detroit Blue, did have on this Old School
tux, you know the kind that's like powder blue or somethin' like that
with dark felt or fake silk trim—but instead in the finest Italian-made

suits and brand-named gators in the loudest colors: bright pinks, greens, yellows, purples, reds, and, naturally, combinations of these. On top of that, they sport sleek fur coats, lavish jewelry, and customized classic cars flashier than the grill on Priest's boss hog. Obviously, styles have changed, but the game remains the same; still, it's to be sold not told.

Two female students in my Black Pulp Fiction class who saw the Owens documentary on HBO were intrigued by the spectacle of the pimping game but were, not surprisingly, put off by its objectification of women. Mind you, there weren't any shots with whores serving their tricks or anything sexually explicit, except perhaps for a few lewd dancers in scenes at a strip club and as a sideshow at the Player's Ball. Everybody knows of course that ain't nothin' new 'bout those kind of public displays, even in mainstream America (just check your local listings for a strip club near you).

Now in the rap game these days seem like just about everybody is a gen-u-wine player, a baller, and a veritable scourge to all player haters. Even a blatant denial of that marker such as Big Pun's (may he rest in peace) popular line about not being a player (from "Still Not a Player" on *Capital Punishment*) these days can intimate actual player status. Truth be told, though, this playa thang has been around for some time. As early as elementary school in the late '60s, me and my South Park homies tried to look and act the part. Though we weren't all that conscious of it, I guess pimps had that kind of juice, that kind of hold on our world back then, right along with Hugh Hefner's iconic Playboy bunny. (Just about every aspiring player we knew had that bunny symbol hanging off his rearview mirror.) And for a shy kid like me who grew up on a heavy dose of black-and-white TV movies, I couldn't help but dream of being a suave player like, say, Dean Martin or Elvis Presley. Not long ago the Columbia Video Club I belonged to advertised in its catalog a set of Dean Martin's Matt Helm spy movies. A shot in the catalog from *The Silencers* has Martin pictured with ten bikini- or pajama-party-clad blondes and brunettes. Now think about it, what young boy (or doddering old man for that matter) wouldn't want to be like Martin in that situation, or like the all-American-boy player Elvis was in *Girls! Girls! Girls!* Or even better, like the debonair international player Sean Connery (and the various actors who succeeded him in the role) portrayed in all those James Bond flicks. Shoot, Bond got play on whatever island, country, city, hamlet, backwoods town he tread. Strange, though, I wonder why nobody ever called those characters pimps; they sure had plenty of women under their control like pimps.

Clearly, the kind of player I'm referring to here is more the playboy type, one who, as we used to say, plays the field (of eligible women). But because, as I've indicated before, the pimp is primarily out to get paid,

not laid, the "player" referent most often denotes gaming ability, persuasive power—be it with the dope game, women, pool, or even somethin'
legit like corporate finance or hoops. But then if pimps are responsible
for putting the "play" in player, ultimately to be a real player one has to
possess game with women (or with men if you a female playa like Lil'
Kim claims to be). The reason male rappers fetishize the player role ain't
too hard to figga. As Fernando puts it in *The New Beats,* "In the ghetto,
where reputation among one's peers and the opposite sex is especially
important, the pimp has elevated sexual gamesmanship to a high art.
. . . In a macho culture, the pimp simply represents every brokenhearted
young man's revenge."[49]

As examples of this pimp/player attitude in rap, Fernando cites LA
rap group Above the Law (e.g., "Pimpology 101" and "Pimp Clinic" on
Black Mafia Life) and Too Short (whom I will discuss at length), who
rap about pimping literally and others who simply assume the role like
St. Louis pre-Nelly-era rapper Sylk Smoov, the Geto Boys' Scarface (see
"The Pimp" off of *Mr. Scarface Is Back*), and Big Daddy Kane.[50] Fernando
neglects to mention, however, other artists like Luther Campbell of 2 Live
Crew and LL Cool J who, like Kane, consistently portray themselves as
not so much pimps but playaz. In fact, to showcase his player status, LL
appeared on the cover of one of the earliest issues of *The Source* (June
1989) with six fine young ladies—black, white, Latin, and Asian. And
every Hip hop fan knows how Luke poses with the ladies on his album
covers, even without the "nasty as they wanna be" 2 Live Crew.

To Fernando's list of rap's pimps and players, I would also add these
artists of the '90s: Seattle-based rapper SirMixaLot (see *Mack Daddy,*
1991; *Chief Boot Knocka,* 1994; and just about every other album he has
put out); ATL dynamic duo Outkast (*Southernplayalisticadillacmuzik,* especially their song "Player's Ball," 1993); Bay Area rappers E-40 (tracks
on, for example, *Tha Hall of Game,* 1996) and Richie Rich (the song
"Real Pimp" on his 1996 album *Seasoned Veteran*); Eightball and MJG,
hailing from Tennessee (*Lyrics of a Pimp: Strictly for da Undaground,*
1997); Do or Die (songs like "Pimpology" and "Still Po Pimpin'" on
Headz or Tailz, 1998); longtime Oakland MC Rappin' 4-Tay, who on his
1999 release (*Introduction to Mackin'*) takes inspiration from the Mack
himself, Goldie (Max Julien), and a real pimp-turned-preacher named the
Bishop Don "Magic" Juan (who's also featured in *Pimps Up, Hos Down*
and some of Snoop's most recent records, videos, and public appear-
ances); and finally, Jay-Z, who, as I alluded earlier, comes off as smooth
as silk in "Who You Wit II" and "Ain't No Nigga" (both on *Reasonable
Doubt*). Oh yeah, I almost forgot about Snoop, that G rider from the
LBC who, borrowing (some might say bitin') from pimp scenes in *The
Mack,* crafted the player's creed: We don't love them hos. Snoop also

does a short rap on the pimp game in a song called "Player's Way" with Bobby Womack and Rick James on the latter's 1997 CD *Urban Rapsody.* Even Ice Cube got in the mix not long ago, breaking away from his usual ghetto angst and lettin' everybody know he too is a player and gets his club on (see "We Be Clubbin'" off the soundtrack to Cube's directorial debut, *The Players Club*).

Jay-Z upped the ante, though, when he released "Big Pimpin'" with down South rappers UGK in 1999. The video was hot, I mean sizzilin', for a long minute on the music video airwaves; it even came to symbolize everything morally vacuous about rap music, as the mainstream media was quick to, uh, call a spade a spade.[51] But you know rappers didn't pay them no mind. An Alabama duo by the name of Dirty hit the scene in '01 calling they first CD *The Pimp & Da Gangsta*. And the video that accompanied one of the premier songs on the record ("Hit Da Floe") definitely manifested the pimpin' style. A short (well, rather long in the music business) two years later and e'rybody going bananas about pimps, or so claims the Netscape music homepage, by the close of the summer of '03. 50 Cent's video remix of "P.I.M.P.," Nelly's "Pimp Juice" video, and Mississippi rapper David Banner's video for "Like a Pimp" were all duly cited. The Banner song and video are quite unusual, though, because in the video you see images that suggest a critique of southern racism more than the lifestyle of a pimp. "Pimp Juice" and "P.I.M.P.," by contrast, are straight up about macking, even featuring some real-life pimps and those who brought them to life on the big screen.

In the more than twenty-five-year existence of Hip hop, a great many (far more than those I've listed here) rappers have strutted on the mic like they bona fide pimps and playaz. Why, even on one of the first rap records, "Rapper's Delight," the Sugarhill Gang's Big Bank Hank called himself a pimp. (Hmm . . . makes one wonder what grandma in that movie *The Wedding Singer* did when she got to Hank's line, "I'm Imp the Dimp, the ladies pimp.")[52] Anyway, the rap artist who has most consistently and most effectively represented the pimp and the pimpin' game is that LA-born, Oakland-bred, now ATL-transplanted enigma of rap Too Short, a.k.a. Short Dog, or, when he ain't puttin' in work, Todd Shaw. I consider Short an enigma or phenomenon because in spite of his rather simple, no-frills style and the criticism he has often gotten for it, the man has turned rappin' about pimps and hos into big business and high art. Since the early '80s when he sold his raps on cassette from the trunk of his car at somethin' like $5 a pop, Too Short has almost single-handedly popularized the cachet of the ghetto pimp in Hip hop culture. And for a man who ain't never pimped a day in his life, that's no small accomplishment. Yet over the course of a rare twelve-album (and counting!) stint, Short Dog has done it with apparent ease.

Discographies of all eleven (and more) of these releases are, I've found, difficult to come by, but one of the earliest recordings is, according to one source, a 1983 album called *Don't Stop Rapping*.[53] Two others, primarily positive raps according to Short, were released circa '85,[54] but I haven't found the titles for these. The other eight albums are well documented and represent vintage, "freaky tales" Too Short: *Born to Mack* (1988), *Life Is . . . Too Short* (1988), *Short Dog's in the House* (1990), *Shorty the Pimp* (1992), *Get In Where You Fit In* (1993), *Cocktails* (1995), *Gettin' It: (Album Number Ten)* (1996), and his recent back-from-retirement releases *Can't Stay Away* (1999) and *You Nasty* (2000). Though many songs on these albums vacillate between pimpin' on one hand and freakin' on the other, Too Short spits some mad game on tracks like "Pimp the Ho" from *Life Is . . . Too Short* and "Pimpology" from *Short Dog's in the House*. In "Pimpology," for instance, Short schools his listeners on game in four quick and easy lessons. He advises would-be players 1) to never fall in love with their ho, 2) to act cool, 3) to not be a trick, and 4) to keep your ho. Short gives more explicit insight and advice on game in a recent *Source* interview:

> I always thought game was just a replacement word for knowledge when you're in the streets. I analyzed it in and out, through and front. To say you have game means that you know; been there and experienced it. People can point things out to you, show you little different angles to make money and all that kind of stuff. But nobody can really give you the game. You gotta go out there and acquire it yourself.[55]

Thus, Short's handy tips for getting game are: 1) "Work and play can go hand in hand. It just depends on how much 'game' you have"; 2) "You should already know this, but the game is always to be sold if there is a chance for profit . . ."; and 3) "Don't let the game trick you into thinkin' it's all about the limelight. At the end of the day, all that matters is bein' able to keep playin', no matter who recognizes."[56] What Short alludes to here seems to me to be a key ingredient in ghetto realistic fiction: game attitude. It's what Iceberg Slim had as a pimp and what he brought to his career as a professional writer. Short similarly appears to be transferring the pimp's game attitude to his vocation as a rapper.

Todd Shaw has never claimed to be anything like the Too Short character he so vividly portrays in his music, but clearly to create his ghetto realistic raps Shaw draws practical knowledge and strength from his pimp alter ego.

Although rapper and actor Ice-T (Tracy Marrow) has only on occasion rapped literally about pimping (e.g., "Somebody Gotta Do It [Pimpin' Ain't Easy!!!]" off his debut album *Rhyme Pays*), he too draws from the pimp's sense of game,[57] having at one time, unlike Shaw, actually pimped for some bread. In his introduction to Iceberg Slim's posthumously published novel *Doom Fox,* Ice-T reveals that he took his moniker in tribute to Slim because he aspired to emulate the one-time superpimp: "There were other rappers out there, but none that came directly from the game. I was the real thing: a robber, pimp, burglar, etc, well known in L.A. and respected in the street by the shot callers, drug dealers, and gang members."[58]

Elsewhere in his introduction to *Doom Fox,* Ice-T comments on his taking Slim as inspiration for his move to become a player in the legit game of rappin'.

> I was embracing the pimp lifestyle. I wanted to be one more than anything in the world. Then I turned back to Slim's works and realized that after all the real-life experiences that pimping gave him, he defied the odds and became an important writer. He took his experiences on the street and used them to elevate himself to immortality. It was a revelation, because nobody tells you when you're young that being a criminal or a pimp or a gangster can lead to any thing positive.
>
> I realized, if I'm idolizing this guy, I should follow in his steps and change my game. Like him, I wanted to be somebody who didn't just die there out on the streets. I decided that though I was out on the street doing wrong, I could take my experience and turn it into something else, possibly something constructive.
>
> I knew I couldn't be a writer like Slim, but when rap music came along it hit me: The same way he could take his experiences and put them on the page, I could take mine and bring them to the mic. So by the same method he became a writer, I became a rapper. I even took on the name Ice in tribute to him. My job was to show the hustlers from my generation what he showed me: that they too can take it to the next level.[59]

I don't know for sure whether rappin' 'bout pimps and hos counts as higher game, since few rappers seem to be discouraging, as Iceberg Slim does in his books, young brothas from actually trying to pimp. Yet it's hard to imagine any shorty in the ghetto these days choosing to pimp because Too Short does so on his records—except that there is one young woman in *Pimps Up, Hos Down* who says that she became a pimp because of Short's influence, along with the influence of a female friend who introduced the pimpin' game to her and later became one of her girls. Still, I'd say, postmodern playaz like Too Short, Ice-T, Ice Cube, Jay-Z, and Nelly (among others) well know that "It's all game," that in most of life's endeavors, legit or otherwise, there's "only one game, that's pimpin',"[60] and if you ain't playing then you gettin' played. Given these odds in our secular world, what else can you do but be a player in this dirty game? You can play it for righteous ends, no doubt, but unrighteousness will confront you at every turn 'cause that's part of the game. So, however you chose to play, playa, play on; play on 'til the real break of dawn.

A White American college student on entering a room full of socializing professors might concentrate his energies on trying to understand words and phrases which are unfamiliar to him. A young ghetto Black man in the same situation would be more likely to try to unravel quickly the games and human interactions behind the words. He wants to know what is going on in the room in terms of the people in it and their objectives rather than in merely "understanding" the semantic content of what is being said. The ability to do this successfully is called "street knowledge."

Christina and Richard Milner, *Black Players*

Brother, I live in the ghetto and have no desire to break its bonds, for I am after all a street nigger learning to write, who is incidentally being blessed with an increasing audience for his efforts. Materially, I dream at the moment of more living space and less wobbly furniture. I experience and view the ghetto as a savagely familiar place of spiritual warmth rich in the writer's treasure of pathos, conflict and struggle. I am convinced that for me it was the only place where I could discover and keep an awareness of who I really am and where I could find my haven, my purpose as a writer and a nigger in this criminal society.

Iceberg Slim, *The Naked Soul of Iceberg Slim*

5

They Got Game: African American Students, Hip Hop, and Literacy in the Zone

Who got game? In the contemporary arts of the academic contact zone, I say African American students got game! But by African American students I don't mean every Tom, Dick, and Juwan (or Shaniqua) attending an American college or university. Nor do I mean every African American student of the *lower class*—especially not those who (as I did) enter college with definite academic and material disadvantages vis-à-vis many middle-class students but without qualitative institutional labels (*developmental, basic, underprepared*). The African American students I refer to in this essay *are* labeled, are distinguished by their below-standard qualifications for higher education (low SAT scores and low to average GPAs, thus, requiring additional course work in math and English). More specifically, they are the relatively small number who come from one of America's many inner cities and who (and this qualification is critical since some "ghetto" kids *do* defy the odds throughout their years of schooling) enter a four-year, predominately white college or university with the designation (stigmatization?) "student at risk." They are, furthermore, those students who (in a way quite different from their suburban counterparts who may consume the same print, audio, and visual literacies) bring with them to the academic contact zone a unique literate sensibility, one that stands at the margins of literate culture at the same time that it mirrors the core of that culture. These students, they the ones I say got game.

Why them? Why this single group of African American students? Why another "liberal" academic article bemoaning the plight of the economically disadvantaged, academically underprepared African American student from some unspecified public school system in some ill-defined inner city? Well . . . not much done changed, that's why. No real substantive change in curricula and in the mandate of academic writing programs that would accommodate such students. And whenever genuine change is proffered (witness the University of Texas case in the early '90s and the Oakland School District Ebonics brouhaha in '97), lightning strikes from Mount Olympus until all is calm, order restored, all radical pedagogues brought low. The college basic writing course or any of those other traditionally ghettoized courses (a double jeopardy for ghetto kids, as it is) don't count as profound curricular change. Writing programs themselves are what's at stake. But then, my cynical self reminds me, how can one reasonably expect substantive curricular change when most of us in the academy—faculty (the tenured ballers) and administrators (the highly paid shot callers)—don't even understand (and often don't care to) what it means for a kid from an urban ghetto to come in close contact with us, folks who often represent the hegemony of the dominant culture. Most of us ain't hipped to (or willing to own up to) the games we play in the vast academic arena. Little wonder why many academic institutions refer to inner-city black and Hispanic kids as "students at risk." Consider this phrase for a moment. Is the student *at* risk or is he *a* risk? (In a choice Freudian moment, one can imagine the "t" slippin' right outta "at.") As to the question, though, I would say it's probably a little of both. But, hey, who really cares what the student risks in the grand academic enterprise. The all-important risk is that of the institution, that being whether it can ably transform these erstwhile college rejects into bona fide students and, upon graduation, "responsible" members of the polis, without, of course, compromising its own values and standards of excellence. Why else would the academy invest in the poor and underprepared unless it believed that the system would, as by design, subject them to its ideology and vision of the world?

I'm getting a little ahead of myself here, but just so you understand where I'm coming from: This ain't another one of those hypes about literacy or literacy education being solely a matter of student competence and work ethic; it's just as much about institutions and the power wielded by those who run them.

In any case, I opened with my earlier disclaimer about African American students because recently some of my colleagues in the field of composition have been critical (and rightly so) of how some of us in the field have represented students of color, particularly African American students, in our research. Matter fact, I was the target of some of this criticism. In an essay titled "Fighting Back by *Writing* Black: Beyond Racially Reductive Composition Theory," David Holmes finds fault with my unpublished dissertation because I didn't clarify exactly what I meant by my use of the phrase "black verbal expression" and because I "missed a golden opportunity to recognize the rhetorical value of dialect . . . without ascribing to dialect assumptions about racial ownership."[1] Since I completed the dissertation Holmes refers to ten years ago, it hardly seems worth it now to defend statements I made there. But the identity question Holmes raises is worth serious consideration, especially if in fact I am, or was then, essentializing blackness. The first problem that Holmes cites me for really ain't 'bout nothin' because he himself realizes that the phrase "black verbal expression" is virtually synonymous with the often used referent "the African-American oral tradition."[2] Why he thinks one descriptor is preferable or less essentialist than the other is beyond me, but the context of the phrase clearly shows that by "black verbal expression" I didn't mean black dialect. But of course y'all wouldn't know that unless you peeped the sentence in the dissertation, which goes: "Much like Houston Baker and Henry Louis Gates, I take the vernacular language of African Americans as central to an understanding of black verbal expression in most, if not all, of its forms."[3] My point here is that while the black vernacular isn't the sum total of all language use by African American people, it should be central to any conceptualization of black or African American rhetoric, which hadn't been the case for most rhetorical studies up to that time.

As for the other matter about the golden opportunity I missed, I'm not sure whether Holmes berates me for not correcting one of my African American male tutees on the plurality of black identity or for not making the racial-identity question a major focus in my dissertation. I mean, hey, the dissertation was about African American Vernacular English (then, Black English Vernacular) and African American male speakers of the dialect, not race per se. That was clear from the very start because other African American at-risk students who I had determined did not or did not often speak the vernacular were not included in the study. The students in the study—who all thought of themselves as black or African American (ah, but were they?)—may have wrongly assumed that because I shared their skin color I would be more like them, that I would talk like "the brothers who say nigga";[4] however, their limited view of blackness has little or nothing to do with my interest in their oral and written uses of black vernacular discourses and whether these discourses constitute a distinct African American *vernacular* rhetoric . . . well, except that the students' use of the word "nigga" confirms what I assert later about ghetto culture, Hip hop, and this generation's sense of self. So, while I'm sensitive to the brotha's (oops, maybe that should be *brother's*) concern about (mis)representing the black vernacular as an essential trait of blackness, I'd much rather him deconstruct academic discourse or critique the perceived superiority of discourses that falsely claim the absence of racial and ethnic specificity.

On another front, in the June 1999 issue of *College Composition and Communication* (*CCC*), Jacqueline Jones Royster and Jean Williams raise concerns over representations of African American students in composition research and scholarship, particularly in works like Valerie Balester's *Cultural Divide: A Study of African-American College-Level Writers*. Their criticism of the book prompted a response from Balester, which was published in the September 2000 issue of *CCC*, along with a lengthy rebuttal from Royster and Williams. It would be difficult to summarize here the various arguments and rebuttals expressed in all three publications, so I'll simply concentrate on what I consider the core issue. One of the main concerns Royster and Williams have about Balester's study—about all studies, really—is the vagueness of certain categories: "mainstream (non-mainstream), cultural divide, successful students (but students who exhibited features in their writing that mark them as needing to cross a divide), average (but again marked)."[5] Such categories or conflation of terms, the authors purport, "served to inscribe African American students as those outside the academic mainstream, students who, as Killingsworth says in the foreword to the book, were called upon to cross 'the cultural divide between life in a second-dialect minority and the life of the educated classes.'"[6] Unlike many studies of African American student writing, including my own, Balester's work focuses on successful African American students, not at-risk, remedial, or marginal students. So it is indeed quite strange that the term "basic writing" should come up in the foreword to a book about successful student writers. But Killingsworth eventually (after the second paragraph) distinguishes Balester's focus in this regard, that instead of basic writers she writes about students who have "made it."[7] And yet if these students have "made it," if they are in fact successful, then it would stand to reason that they are in many ways just as much mainstream as their white peers. I don't know whether Balester could have properly addressed this, but that is a question worth raising in much of our research: What constitutes mainstream status among all student writers? Or is the academic mainstream limited to us, the gatekeepers, and to the few students we have allowed privileged access?

Like Balester, much of my work during and since graduate school has focused on African American Vernacular English (AAVE), particularly as a rhetorical resource for teaching writing to African American students who, at least part of the time, speak AAVE. While in my research I have purposely limited my focus to basic writers generally and to African American male basic writers specifically, I realize that I do need to be careful about perceiving and representing this group as a monolith. Since in this essay I focus on the writing of one African American student labeled by the academy as "at risk" or "basic," I don't believe that I've done that. In spite of the fact that the student can be classified as a basic writer and as the product of an inner city, I hope that I have made it clear that for me he represents the potential of many such students, not the standard by which they are to be measured. Hence, I have penned "They Got Game" instead of "He Got Game" to signify the collective potential or capacity of many African American "at risk" students to produce prose (and poetry) that challenges the way literacy is perceived and taught in the contact zone of the academy.

At times, especially toward the end of the essay, I refer to undergraduate students generally because the composition course on rap orality and literacy that I've taught in the years since the study has enrolled male and female students of many races, cultures, and ethnicities. And besides, the topic I'm dealing with in the course—Hip hop—accommodates a wide variety of racial, ethnic, social, and cultural groups. Why, in spite of the pervasive homophobia in much of rap music, there's even a small contingent of gay rap artists and fans.[8] My interest in the main then is African American youth expressive culture, but more generally popular culture among American youths. Much like Jabari Mahiri does in *Shooting for Excellence: African American and Youth Culture in New Century Schools,* I propose that "aspects of popular youth culture can act as unifying and equalizing forces in culturally diverse classrooms and that African American and youth cultural sources for curricula can motivate learning of traditional subject matter."[9] However, as I address curricular and pedagogical issues here, I'm not proposing the use of youth cultural sources or pop culture just to ease students into learning traditional academic material. I'm more interested in what students and their teachers can learn from nontraditional literate practices like Hip hop. After all, American youth culture often comprises traditional and nontraditional discourses, for even in Hip hop the two are hardly separable.

Given rap's oral and literate modes, its riveting narratives of life in America's urban ghettos, its caustic critiques of American racism, classism, and sexism (albeit the latter by a precious few female and male artists), and its broad appeal among youth of all races, genders, and classes, I argue that Hip hop music and culture should figure into literacy studies and composition pedagogy for all (that's right, *all*) students, but especially for urban black students in a predominantly white college or university. For Hip hop has turned oral street-corner rapping into literate art. The African American student whose Hip hop–inspired writing I discuss in what follows demonstrates the literateness of rap in the contact zone of the academy.

And Y'all Thought Shakespeare Had Mad Game

In the course of an interview I had with "the E"[10] about his writing in high school, he showed me several "raps" he had drafted onto the pages of a spiral notebook. He and his boys had composed raps in their English class, often on days when they were shown films on the literature of Shakespeare. To relieve themselves of boredom with this class activity, the E confessed to me, they sat in the rear of the class and composed raps. In the following excerpt, I quote in its entirety (and with the student's spellings and phrasings intact) one of the more intriguing examples of the E's raps. Like most gangsta/reality rap lyrics, the E's rap is tinged with the occasional sexist and homophobic slight—which of course wouldn't be appropriate subject matter for many classrooms or certain public spaces—yet it exemplifies the literate practice of one young black male who is invested rhetorically in urban street sensibilities. Like most raps, this piece possesses rhyming couplets, but note that the E wrote it as if it were a work of prose.

> The Average Nig
> Now the E will never quit, I just go in a rage You wanna see the Mack come and step on the stage Then I bring forth, a new type of style, the Suckas fruntin and runnin when they see I'm not a Juevinile Hoe out on me! Then nigga ya hit Catch ya on the street grab [a] 9 and yo thats it, cause I don't play when its time to get way to real just grab the gat and ya cap I'll peel. I don't Bang I don't Slang I'm just out for surviven It's hard not to serve when ya strugglin and striven, To be on the top ya gotta be on ya own physically with ya bro's and mentally alone.
> Alway Fuckin' hoes I will never be gay and front any Muthafucka that has somethin' to say. you said that I was wrong, I really don't give a fuck not steppin' to fiens my Bitches got to have some type of butt and some class if they don't I cold get in that ASS. Not jokin' just strokin the girls can't be [smokin?] I always enhance cause I'm a vigorous man. Strong and able with some tricks I can do throw me that ASS and the Pussy I'll run through. Hoes say I'm crazy niggas think I'm cool I'll just shakem and Bakem and takem all to school. My Bro's know me they know I don't a fuck tryin' to be down nigga dont press ya luck. See I have a goal in life to get fully paid Its hard for a brother in this day and age. I have to go through the system and get good grades, or be six feet under with soil collecting sunrays.

Though I don't condone the E's use of obscene and misogynistic language in the piece, I am intrigued by his motivation to choose a popular art form to express himself (or a certain self) in writing. Like many youth these days, the E was inspired by rap artists to write, to engage in a unique form of literacy associated more with urban street culture than the culture of American schools. Mind you, I'm not disputing his lack of facility with standard academic prose. Truth be told, at this very early stage in his college career, his freshmen year at college, his prose is quite far from meeting the standards (both grammatical and rhetorical) of college-level writing. What I am disputing or calling into question, though, is the "primarily oral" (and, thus, nonliterate or subliterate) marker often (still) ascribed to young African Americans from the inner city.[11]

Some years ago, Walter Ong, author of several highly influential articles and books on orality and literacy, argued that in a black urban ghetto—it being *primarily oral*—"intensive analysis is not practiced, and not even thought of."[12] Ong goes on to say that "in a primary oral culture education consists in identification, participation, getting into the act, feeling affinity with a culture's heroes, getting 'with it'—not in analysis at all."[13] Now, I ain't gon lie; brothas be primed to *get with it,* but how a brotha gon get wit it if he don't know what's goin' down in the first place. I mean part of the process of gettin' with it (at least as I see it) is *analyzing,* breaking down a situation (yours and other folks') so that you can *get with it* properly—knowwhatI'msaying? The problem with Ong's community college student (oddly enough, not one he taught but one whom he conveniently uses as an example of *all* black, inner-city, "primarily oral" students) is not his deficiency in the analysis department, but rather his disinterestedness in the question as it was put to him. What red-blooded, American college freshman, whether in the mid-'80s (the time of Ong's study) or today in the new millennium, would have any real, substantive response to the question, What do you think of Nixon's action in Cambodia? In retrospect, our assessment of the man himself (his *ethos* as president) has been far more important than any single policy or political act he authorized. Besides, even a poor answer to such a question in and of itself doesn't mean a student lacks the ability to analyze. If anything, an example like that could simply mean that the student isn't privy to the ways of analyzing (speaking to and about) texts that we so dearly cherish in the academy. Of course, this is an old argument in the orality/literacy debate. About fifteen years ago, in fact, after a detailed review of such literature, James Gee arrived at the illuminating conclusion that

> language and literacy acquisition are forms of socialization,
> in this case socialization into mainstream ways of using

language in speech and print, mainstream ways of taking meaning, of making sense of experience. Discourse practices are always embedded in the particular world view of a particular social group; they are tied to a set of values and norms. In learning new discourse practices, a student partakes of this set of values and norms, this world view.

. . . Literacy in and of itself leads to no higher order, global cognitive skills; all humans who are acculturated and socialized are already in possession of higher order cognitive skills, though their expression and the practices they are embedded in will differ across cultures.

Essay-text literacy, with its attendant emphasis on the syntactic mode and explicitness, while only one cultural expression of literacy among many, is connected with the form of consciousness and interests of the powerful in our society.[14]

Had he considered it, I suspect that rap would be one such literacy practice that Gee could see expressing some of these higher-order thinking skills, though in a different way from essay-text literacy. However, for Ong (and perhaps many like-minded writing teachers today), the E's rap wouldn't make the grade, wouldn't qualify as, say, "intensive analysis"—for it doesn't subscribe to the same values (idle boasts over self-effacing discourse) and discursive practices (AAVE speech patterns and street slang as opposed to "standard" English grammar and usage, emotive rather than "reasoned" discourse) of the mainstream. Yet I would argue that the E has *analyzed* his subject (his own rhyming skills, survival instincts, desires/preferences, reputation, and goals) quite well. He knows for one thing that to be successful in life ("get fully paid") he has to "go through the system and get good grades." Coming from the streets of inner-city Cleveland, though, he also knows you gotta walk a fine line between the hood and the mainstream world, between being "physically with ya bros" and "mentally alone." Now if that ain't some heavy analysis, then I'm in the wrong game, baby.

Let me break it down to y'all like this. What the young brotha tryna say is that life in the ghetto is all about game, about trying to play the game and hustle for cream (chedda, scrilla, paper, and so on) however you can, legal or otherwise. But see, the E, he not down with the otherwise—at least not at this point in his life. According to the last lines of the first stanza—which, by the way, he probably adopted from an N.W.A. tune called "Gangsta Gangsta"—life in the ghetto is not (ultimately) about gang banging or slanging rocks but about dealin' with the hand that's dealt you and, like Curtis Mayfield once crooned, *tryin' to get over.* But the key for the E and for many (though not all) individuals of similar background is to maintain a safe balance between aspirations and origins—that is, between doing yo own thang and still being down with the brothas on the block.

With the E's analysis, as such, I think that there's little question about the "literateness" of his rap in particular and of rap music in general. Since raps are typically written first and later transmitted orally via electronic media, Ong might, however, consider them examples of "secondary" or "post-literate" orality. True, they are secondarily oral but only to consumers of the music, not to those, like the E, who produce it for very limited oral consumption. Hip hop critic Tricia Rose, in fact, sees rap not as a primarily oral practice but a literate one.

> Although power is located in the oral presentation of rap, rap rhymes are not the "fixed, rhythmically balanced expressions" that Ong refers to in his description of oral cultures but rhymes constructed in linear, literate (written) patterns. . . . By comparison [to oral cultures], rap lyrics are oral performances that display written (literate) forms of thought and communication.[15]

One can't, of course, equate the E's rhyming skills with that of most professional rappers; yet, even his rap adheres, for the most part, to the linear, written patterns Rose speaks of. "The Average Nig" begins with the E's introduction of himself. He identifies himself as a "mack" and one who is about to put forth a new style of rap. From there, he establishes his rep: Even though he doesn't "bang" or "slang," he's the type of dude you can't "Hoe out" on because he knows how it is when things get real. The second verse of the rap discusses the E's sexual tastes. He tells us he's quite the virile man, a playa (but what rapper isn't?), and that he prefers women (I'm giving him the benefit of the doubt with this polite substitution) who have a butt and (thankfully) some class. Following this, the E appears to sum up what he has said about himself, or rather, what others ("hoes" and "niggas") do. And like the first verse, he ends this one on a serious note, with the sobering option of either taking on the system (primarily education) or an early death. So, the E's lyrical pattern is pretty direct, I think, and the content is consistent with the topoi of gangsta/reality rap.

Besides linearity, "literate forms of thought and communication" include, according to Rose, the fact that "in rap the rhymed word is often in the middle of a long sentence, and punctuated short phrases are worked against the meter of the bass line. . . . The music, its rhythmic patterns, and the idiosyncratic articulation by the rapper are essential to the song's meanings."[16] Deceptively simple on its surface, especially sans the rapper's characteristic laid-back manner of articulation, Snoop Dogg's lines in Dr. Dre's "Nuthin But a 'G' Thang" (on *The Chronic*) demonstrate the complexity of thought and meaning often masked by rap's facile association with orality.

> She could be earnin' her man
> And learnin' her man,
> And at the same time burnin' her man[17]

Anthony DeCurtis's gloss on these lines in his essay "Word" highlights Snoop's use of language that is "sometimes reinforcing, sometimes contradictory" in meaning.[18] He suggests that the "she" spoken of here "could be making herself worthy of her man; making money for him; trying to understand him; teaching him; ripping him off; infecting him with a sexually transmitted disease."[19] The complexity of these lines alone should show the kind of literate thought (if there is such a thing so completely divorced from *oral thought*) rappers are capable of. But the lines after the DeCurtis quotation evince even greater complexity of meaning, for, unless we read it as some kind of non sequitur, then Snoop must be using "pussy" as a multilayered metaphor—sort of like the pimp's mantra not to be pimped by his hos, or the player's resolve not to be "pussy whipped" or "pussied" by the women he plays. Now this kind of critical thought might be too scatological and chauvinist for some, and rightly so, but we shouldn't deny the baby (the levels of abstraction) 'cause the bathwater be fonky.

In any case—whether primarily literate or secondarily oral—rap lyrics demonstrate the linguistic versatility and the keen rhetorical and analytical skill of young men and women from America's inner cities. In a word, G, they got game we don't think they got because the game they play don't adhere to our superficial rules. Some folks—some wannabe black public intellectual itching to "save" the race from its destructive Hip hop self—no doubt will deny the value of this kind of rhythmic repartee. Nonetheless, whether we acknowledge it or not, rap and Hip hop represent inner-city youths' most intense engagement with literacy, with literate production and consumption. In "Juicy," the Notorious B.I.G. stated that he read *Word-Up Magazine* (see *Ready to Die*). And every Hip hop head out there knows what a phenomenal wordsmith he became after he soaked up some of the culture through print, audio, and visual media. Rap music and Hip hop culture have turned youth across the nation and around the world on to not only a new kind of sound (by way of finely honed deejaying and production skills on sophisticated musical technology), but to writing and performance. (Witness the resurgence of performance poetry at clubs in New York City, Los Angeles, on college campuses across the country—my own small liberal arts college included—and of late on Russell Simmons's *Def Poetry Jam*.) For inner-city African Americans and Latino/as, this new interest in poetic expression likely exists for several reasons but perhaps most significantly because rap ardently resists what many of us willfully ignore: the tremendous silencing potential of the dominant culture's forms of oral and literate practice.[20] Rap breaks, or rather bum-rushes, this literate silencing. It gives voice to youth who because literacy education is largely based on Eurocentric models like Shakespeare or Hemmingway rather than Zora Neale Hurston, Sandra Cisneros, or Rakim often see literacy and literacy education as a white thang.

Bringing Game to the Zone

Given my assertion regarding the literateness of rap compositions and the unique rhetorical skill of its creators, I want to go on to characterize rap, or rather African American student writing imbued with rap sensibilities, as what Mary Louise Pratt calls the "literate arts of the contact zone."[21] Contact zones are, as those of us in Composition/Literacy Studies well know, "social spaces where cultures meet, clash, and grapple with each other, often in contexts of highly asymmetrical relations of power."[22] The most obvious historical examples of Pratt's "social spaces" are African slavery in the Americas and European colonialism throughout much of the non-Western world. A more recent site of cultural contact, I propose, is rap and the American academy, or, more precisely, Hip hop youths (some inner city and others, increasingly, suburban and rural) armed with black, ghettocentric lyrics and the universities that attempt to educate or, shall I say, mainstream them.

In her essay, Pratt offers as an example of a contact zone seventeenth-century Peru, at which time an Andean by the name of Felipe Guaman Poma de Ayala composed a rather subversive twelve-hundred-page letter addressed to the king of Spain, Philip III, who had conquered the massive Inca empire years earlier. Titled *The First New Chronicle and Good Government* and written in a mixture of Quechua, the language of the Inca, and "ungrammatical, expressive Spanish," the letter undermines the standard Spanish conquest narrative to construct in its place "a new picture of the world, a picture of a Christian world with Andean rather than European peoples at the center of it."[23] Pratt refers to the letter as an *autoethnographic* text, one in which "people undertake to describe themselves in ways that engage with representations others have made of them."[24]

Besides autoenthography, some of the other literate arts of the contact zone are "transculturation, critique, collaboration, bilingualism, mediation, parody, denunciation, imaginary dialogue, and vernacular expression."[25] Clearly, not all of these apply to rap compositions, but I believe one can find, in particular, elements of autoethnography, transculturation, critique, denunciation, and, of course, vernacular expression. In fact, though it may seem enormously reductive to do so, one could say that all of these literate arts are subsumed under the African American vernacular discursive forms *rapping* and *signifying*. Since rapping and signifying involve boastful talk and ritual insult, performance and self-expression, it's quite akin to Pratt's arts of the contact zone. As an example, one might consider Ice Cube's use of signifying in the acknowledgment section of his CD *The Predator* as a process in *transculturation,* which denotes "processes whereby members of subordinated or marginal groups select and invent from materials transmitted by a dominant or metropolitan culture."[26] Against the backdrop of the formal, literate genre of acknowledgments for published works, Cube appropriates the form but substitutes his own critical content. Note especially the sardonic tone of the portions I've italicized.

> Ice Cube wishes to *acknowledge the failure* of the public school system to teach all of its students about the major contributions made by our African American scientists, inventors, artists, scholars and leaders (*with all due respect for your lectures on the peanut*). *Without the role of state funded education in the conspiracy, the Predator album might not have been made.*[27]

Obviously, a political proposition is being put forth here, one that specifically targets the alleged miseducation students receive in American public schools. Quite in keeping with literate art in the racially charged contact zone of America, on the backhand of a denunciation of the hegemony of the dominant culture comes recrimination and perhaps reconstitution— *The Predator* authored and published for mainstream public consumption. Other examples abound, especially with the added visual effect of the now-ubiquitous music video. While video programs like BET's *Rap City* have been (especially in the late '90s, but then also in 2000, '01, '02, '03, '04 . . .) heavy on the "booty" videos (which, nonetheless, could be the object of serious feminist critique in writing classes), the production of these videos can be surprisingly transcultural or layered in signifying language. Select portions of P. Diddy's "Bad Boy for Life," Trick Daddy's "I'm a Thug," Eve's "Let Me Blow Your Mind" and "Love Is Blind," Ludacris and Jermaine Dupri's "Welcome to Atlanta," Nappy Roots' "Po' Folks," and David Banner's "Like a Pimp" all readily attest to this.

To demonstrate how Hip hop (or rather, the topoi in reality rap) and academic modes of literacy can converge in the contact zone of the academy, I'll again refer to the E's writing, only this time some informal prose pieces he wrote in his college basic writing course. In this first-semester course, the E wrote some rather provocative journal pieces. Two of his entries cover subjects rarely included among topics in college writing courses: jacking people for their cars and making crack cocaine. The first entry—titled "How to Pull a Jack Move!"—is a short how-to exposition providing, as one might expect, detailed instructions on committing a robbery. But the unique, street content of the prose here makes the entry so fascinating, for it suggests lived experience antithetical to that of the traditional college student (black or white). The E first enlightens his readers on the key terms: "First of all a Jack Move or a Jack is a robbery by gunpoint. There are many slang words for a robbery or something being taken off one person by another they are: gafflen; ganging (or a gange), and PD rolled. The only differences is that a Jack is by gunpoint." From here he goes on to explain how one goes about pulling one of the most famous jack moves, jacking someone "for their car and money."

> First you wait till they pull up at a red light or any kind of stop. Run up on the car with your gun in hand and ready to shoot. Any kind of gun can do the job a Ak 47, 9mm, 12 gauge anything. Just simply tell the persons who are in the car to empty there valuables on the car seats quickly, (because there is no time to wait). Tell the persons to get out or even pull them out. Then get in there vehicle and drive off. Do what you want with [the] car, sell it, sell the pieces, rims, stereo equipment or just profile in the car until the gas runs out.

A "jack move" is, thus, street talk gangsters or *gangsta rappers* (like Biggie Smalls in "Gimme the Loot" or, more recently, M.O.P. in "Ante Up") use to refer to robbery with a gun. In addition to providing this precise definition, the E clearly offers quite explicit and detailed instructions on pulling a jack. He tells his readers (or would-be jackers) both what to do and what to say, and he even provides alternatives for how they might make use of their rewards. They can either sell pieces of the car for money or "profile in the car until the gas runs out." The idea of *profiling*[28] in a car, though the term is, I believe, of fairly recent vintage, is central to street culture. The value (some) young brothas place on their status associated with a fancy car or ride is summed up in the word *pro-filing*. One's image or profile appearing behind the wheel of a car as it cruises through the hood (with a booming stereo system, of course) can mean everything to some young men (and women) in the bleak landscape of the urban ghetto. And for a kid to go to such lengths to profile in, say, a stolen Benz 'til it runs out of gas says a whole lot about how American materialism has warped the younger generation's value for life and sense of self.

My second example comes from the E's journal entry called "The Rocking and Cutting of Cocaine," wherein he unabashedly instructs his readers on how to make crack cocaine.

> When you are rocking or cooking up cocaine, you first need Baking Soda, a Tube of some sort and a pot and of course you need the cocaine.
>
> First you take a little bit of the cocaine not that much, then add a little bit of backing soda just a touch of it. You can only do it by the eye, That's why you have to do it slow. While the cocaine, backing soda and the water are in the tube you shake it over the pot of boiling water.
>
> Then you wait for a egg shape to form in the testube this is called a "cookie" or a "chop." After you see this, pour the water into another pot and save it because some of the cocaine is still in the water and can be used again.
>
> Take the cookie and cut them into desired pieces. The most famous are 20's, 10's and 5 pieces but there are some addicts that ask for 7 pieces.

The E's entry here predates Ice Cube's "What Can I Do?" (*Lethal Injection*, 1993) and Master P's "Ghetto D" (*Ghetto D*, 1997), but it's interesting how similarly didactic they are, especially Master P's business-like instruction on ghetto dope dealing in his song. Somewhat like "What Can I Do?" and Cube's *Predator* acknowledgment cited earlier, P's song is set up, on the one hand, as a critique on the established law enforcement authorities and, on the other hand, as a lecture for all playaz and ballaz. For instance, in the intro, P credits the song or record to a highly improbable association between his record label and, presumably, the ATF (Bureau of Alcohol, Tobacco, and Firearms)—only he substitutes "freedom of speech committee" for "alcohol." No Limit Records . . . Ghetto Dope . . . Freedom of Speech committee—hmm, no analysis at all?!!! By the end of the song, P instructs his would-be souljas for the long haul to switch up they game. Situated between these critical points are rather detailed steps on handlin' yo bi'ness, be it music or crack. Actually, P's younger brother, C Murder, who takes the mic first, offers the unlearned instruction not unlike the E does in his journal.

Now, I have offered the preceding student examples not to assert, as some would have it, black male pathology but to show how the E's use of rap and street culture converged in interesting ways with the academy, with academic writing; that is, through these examples I wish to show how the sensibilities of urban street culture came into direct contact (and conflict) with those of the university. This type of writing, I believe, allowed this student to resist, as I stated earlier, the silencing effect of standard academic writing topics and modes. Not that the E *couldn't* have written about a more palatable subject for academic audiences, say, something like "how to play a musical instrument," "how to perform CPR," or "how to repair a flat tire"—all of which may well have been within the sphere of his knowledge and experience. In fact, some of the E's other entries do cover less controversial topics in Hip hop such as "How to make a Sample and Loop it into a song" and "Why I like Rap and R&B Music." Interestingly, the latter entry provides what could serve as a strong rationale for the study of Hip hop: "I like rap and R&B music in that it teaches young black youth about what and what not to watch for in todays society. It helps us learn about our culture and history. It also helps us relate to others that have a problem that we might have already faced."

But the very fact that the E *chose* carjacking and making crack as topics for his journals says something not only about the nature of his social experience and knowledge (that is, again, his consumption of reality rap and street culture) but, more important, the nature of ours, the limits of our knowledge and understanding of the worlds (real and imagined) our students inhabit and the identities they construct for themselves in dialectic with those worlds. Clearly, student writing about such kind of lived experience will likely challenge, even threaten, the values the academy seeks to inculcate in its charges. But, hey, that ain't necessarily a bad thing. After all, many of the values academic institutions promote can also be deeply hegemonic and psychologically damaging to some of the constituents they claim to serve. And here I don't mean that it would threaten our values of morality and adherence to law; rather, I mean the academy's value of certain kinds of knowledge (objective, abstract, rational, impassive, impersonal) or sources of knowledge (the lived experience and consciousness of a hyperliterate Euro-American citizenry) and certain ways of demonstrating these (such as the linear, thesis-driven expository essay on largely innocuous subject matter). In *Electric Rhetoric: Classical Rhetoric, Oralism, and a New Literacy,* Kathleen Welch believes that contemporary media/technology, the new orality she calls it, is changing our consciousness from a linear to a more associative frame, but I doubt that it has or will have much effect on writing programs and the way most faculty (in and outside of said programs) teach the expository essay any time soon. And yet if we genuinely expect serious critical reading, writing, and thinking to take place for *all* students in the academy, the clash between academic culture (including middle-class suburban culture, a slightly different thing) and urban vernacular culture must inform writing theory and pedagogy.

How specifically might urban vernacular culture or the clash between it and the mainstream university inform writing instruction? Pratt's pedagogical arts of the contact zone may provide some answer. They consist of the following:

> exercises in storytelling and in identifying with the ideas, interests, histories, and attitudes of others; experiments in transculturation and collaborative work and in the arts of critique, parody, and comparison (including unseemly comparisons between elite and vernacular cultural forms); the redemption of the oral; ways for people to engage with suppressed aspects of history (including their own histories), ways to move *into and out of* rhetorics of authenticity; ground rules for communication across lines of difference and hierarchy that go beyond politeness but maintain mutual respect; a systematic approach to the all-important concept of *cultural mediation.*[29]

Though some of these pedagogical arts seem particularly designed for the Americas course at Stanford, where Pratt first introduced the notion of contact zones more than ten years ago, quite a few of them could also be adapted to a course on writing and Hip hop. In particular, three of these pedagogical arts could, I believe, critically engage at-risk (as well as non-at-risk) students in the literate arts of the contact zone. Below, I list each of the three arts and discuss how they might be employed in a zone where Hip hop shares center stage with academia (that is, at least, with instruction in expository writing).

Exercises in Storytelling and in Identifying with the Ideas, Interests, Histories, and Attitudes of Others

While many students come to college these days overly stimulated and too easily distracted by the latest version of Playstation; MTV and VH1; ads for Tommy Jeans, DKNY, and Esprit; Net surfing and emailing; cell phones and pagers; body piercing; drugs; and alcohol; *Glamour* and *Sports Illustrated;* the hottest CDs and DVDs—as well as the usual college fare: frat parties, barhopping, dating, sex, sports, and the latest trend, goin' buck wild (I mean butt naked in front of MTV cameras) on spring break in Miami, the Bahamas, Cancún, or wherever else—they also come to us with a virtual gold mine of knowledge and experience involving various oral and literate media. That is to say, they possess a wealth of cultural knowledge in desperate need of serious intellectual inquiry and critique. Just consider what many of these students consume from Hip hop alone: besides the music and videos (oral and visual media), there's Hip hop Web sites; song lyrics on CD covers and on the Internet; magazines like *The Source, XXL, Murder Dog,* and *Vibe;* and—a Hip hop basic—graffiti art on public spaces throughout the country (all various forms of print and graphic media). Added to these oral, visual, and print media are others—dance (breakin', in particular); the spoken word (rappin'); the sound (a deejay's mixes and scratches, which in itself is a kind of art requiring specialized knowledge); the clothes; the cars, with their elaborate sound systems, rims, and hydraulics; various types of hairstyles, handshakes, swagger, poses, attitude, and way of conversatin'—and you got a whole 'nother way of being or, as KRS-One would have it (see his "Temple of Hip Hop" web page or his recently published book, *Ruminations*), a whole 'nother consciousness taking shape in contemporary urban America. In *Hip Hop America,* Nelson George refers to this cultural shift as a set of post–civil rights, postmodern cultural forms:

> At its most elemental level hip hop is a product of post–civil rights era America, a set of cultural forms originally nurtured by African-American, Caribbean-American, and Latin American youth in and around New York in the '70s. Its most popular vehicle for expression has been music, though dance, painting, fashion, video, crime, and commerce are also its playing fields. It's a postmodern art in that it shamelessly raids older forms of pop culture—kung fu movies, chitlin' circuit comedy, '70s funk, and other equally disparate sources—and reshapes the material to fit the personality of an individual artist and the taste of the times.[30]

Hip hop a postmodern art? Surely, George musta stuttered. All this time academics been thinking and writing about postmodernity, postmodernism, postmodern this and postmodern that . . . and come to find out we didn't have a clue about the postmodern theory in practice in the ghetto. Postmodernism right there on the gritty streets of the Bronx where Herc, Bam, Flash, Grand Wizard Theodore, and them cats was mixing records, painting trains, and busting moves in the mid-'70s. Twenty-five-plus years later, and Hip hop ain't missed a postmodern beat. To get a bit mo' insight on this, check out Russell Potter's take in *Spectacular Vernaculars: Hip-hop and the Politics of Postmodernism.*

Anyway, as far as storytellin' goes, students have a whole lot to draw on, a whole lot to teach us in the contact zone of the academy. As Hip hop storytellers Slick Rick, Outkast, and others exhibit in their raps, students in the academic/Hip hop contact zone can write accounts of their lived experience as inner-city, rural, or suburban youths in postmodern America. If writing is, after all, about discovery and knowledge making, then what better way to generate knowledge—real, local knowledge—than to have students narrate meaningful aspects of their lives in the public sphere. Because Hip hop's narratives are rarely just personal, mere self-disclosures, they tend toward the autoethnographic, or what you might call personalized public narratives, in that they present as public issues what many see as private or personal problems (like fatherlessness, criminal charges, living on welfare, sexual habits, premature deaths, homey love, baby mama or daddy drama).

Of course, students should learn how to write, say, effective arguments (the mantra at my old, old job), but our personal lives are in fact arguments, are embedded in argument. And besides, an argument is so much more meaningful when the writer's personal knowledge and experience, her subjectivity, suffuse it. Now, tell me, what kind of sense do it make to have students write arguments about, say, the causes of terrorism without reference to their personal thoughts and feelings on the tragedy of 9/11? Instead of trying to get students to look objectively outside their own personal spaces, Hip hop shows us that that's precisely where we should have them look, at the places and spaces where much of their most thoughtful, creative, and impassioned arguments live and breathe.

Now about the relative substance of these narratives coming from students on the right side of the track—well, I think that they could even teach us a thing or two about coming of age in Gen Y, Gen Next, or Gen Whatever-Else-We-Old-Folks-Can-Come-Up-with-to-Label-Them. So while students from the 'burbs may not have, as many rappers do, a ghetto-fabulous, rags-to-riches story to tell, they probably got enough drama going on in their lives and communities to produce a riveting literary episode or two. *American Beauty* may not be the quintessential white suburban American tale, but it's not an absolute aberration either. Columbine and a dozen other suburban school shootings not long ago sufficiently attest to that. And if nothing else, there's a story, maybe a mildly subversive one, behind their relative interest and participation in Hip hop. I mean, think about it—what in their lived experience (their right mind, some parents might say) would induce (a growing number of) suburban white teens to identify with (or try to anyway) niggaz in Brick City, The Mil, ATL, Philly, The Lou, LBC, or any other ghetto in urban

America? Bound to be some mighty interesting commentary on whiteness in this recent wave of wiggermania. But then let's be real; who wanna talk about wiggers or whiteness with white kids in a writing class when you can talk about professional writing, service learning, or hypertexts with absolutely no regard to the subtext of whiteness that pervades them?

As for the part about having students identify with others' ideas, attitudes, interests, and histories, well, I don't know how much you can expect students to do that in a one-semester course. I guess that I would first want to get students to think critically about the ideas, interests, and so forth they already identify with. (See, this kind of narrative writing ain't just about telling lighthearted anecdotes; it's also about self-reflection and self-criticism.) Having examined these carefully, I would then ask them to connect their ideas, interests, and histories with those of others, particularly Hip hop's others. Greg Dimitriadis makes an interesting assertion in this regard. Drawing on the work of scholars in media/popular culture and education (like Henry Giroux), he writes, "In many respects, popular culture provides the key narratives or stories—around love, respect, friendship, adventure, etc.—that people make use of in coming to inhabit validated identities. Increasingly, in fact, young people are turning to popular culture to inhabit particular identities, often in lieu of narratives available in traditional institutions such as school and family."[31] I haven't asked students to identify with, say, the attitude of Hip hoppas (the irreverent, keeping-it-real stance toward life), but it would definitely add new life to an often very tired and humdrum comp class. And this way, white kids might learn a thing or two about the myths of black identity and black kids might see how those myths are in constant dialectic with the more insidious myths of not only white maleness but also white femaleness (for example, the "SOUTHERNBELLE").[32] One rather small thing I have tried to do in my rap/comp classes, though, is to have students invent Hip hop aliases for themselves, nicknames reflecting their would-be Hip hop alter ego. Hip hop culture, like African American vernacular culture generally, relishes in naming, in (re)inventing the self. By adopting their own Hip hop aliases, students might begin to engage in the creative process of self-invention and self-construction that rap artists are masters of. But the Hip hop alias is merely an extension of the creative process, for without the Hip hop artists' raps, turntable and/or production skills, tags, or breaks, naming almost becomes superfluous. So, to give students a feel for the creative process of rapping in particular (and writing and wordplay generally), I have had them write their own raps and perform them before the class. Now, of course, some students get nervous about the performance part, but, in the end, they get to feelin' it and some even go so far as to make it a memorable event by adding dance routines, specially recorded beats, and comic sketches. The exercise doesn't adequately represent rappers' creative work, but it's my hope that students gain a fresh appreciation of rap not only as recorded music but also as literate art (such as imaginative storytelling, clever wordplay, intimidating boasts, caustic quips, and amusing anecdotes). If students ("at risk" or otherwise) could learn to treat their prose with the dedication and passion that many rappers do in the composition of their lyrics, then who you think would be singing Hip hop's praises?

Experiments in Transculturation . . . and in the Arts of Critique, Parody, and Comparison (Including Unseemly Comparisons Between Elite and Vernacular Cultural Forms)

Earlier, I mentioned what I thought might be examples of transculturation and critique in rap music. Because of rap music's roots in African American street vernacular forms like rapping and capping, the dozens, and signifying, the pedagogical arts of critique, parody, comparison, and transculturation are rife in Hip hop culture. While no explicit evidence suggests that any of these arts constituted the E's rap or journal entries, one could make the case that his no-nonsense instructions on carjacking and making crack cocaine may be a mild subversion of the standard how-to essay. However, a stronger case of this kind of prose experimentation can be made with the writing of other "at risk" students whose work I've discussed elsewhere.[33] In these students' formal and informal writing, there are several examples of signifying language, and certainly, as I argue there, this could serve as a rich pedagogical resource for teachers to use to help some African American ("at risk") students appropriate academic discourses. Others have argued more compellingly for signifying as a resource in the classroom—namely, Carol Lee, focusing primarily on signifying to teach reading in secondary schools (Signifying as a Scaffold), and Valerie Balester, concentrating on African American discursive practices generally to teach college-level writing (Cultural Divide).

Neither Lee nor Balester discusses her work in terms of Pratt's arts of the contact zone; yet, much like Pratt, they seek to bring the vernacular into full contact with elite or academic cultural forms. A. Suresh Canagarajah, on the other hand, does make significant use of Pratt's work, particularly her notion of safe houses, which she defines as social and intellectual spaces where groups are protected from oppression by a dominant culture.[34] In his article "Safe Houses in the Contact Zone: Coping Strategies of African-American Students in the Academy," Canagarajah claims that safe houses provide "a forum within the classroom where minority students can keep alive, practice, and develop their own vernacular discourse."[35] By analyzing texts constructed in the safe houses—"transcripts of electronic conferences, verbal disputes in the mail, and drafts of essays"—students can, according to Canagarajah, learn strategies that would help them negotiate the differences between academic and vernacular discourses.[36] Canagarajah's point about safe houses makes a lot of sense, but I question to what extent these kinds of safe-house texts can constitute class curricula. What will become of them once the final draft of a paper is due? Will oppositional, vernacular discourses generated in the safe house find their way into the formal, graded work produced in the contact zone?

These days, in fact, I wonder about pedagogical approaches (mine included) that center on the use of African American vernacular discourses as a bridge to mainstream academic discourses, because the concept behind the approach still implies the deficiency of the former vis-à-vis the latter. When all is said and done, our pedagogy (not to mention our theory) still privileges elite discourses, or put more bluntly, discourses that reflect and sustain white hegemony. I mean, once, say, a Hip hop–inspired basic writer gets through the sympathetic accommodation phase of a semester- or year-long basic writing course, then it's time for mainstreaming and, quite possibly, even she will be inclined (that's the game behind the game, as Chuck D would say) to repudiate the vernacular and its culture. But don't get it twisted, yo; I'm not out to eradicate (not like what some folks is tryna do with Ebonics) the teaching of standard English or academic discourses in college writing classes. I just wanna keep inner-city kids from trading in their ghetto pass for the patronizing acceptance or approval of a shamelessly self-righteous (black and white) mainstream. But, Gloria Anzaldua reminds us, "it is not enough to stand on the opposite river bank, shouting questions, challenging patriarchal, white conventions. . . . At some point, on our way to a new consciousness, we will have to leave the opposite bank, the split between two mortal combatants somehow healed so that we are on both shores at once."[37] I doubt that we will ever get to that point, honestly; given the growing corporatization of the academy, especially writing programs, the culture of the university is getting more conservative and prescriptive, not less. Until we switch the game, or expose the game behind the game, the university writing class will still be about conformity to the American mainstream. As Victor Villanueva eloquently states, "A curriculum that conceives of empowerment as enabling access to the middle class is fundamentally traditional, no matter the doffs of the hat to women's studies, minority literature, multiculturalism. At bottom, there is still hegemony."[38]

So, what do we do? How do we go about changing the game? Well, short of completely altering our worldviews and reconstructing our identities as writing teachers and administrators, I would say that one thing we can do is to try playing the game on a different field—one that we construct with our students based on their culture's terms and not our own. For even when we try to resist, say, the hegemony of the traditional canon of language and literacy, we come up with course materials (like the in-house freshmen reader used at my recent old job) that cater to *our* interests, be it affirmative action, feminism, technology, education, or gay rights. We assume that topics such as these, in and of themselves, will make academic discourse accessible to students of diverse backgrounds, when really they deny students the opportunity to make sense of academic discourses in a way that legitimizes their own lived experience and identity constructions. I think Jabari Mahiri was on point when he stated in *Shooting for Excellence* that "the best way to build on [students'] lived experiences was to provide ways for students to identify, explore, and affirm the things that were important in their lives, and to provide many avenues and opportunities for those things to surface in the context of our classes and in the topics of our writing."[39] Not that we shouldn't at some point introduce students to the aforementioned topics. We just need to do so from a different perspective, to try seeing these matters through a different screen, as Kenneth Burke might say.[40] Take feminism, for instance, a subject that comes up fairly often in rhet/comp circles, more so, it seems, than race or class ever does. Gloria Steinem and bell hooks are both fine choices for reading (especially hooks because she does know her Hip hop), but there you're talkin' 'bout an earlier generation of feminists who ain't come of age in the Hip hop generation. Not like self-proclaimed Hip hop feminist Joan Morgan has. As the sista says in *When Chickenheads Come Home to Roost* (and how many self-proclaimed rhet/comp feminists know anything about a "chickenhead"?), "More than any other generation before us, we need a feminism committed to 'keeping it real.' We need a voice like our music—one that samples and layers many voices, injects its sensibilities into the old and flips it into something new, provocative, and powerful."[41] In Pratt's terms, I guess you could call this a comparison of elite academic discourses on feminism and a vernacular, street kind of feminist discourse.

Redemption of the Oral

If I have consciously focused on any of these approaches on Pratt's list of pedagogical arts, this has to be it. I haven't actually called what I do a "redemption of the oral" (whatever that means for her), but it sounds like what I do when I emphasize oral expression in the writing classroom. But even personally, since at least '94 I've tried to mingle the written with the oral—which for me means a casual, conversational approach to writing and, as you've witnessed in this book, a liberal use of the black vernacular (including a bit of Hip hop slang). I make no claim that writing in such a way enhances the reading of my work (you'll be the judge of that, I'm sure), but I find the approach liberating and empowering. It unleashes facets of the self that often are suppressed by my more frequent use of academically sanctioned forms of speech and writing. And as a writer (not just an academic), this is important to me if I'm going to claim any kind of meaningful ownership and authority over what I write.

As for my students, well, I do not require them to write in an oral style or in slang because I know that most of them aren't used to doing so and that some may even subconsciously resist it. All I ask is that students loosen up their prose a bit, try to express themselves in a way that's less rigid and conventional than the stale academic models etched into their brains from high school or (re)produced in college textbooks. But if they comfortable using it, then I let 'em rip with some Hip hop slanguage or their own brand of colloquial speech (especially if it's done tactfully, with rhetorical effect). "Get yo slang on, baby, and make us feel you!" is my motto these days. The students who have tried writing this way don't necessarily write a better overall paper than those who haven't. Slang or no slang, they gotta make a point and, depending on the assignment, put forth some sound reasons to substantiate it (that's the game again, man, what can I say?). And all the Hip hop slang in the world won't help you if you ain't got nuthin' meaningful to say. But what Hip hop slang or colloquial speech can do, I think, is brighten up students' often dull, emotionless prose, let them assume a different writing voice and identity for a change, and, most important, give them a definite sense of rhetoric, a sense of the transformative power of the word—oral and written.

Real professional writers (not just those in the fields comp folk glorify) in published periodicals do it, after all. Take the Hip hop magazine *The Source,* for example. The articles in it are not all written in Hip hop slang or in the black vernacular (which I personally take umbrage to), but one-time editor Carlito Rodriguez faithfully set the tone for each issue by writing in a way that, on the one hand, conveys the necessary information and, on the other hand, legitimizes the collective Hip hop identity. Here's how he put it down in an excerpt from a piece he calls "The Boys of Summer." It isn't written entirely in the vernacular; in fact, it shows a nice mixture of vernacular and standard language styles: "Reminisce with me. Last time we kicked it, I was gassin' you up on the joys of summa'time. Some of you might have interpreted it as me complaining about having to spend most of my time holed up in an office, hackin' away at a computer keyboard. But whatever the case might be, consider this diatribe as the latest in my never-ending thirst for an eternal summer."[42]

Elliot Wilson, editor-in-chief of *XXL,* uses a similar style in his "Still-stupid" editorial in the January–February '02 issue, though for one of my students Wilson's use of slang was way too heavy-handed. Even more impressive than the editorial are the letters to the editor. Mostly young folks, probably all in their teens, write in to comment on an article, expressing their personal pleasure or distaste and doing so in Hip hop style. Here's an excerpt written by a young sista in NYC: "I just wanna give y'all props for the best issue I've ever read. I'ma cop like five to help y'all sales with this one. I attend Stuyvesant High School and after all that terrorist shit at the WTC and being evacuated from the school, seeing the issue a few days later and reading the cover story on my favorite rapper, Ja Rule, helped a lot."[43] Granted, this is merely a letter—a far more informal type of writing than a school essay—but the young sista's command of language, her conscious manipulation of words and letters, is priceless.

Way befo Rodriguez, Wilson, and all of these pups set down their Hip hop prose styles, though, journalist and cultural critic Greg Tate had done so in the late '80s and early '90s. Matter fact, he may well have set the precedence for a Hip hop vernacular prose style with his collection of essays titled *Flyboy in the Buttermilk: Essays on Contemporary America*. I mean, back then the brotha even broke down hermeneutics with Hip hop flava:

> Word, word. Word up: Thelonious X. Thrashfunk sez, yo Greg, black people need our own Roland Barthes, man. Black deconstruction in America? I'm way ahead of the brother, or so I think when I tell him about my dream magazine: I Signify—The Journal of Afro-American Semiotics. . . .[44]
>
> And white folks thought black people only had the edge on them in primitivism; uh-huh, brothers and sisters got deconstruction racing through their veins too. Matter of fact, one of the hippest essays in the collection, James Snead's "Repetition as a Figure of Black Culture," gives the granddaddy of dialectics (that's Hegel y'all) a run for his modernism.[45]

Of course, I am aware that Tate and everybody else who writes this way (including me) are coming at it from the flip side compared to the average student in a basic writing or first-year composition class; that is, long after most of us have become fluent writers of some "standard" variety of English (be it journalistic, academic, or something else) we then flip the script, begin switching linguistic codes and using vernacular expressions in our writing. (Then again, I can't really speak for the younger generation, those who write in to *The Source* and *XXL*. They may have begun mixing up vernacular and standard codes soon after learning to use a pen or a computer keyboard.) In any case, for me it's not just about switching codes or peppering the pages of my text with slang. It's about alternative ways of representing and affirming the self in the face of the still pervasive linguistic and cultural imperialism in the academy (the Lino Graglias of the academic world are still at large). Though he didn't put it quite in these terms, Iceberg Slim touched on this idea when he queried a young fan and an aspiring writer: "what kind of writer do you want to be, that you want the world to hear and pay attention to?"[46] Here, Slim's talking specifically about writing as a literary career; however, the question is pertinent, I think, to students in college composition classes because even these students are intuitively aware of the close connection between language use and social or cultural identity. In the sphere of television broadcasting, for instance, they are well aware of the differences between, say, the dramatic, Hip hop–inspired style of ESPN sportscaster Stuart Scott (among other New School sports anchors) and veteran ABC news anchors Ted Koppel and Diane Sawyer. But then, these days the networks seem to allow a "nonstandard" code or mode of presentation in sports television and radio announcing but not so much in news, not even on most BET or MTV news programs (with the one exception of talk show host Ed Gordon on the now-defunct *BET Tonight*).

Anyway, Slim advises this young brotha about what kind of writer he might choose to be. Remember this was back in the '70s and there weren't a lot of dudes tradin' in street hustles for a pen. Slim was unique among black writers at the time, and he wants his young fan to know that he can stay true to himself, to his background as a published writer.

> Let's look at a much different kind of black writer, say one from a lifelong middle-class background, whose writings you admire and respect because you are a different kind of brother. Like a certain older black writer whose writings are virtually unknown to the black masses, I am gifted, craven, cunning or perhaps simply repressed enough to have created a novel dealing with the condition of blacks in America that has won admiration from some white critics and charms even the white racist. "Magnificently detached and objective," "unmatched aloofness from bitterness and accusation," say the white critics in gratitude for unpricked conscience. And the white racists will spread the word, "The Nigger is a genius . . . ," "What a truthful look into the black ghetto," to close with the final damning, "He writes like a white man."[47]

Slim's disdain for the middle-class black writer is blatant enough. But in fact his slight has less to do with the middle-class status of black writers and more to do with the fact that the work of these writers is often used to reify white hegemony in the name of some bogus objective standard of literary excellence. Unlike Slim does with his young fan, we don't typically ask students what kind of writer they want to be; we often don't even tell them that they have a choice. Thus, students (especially students of color from underprivileged backgrounds) aren't typically made aware of the fact that the writing we teach them reflects the ideology of the privileged classes and that to give way to it uncritically may lead to a heightened sense of double-consciousness. Keenly aware of this in the literary world, Slim warns the young blood to

> Watch out! Take my hand, young Brother, as we avoid that gilded glob of bullshit about the ideal of the colorless black writer and the superiority of his purely objective art. I believe that in these times a black writer is a success only when the black masses can relate to his work and to him with respect and a strong sense of kinship. I believe a black writer in these times who shuns or loses kinship with his people is early doomed to dry up and die as a writer. He needs for his creative survival a living, throbbing lifeline to his people, for with only the impersonal white critics' cold pats on his nappy head and the fawning quicksand favor of the white public, his writer's juices will drain away.[48]

Some may not buy the dichotomy Slim draws between mainstream black writers and writers like him, a ghetto-pimp-turned-writer. But if you read his works and that of other writers of his time, you'd have to agree that he surely wasn't penning his urban sagas to appeal to the literati or, like Morgan say, *niggerati*.[49] And yet the issue Slim raises about the writer who best represents the black masses is a tricky one, especially now when, according to Hip hop critic Michael Eric Dyson, even ghetto culture is fragmented.[50]

Still, the issue that Slim raises reflects more so on the establishment, on established expectations for literacy production in the literate community. Or in, as I been sayin', the composition classroom. Clearly, we've come a long way from the five-paragraph theme and the current traditional model of writing, but I think that William Upski Wimsatt, a young white writer and self-professed Hip hop junkie, has a point when he associates current writing practices (namely, our books) with a characteristically suburban American mindset. In *Bomb the Suburbs,* he states:

> The suburbs is more than just an unfortunate geographical location, it is an unfortunate state-of-mind. It's the American state-of-mind, founded on fear, conformity, shallowness of character, and dullness of imagination.

> Most books are suburban books. Neatly designed, neatly packaged, and automatically produced. The author chooses one topic, one voice, one style, one audience, one point of view, then lays out the book according to plan.[51]

That's an oversimplification, of course, given some of the stuff that's out there from writers who do their own thing (like Wimsatt) and publish their works independently. But the point here is to find ways to redeem the oral in the academic contact zone. Organized, as he says, like a "cluttered and dense" city with "home-made, one-of-a-kind items,"[52] his book could serve as one way of accomplishing this redemption. And redemption of the oral is possible in the oral traditions of Native Americans, Mexican Americans, African Americans, and certain ethnic Caucasian American groups. Yet as an art based on the oral and written word, on poetic expression and performance, Hip hop on its own might be our best hope of redeeming the oral for a generation that is increasingly being defined by it.

GETTIN' MY TEACH ON CUZ, HEY, I GOT GAME TOO

To be perfectly honest, though, prior to piecing together this chapter I hadn't really given much thought to using contact-zone theory as a kind of pedagogical model or as a way to structure a writing class. Even after reviewing a number of such studies in *Theorizing Composition* a few years ago, I didn't consider contact-zone theory as easily applicable to pedagogy or curricula. Originally, I caught hold of the idea because I saw it as a way of recognizing and affirming the literate practices of those whom the academic community regards as (à la Ong) nonliterate. In fact, the comp class on rap that I created ten years ago grew out of my interest in nonmainstream literacy practices and my desire to meet students where they are, or at least where I believed some of them to be, given my work with students like the E. And after ten years of teaching this class, I gotta say that the oral-literate art of Hip hop is one of the few things that inspire me to teach writing. Lately I've been feeling a lot like Geoff Sirc did in '98 when he wrote: "I really don't know what to do in a writing class anymore, what makes real sense, except to play 2Pac records."[53] Along with playing Pac records (and many others, of course) in a writing class, I would also want the class to bust a few moves, to get students completely out of traditional classroom mode. I haven't quite pulled this off in my classes yet, and maybe I'm dreaming, but if former secretary of state Madeleine Albright (among others) can bust some moves to Aretha Franklin's "Respect" on CNN, then I know dreams can come true. (I guess I got to tune into CNN more often. You never know; I just might

catch C. Delores Tucker, William Bennett, and Bill O'Reilly—well, maybe
not O'Reilly—cuttin' up when the next episode airs.)

If I can't get students to bust a move, if I can't get 'em out of the
traditional way of thinking and behaving in the classroom, then perhaps
the best thing I can do is get myself out of that mode. I'm not quite there
yet, haven't busted a whole lotta moves up to now, but I do what I can to
understand and appropriate aspects of contemporary youth culture. But
of course, I don't front like I'm eighteen or twenty and share the same
values and tastes that my students do. I mean, I can rock right along wit
'em to DMX, Eminem, Missy, or Chingy; I can floss in some Timberland
boots and some Mecca or Iceberg carpenter jeans; I can even sport a do-
rag (oops I guess it don't really count if you sportin' it at the crib) and
all that, but you ain't gon see me wearing jeans halfway down my butt,
or see me sportin' gold teeth and cornrows, or tattooed and pierced up
like rappers do on they videos. I got mad respect for the style these young
brothas and sistas be innovatin', but I got my limits, you know. Gotta
stay true to myself, as any keeping-it-real Hip hop head must. Besides, G,
not even all Hip hop heads are alike. Gangstaz and playaz abound, but
there are quite a few intellectuals and activists too. And then you got a
few Old School cats like me.

But yo, one day this Old School cat is gonna bust some moves on all
them young bucks. One day, I'm gon roll up in class, give 'em a gangsta
glare, and spit a little somethin' like:

Hip-hopology 101

> *What up, people! Check your registration, make sho you*
>   *have a seat*
> *You in Hip-hopology 101, the class on readin' and writin'*
>   *to the rhythms of the phattest Hip hop beats*
> *Syllabus designed to stimulate yo mind and yo body to the*
>   *sounds of the ghetto streets*
> *I'm the prof, as you can see*
> *The name is Campbell, Phd*
> *But, yo, no need for the formality*
> *You can call me Doc, or better yet, Prof e. c.*
> *Prophecy, that is, y'all feeling me?*
>
> *Rhetorician, orator, critic, and sometime prophet, I pro-*
>   *fess*
> *Charged to speak the cold, hard truth always from the*
>   *chest*
> *And like Ra I tends to bless, to put the mind to rest,*

To relieve stress from the troubled breast
Confess and I'll take you highER
Baby, baby, baby light yo fiRE
More than, let me guess, the cess you ingest

One-hundred proof product of the Lone Star State
Sealed by fate, '60 the date, flesh did flesh create
20 plus did blood propitiate, spirit regenerate
Check the plates, playa, but spare the hate
You Yankees cain't relate, cain't even contemplate
That Southern gravy and chicken fried steak
Don't mean to denigrate
Just aim to penetrate
With my rhyme
Yo' New York state of mind
And impart (in)sight to the blind
Seek and you shall find
As it is written
Destiny manifest, the seasons and the times

Sent on a mission to the East to teach
You new millennium yups how to write wit rhythm in yo
*   soul*
And fire in yo speech
Picture Malcolm rappin' to a fonky Dre beat
Or Cee Lo harmonizing while Dr. King preach
I got a dream today, brothas and sistas, I beseech!
Dig deep befo' you sleep
Education come dirt cheap
When seeds sown don't reap

Yo check your first impression
Boys and Girls, class is now in session
Doggin' me out, thinkin' that nigga too preppie and proper
*   for mic aggression*
Flossin' in yo Fubu and Sean Jean, youse a real nigga, rep-
*   resentin' Hip hop*
Now, now son don't get it twisted, Hip hop not 'bout
*   what you cop*
But the science you drop
And innovation like Dizzy with bop
No Tommy to my name, no Lugz or Timbs I can claim
But I'm mo' Hip hop than you, fool, cuz I'm an old school

> *representative of the game*
> *And still got enough playa in me to put yo mama to*
>   *shame*
> *Boy, what's my name?*
> *Peep the picture I'm paintin' in yo frame*
> *And recognize the source of the game you claim*
> *Take heed to the Prof e.c., for therein lies the true*
> *Class dismissed after a moment of silence for my H-town*
>   *homie DJ Screw*

I call this little ditty "Hip-hopology 101." Naw, I ain't quittin' my day job, so don't think I'm trippin' over this. After a long minute of hounding from my students, I finally got it together and laid down some lines. In spring '01, I presented to my class an earlier version of what I've written here. My students didn't say a whole lot after I performed it, but judging from their reactions during the performance they were amused by a few lines (in particular, the one about chicken-fried steak got a few laughs). But regardless of what they thought about it, I got turned on to the whole creative process of writin' and rappin'. Much like Erick Sermon spoke of in "Music," I guess the rhythm just got me in a zone. And maybe that's what writing should do, get students into a zone. Maybe if we treated writing more like rapping, taught writing like it was something you felt and got a groove to, then students like the E could really show us how much game they got.

That's it. Peace! I'm out.

Notes

Chapter 1

1. See Rickford and Rickford's *Spoken Soul* for a thorough rundown on what all those "enlightened" minds had to say.
2. Folks interested in this literature should check out Mufwene et al., *African-American English,* as well as two other edited collections specifically focusing on the language education of young African American Vernacular English speakers—Adger, Christian, and Taylor's *Making the Connection* and Perry and Delpit's *The Real Ebonics Debate.* Three well-respected African American linguists/language educators have also put together in a single volume many of their earlier articles on the vernacular. John Rickford has published his *African American Vernacular English;* John Baugh has collected some old and new essays in *Out of the Mouths of Slaves;* and language and language policy expert Geneva Smitherman has reproduced many of her essays on the social, legal, and educational ramifications of black speech in *Talkin That Talk.* Baugh and Rickford have also published books specifically on the recent Ebonics controversy. Baugh's *Beyond Ebonics* covers the Ebonics controversy from a linguistic, educational, and legal perspective. Rickford, along with his coauthor and son Russell John Rickford, covers similar ground in *Spoken Soul,* only his reference to Ebonics or the vernacular as Spoken Soul—a label offered by writer Claude Brown in the '60s—speaks to the intrinsic significance of the vernacular to African American life and culture.
3. See chapters 1 and 2 of my dissertation, "The Rhetoric of Black English Vernacular," for this review.
4. Based on Williams's statement from the St. Louis conference, according to Baugh, "Ebonics is an international construct, including the linguistic consequences of the African slave trade" (*Beyond Ebonics,* 74). According to Tolliver-Weddington's definition, "Ebonics is the equivalent of black English" and is a dialect of English (ibid.). Ernie Smith's more recent definition posits that "Ebonics is the antonym of black English and is considered to be a language other than English" (ibid.). And finally, based on the work of Blackshire-Belay, "Ebonics refers to language among all people of African descent throughout the African

153

Diaspora" (ibid., 74–75).

5. Royster, "When the First Voice You Hear," 37.
6. See Rickford and Rickford, *Spoken Soul,* 5, for Jackson's complete statement.
7. Ibid., 3–10.
8. Personal communication from student.
9. X, *Autobiography,* 310.
10. Angelou, *The Caged Bird,* 6.
11. Rickford and Rickford, *Spoken Soul,* 37–38.
12. Madison Searle, email message to author containing excerpt of an article from the *Houston Chronicle,* October 17, 2000.
13. Rickford and Rickford, *Spoken Soul,* 64–65.
14. Cosby, "Elements of Igno-Ebonics Style."
15. Anzaldua, *Borderlands/La Frontera,* 59.
16. Cosby, "Elements of Igno-Ebonics Style."
17. Ibid.
18. Angelou, *The Caged Bird,* 2.
19. R. Jones, "Not White Just Right."
20. See "True to the Game" on Ice Cube's *Death Certificate.*
21. "Big L: R.I.P."
22. Matthews, "Book of Rhymes." Writer Adam Matthews interviewed rapper A.G. on his favorite verse from Big L's "Ebonics."
23. Rodriguez, "Gift of Gab."
24. McGregor, "The Source's New World Hip-hop Dictionary," 49.
25. McClendon, *Better English,* 69.
26. Rice, "King of Slanguage," 151.
27. Hold up! Word has it, courtesy of the underground rap mag *Murder Dog* ("Murder Dog Magazine Presents E-40's Book of Slang Volume One"), as of fall '03 E-40 got his own slang book in the works. So stay tuned!
28. Parker, "Home Grown Love," 170.

Chapter 2

1. Two additional African American texts appear, however, in the second edition of Bizzell and Herzberg's *The Rhetorical Tradition.*
2. Brown, H., *Die Nigger Die!* 27.
3. Smitherman, *Talkin That Talk,* 283.
4. Sparks, *Mind of South Africa,* 8.
5. Ibid., 9.
6. Hrbek, *Africa,* 75–85.
7. Niane, *Sundiata,* 60–61.
8. Sparks, *Mind of South Africa,* 100.
9. Niane, *Sundiata,* 60.
10. Smitherman, *Talkin and Testifyin,* 79.
11. Ibid.
12. Brown, H., *Die Nigger Die!* 27–28.
13. Ibid., 28.

14. Ba, "The Living Tradition," 62n. 67.
15. Ibid., 62, 69.
16. Ibid., 67.
17. Hale, *Scribe, Griot, and Novelist*, 36.
18. Ibid.
19. Ibid.
20. Ibid.
21. Ibid., 37.
22. Niane, *Sundiata*, 1.
23. Ibid.
24. Ibid, 96.
25. Ibid., viii.
26. Ibid., 62–63.
27. Hale, *Scribe, Griot, and Novelist*, 37.
28. Ibid.
29. Ibid., 38.
30. Edwards and Sienkewicz, *Oral Cultures*, 18.
31. See Abrahams's *Deep Down in the Jungle*.
32. Edwards and Sienkewicz, *Oral Cultures*, 1.
33. Ibid., 162–63.
34. Though likely unaware of Major's definition of rap—the version in the 1970 edition of the *Dictionary of African American Slang*, that is—William Safire takes the origins of the term back even further to the fourteenth and sixteenth centuries in Europe. For instance, Safire writes that "as a verb rap has long meant 'to express orally.' The poet Sir Thomas Wyatt wrote in 1541, 'I am wont sometime to rap out on oath in an earnest talk.' British prison slang used rap for 'say' as early as 1829 . . ." (Safire, "The Rap on Hip-hop," 40–41).
35. Major, *Dictionary of African-American Slang*, 376.
36. Ibid., 1732.
37. Ibid., 1753.
38. Ibid., 376–77.
39. Ibid., 377.
40. Smitherman, *Black Talk*, 190.
41. Ibid.
42. See Kochman's 1969 essay, "Rappin' in the Black Ghetto."
43. Ibid., 27.
44. Ibid., 28.
45. Ibid., 27.
46. See Diawara, "The Song of the Griot."
47. Kochman, "Rappin' in the Black Ghetto," 27.
48. Bizzell and Herzberg, *Rhetorical Tradition*, 1198.
49. Abrahams, "Black Talking," 257.
50. Smitherman, *Talkin and Testifyin*, 78.
51. Ibid., 79, emphasis added.
52. Ibid., 79–80, emphasis added.
53. Cross, *Not about a Salary*, 10.

54. Ibid., 11–12.

55. Shabazz and Shabazz, *Dolemite,* 2.

56. Ibid., 36.

57. Ibid., 9.

58. Ibid., 11.

59. Ibid., 28. Louis Jordan also did a rendition of this song in 1947 (see *Five Guys Named Moe*), though Fletcher was probably the one who wrote it and originally performed it.

60. Cross, *Not about a Salary,* 12.

61. Ibid.

62. Salaam, "Wordsmiths for Your Shelf," 48.

63. James, *That's Blaxploitation!* 9.

64. See the album's liner notes.

65. Fernando, *New Beats,* 130–32.

66. Collectables released in 2002 another Poets album titled *Poetry Is Black.* It includes many of the poems that appear on *Right On!* but it also features five poems performed by Gylan Kain. For the compilation, these poems may have been taken from Kain's 1990 album *The Blue Guerilla.*

67. See Campbell, "Real Niggaz's Don't Die."

68. O'Hagan, "Bardcore!" 6

69. Ibid., 7.

70. The Last Poets, *Vibes from the Scribes,* 37.

71. O'Hagan, "Bardcore!" 7.

72. Fernando, *New Beats,* 132.

73. Scott-Heron, *Now and Then,* xiv.

74. Ibid., 78–79.

75. Cross, *Not about a Salary,* 13. During a recent Internet search, I came upon an apparent second album published in 1971. Reissued in 2002 on the Acid Jazz label, the album is called *The Black Voices: On the Street in Watts.* According to Cross, the album was actually cut before *Rappin' Black in a White World.* But *Black Voices* is a compilation album that Anthony Hamilton (none of the other Prophets) got persuaded to do by Talmadage Spratt, the then-director of the Westside branch of the Watts Writer's Workshop (see the album's liner notes). Three other poets, presumably all participants in this branch of the Watts Writer's Workshop, appear on the record: Odie Hawkins, Emmery Lee Joseph Evans, Jr., and Ed Bereal. In 1996 (with FFRR; 1997 with Acid Jazz), the Prophets apparently released their second album titled *When the 90's Came.* Except for the more rap-music-oriented production of tracks like "trippin" (courtesy of West Coast rapper DJ Quick), the latest album is reminiscent of *Rappin' Black.* Noticeably absent from this CD, however, is Dee Dee McNeil, who contributed significantly to the first album.

76. Unfortunately for me since my purchase, *Rappin' Black in a White World* has come out on CD and is a lot more affordable.

77. See Fernando, *New Beats.*

78. Toop, *Rap Attack 2*, 19.
79. Fernando, *New Beats*, 32.
80. Dyson, *Reflecting Black*, 12.
81. Ba, "The Living Tradition," 69.
82. Toop, *Rap Attack 2*, 32.
83. See the album's liner notes.
84. Medina, *Bum Rush the Page*, xix.
85. Small, *Break It Down*, 12.

Chapter 3

For heads familiar with Todd Boyd's *The New H.N.I.C.* let me set the record straight. I ain't bitin' off the brotha's chapter that goes by the title "Can't Knock the Hustle." His book beat mine to press (I cain't knock that), but my earliest drafts of this chapter back around '97 and '98 employ the phrase in the title to capture a key concept in Hip hop—the ghetto hustling ethic.

1. Lightnin' Rod, "Hustlers Convention." Subsequent quotations are from the same source.
2. Jackson, "Play On," 101.
3. Stanley and Morley, *Rap: The Lyrics*, 152.
4. Brown, *Life and Loves*, xxxiii.
5. Fernando, *New Beats*, 84.
6. Ibid.
7. Ibid., 85.
8. Ibid.
9. See John Roberts's *From Trickster to Badman*.
10. Smitherman, *Talkin and Testifyin*, 52.
11. Harris, "Eazy-E," 256.
12. Ibid.
13. Quoted in Mills, "The Gangsta Rapper," 32.
14. Abrahams, *Deep Down in the Jungle*, 136–37.
15. White, *Rebel for the Hell of It*, 139.
16. Lassiter, "Talkin' Trash," 22.
17. As the tale would have it, that is. In real life, however, Stag-O-Lee appears to have been far from inarticulate. According to Cecil Brown's recent book *Stagolee Shot Billy*, Lee Shelton, a.k.a. Stag-O-Lee, was both the leader of a political and social organization called the Black Four Hundred Club and a pimp or mack in the red-light district of St. Louis. Given these two high-profile social positions, the real Stag-O-Lee had to be a man of words as well as action.
18. Pelton, *Trickster in West Africa*, 5, 24.
19. Abrahams, *Deep Down in the Jungle*, 115–16.
20. Hannerz is quoted in Jackson, *Get Your Ass in the Water*, 14.
21. Wepman, Newman, and Binderman, *The Life*, 17–18.
22. Ibid., 18.
23. Ibid., 47.
24. Jackson, *Get Your Ass in the Water*, 57.

25. Ibid., 58.
26. Ibid., 60.
27. Ibid., 57.
28. Ibid.
29. Roberts, *From Trickster to Badman*, 174.
30. Jackson, *Get Your Ass in the Water*, 59.
31. Shabazz and Shabazz, *Dolemite*, 45.
32. Roberts, *From Trickster to Badman*, 197.
33. Ibid., 199–200.
34. Dyson, *Between God and Gangsta Rap*, 181.
35. Roberts, *From Trickster to Badman*, 212.
36. Hudson, "The Hustling Ethic," 424.
37. Roberts, *From Trickster to Badman*, 203–4.
38. Ibid., 204.
39. Ibid., 212.
40. Singleton is quoted in Armond White's *Rebel for the Hell of It*, 95.
41. Ibid., 167.
42. Ibid., 165.
43. Giddings is quoted in ibid., 171.
44. Ibid., 51.
45. McWhorter, "How Hip-Hop Holds Blacks Back," 1.
46. Ibid., 2.
47. Ibid.
48. Levine, *Black Culture*, 419.
49. See Samuels, Croal, and Gates, "Battle for the Soul of Hip-Hop."
50. See, for example, the selections on the audio *Copulatin' Blues Volume One*.
51. Lhamon, *Raising Cain*, 6.
52. Dyson, *Holler If You Hear Me*, 170.
53. George, *Hip Hop America*, 47.
54. See Cornel West, *Race Matters*.

Chapter 4

1. Newton, "He Won't Bleed Me," 115–16.
2. Ibid., 133.
3. Ibid., 142–43.
4. Goode, "From *Dopefiend* to *Kenyatta's Last Hit*," 43.
5. See the back cover of Goines's *Death List*.
6. Goode, "From *Dopefiend* to *Kenyatta's Last Hit*," 43.
7. Stone, *Donald Writes No More*, 229–30.
8. Goines, *Black Gangster*, 127.
9. Wepman, Newman, and Binderman, *The Life*, 175.
10. Marc Gerald has since teamed up with actor Wesley Snipes to launch the publishing firm Syndicate Media Group. The firm publishes more recent works of urban pulp fiction, some by seasoned vets like Roland Jefferson, author of *The School on 103rd Street*. (*Black Issues Book Review*, September–October 2001: 56–57.)

11. See the Old School Books Web site, http://www.wwnorton.com/subject.osb.htm.
12. The short story is reprinted in *The Black Scholar* 28, no. 1.
13. James, *That's Blaxploitation!* 42.
14. According to Iceberg Slim's pimp mentor "Sweet" Jones, White America's been pimping black folk since the first African stepped off the slave ship. See Iceberg Slim, *Pimp.*
15. Goode, "From *Dopefiend* to *Kenyatta's Last Hit,*" 45–46.
16. Stone, *Donald Writes No More,* 229.
17. Jackson, *Get Your Ass in the Water,* 29–30.
18. Kochman, "Rappin' in the Black Ghetto," 27, emphasis added.
19. Jackson, *Get Your Ass in the Water,* 21.
20. Slim, *Pimp,* 179.
21. Ibid., 218.
22. Ibid., 218–19.
23. Cited in Milner and Milner, *Black Players,* 292–93.
24. Slim, *Naked Soul,* 58–59.
25. Ibid., 58.
26. Ibid., 30.
27. This interview is cited in James, *That's Blaxploitation!* 112–16.
28. Ibid., 113.
29. Ibid.
30. Ibid., 115.
31. Ibid., 115–16.
32. Slim, *Pimp,* 272–73.
33. Ibid., 273–74.
34. Ibid., 274.
35. Ibid.
36. James, *That's Blaxploitation!* 116.
37. See Aristotle's *"Art" of Rhetoric.*
38. Milner and Milner, *Black Players,* 34.
39. Ibid., 34.
40. Ibid.
41. Ibid., 236.
42. Ibid.
43. Ibid., 238.
44. Ibid., 237.
45. Ibid., 238.
46. Ibid., 243.
47. Burke, "Pimpology 101," 108.
48. Voss, "Sugar Daddies," 66.
49. Fernando, *New Beats,* 112.
50. Ibid., 116.
51. See, for example, Samuels, Croal, and Gates, "Battle for the Soul of Hip-Hop."
52. See Stanley and Morley, *Rap: The Lyrics,* for the complete text of the song.
53. Jenkins, "Short Stop."

54. Small, *Break It Down*, 189.
55. Williams, "Shorty the Pimp," 182.
56. Ibid., 181–82.
57. See, for example, the chapter "A Pimp's Guide to Sex, Rap, and God" in Ice-T's book *The Ice Opinion: Who Gives a Fuck?*
58. Ice-T, introduction to *Doom Fox*, ix.
59. Ibid., viii–ix.
60. Ice-T, quoted in *Pimps Up, Hos Down*.

Chapter 5

For what would have been the third epigraph heading this essay, peep the hook for Public Enemy's "He Got Game" from the *He Got Game* movie soundtrack.

1. Holmes, "Fighting Back by *Writing* Black," 60.
2. Ibid.
3. Campbell, "The Rhetoric of Black English Vernacular," 5–6.
4. Holmes, "Fighting Back by *Writing* Black," 60.
5. Royster and Williams, "Reading Past Resistance," 136.
6. Ibid.
7. Balester, *Cultural Divide*, vii.
8. See Touré, "Gay Rappers."
9. Mahiri, *Shooting for Excellence*, 7.
10. The interview was conducted in 1991–92 during the course of data collection for my doctoral dissertation. "The E," as he proudly refers to himself in his rap, was one of five student participants in the study. Given the substantial role that Hip hop plays in this essay, I refer to the student solely by his rap aliases "the E" or "E."
11. See Ong's and Farrell's essays in *A Sourcebook for Basic Writing Teachers*.
12. Ong, "Literacy and Orality in Our Times," 50.
13. Ibid., 51.
14. Gee, "Orality and Literacy," 742.
15. Rose, *Black Noise*, 87–88.
16. Ibid., 88.
17. DeCurtis, "Word," 96.
18. Ibid.
19. Ibid.
20. See Cook, W., "Writing in the Spaces Left."
21. Pratt, "Arts of the Contact Zone," 37.
22. Ibid., 34.
23. Ibid.
24. Ibid., 35.
25. Ibid., 37.
26. Ibid., 36.
27. Liner notes, Ice Cube, *The Predator*.
28. There may be some overlap with the police use of the term *profiling*,

but the meaning here is largely positive and associated with styling before onlookers.

29. Pratt, "Arts of the Contact Zone," 40.
30. George, *Hip Hop America,* viii.
31. Dimitriadis, *Performing Identity/Performing Culture,* 96.
32. See Joan Morgan's *When Chickenheads Come Home to Roost: A Hip-Hop Feminist Breaks It Down.*
33. See Campbell, "*The Signifying Monkey* Revisited" and "Real Niggaz's Don't Die."
34. Pratt, "Arts of the Contact Zone," 40.
35. Canagarajah, "Safe Houses in the Contact Zone," 190.
36. Ibid., 193.
37. Anzaldua, *Borderlands/La Frontera,* 78.
38. Villanueva, *Bootstraps,* 135.
39. Mahiri, *Shooting for Excellence,* 79.
40. See Burke, *Language as Symbolic Action.*
41. Morgan, *Chickenheads Come Home,* 62.
42. Rodriguez, "The Boys of Summer," 34.
43. TAsHa, letter to the editor, *XXL,* 24.
44. Tate, *Flyboy in the Buttermilk,* 145.
45. Ibid., 147.
46. Slim, *The Naked Soul,* 220.
47. Ibid., 218–19.
48. Ibid., 219.
49. Morgan, *Chickenheads Come Home,* 39.
50. Herbert, "The Making of a Hip-hop Intellectual," 49.
51. See the book cover of Wimsatt's *Bomb the Suburbs.*
52. Ibid.
53. Sirc, "Never Mind the Sex Pistols," 106.

Works Cited

Abrahams, Roger D. "Black Talking on the Streets." In *Explorations in the Ethnography of Speaking*, edited by Richard Bauman and Joel Sherzer, 240–62. London: Cambridge University Press, 1974.

———. *Deep Down in the Jungle: Negro Narrative Folklore from the Streets of Philadelphia*. Hatboro, PA: Folklore Associates, 1964.

Adger, Carolyn Temple, Donna Christian, and Orlando Taylor, eds. *Making the Connection: Language and Academic Achievement among African American Students*. McHenry, IL: Center for Applied Linguistics and Delta Systems, 1999.

Aristotle. *"Art" of Rhetoric*, translated by J. H. Freese. Cambridge, MA: Harvard University Press, 1926.

Angelou, Maya. *I Know Why the Caged Bird Sings*. New York: Bantam, 1969.

———. *Singin' and Swingin' and Gettin' Merry Like Christmas*. New York: Bantam, 1976.

Anzaldua, Gloria. *Borderlands/La Frontera: The New Mestiza*. San Francisco: Aunt Lute, 1987.

Ba, A. Hampté. "The Living Tradition." In *Methodology and African Prehistory*, edited by J. Ki-Zerbo, 62–72. Vol. 1 of *UNESCO General History of Africa*. London: James Currey, 1990.

Baker, Houston, Jr. *Blues, Ideology, and Afro-American Literature: A Vernacular Theory*. Chicago: University of Chicago Press, 1984.

Balester, Valerie M. *Cultural Divide: A Study of African-American College-Level Writers*. Portsmouth, NH: Boynton/Cook, 1993.

———. "The Problem of Method: Striving to See with Multiple Perspectives." *College Composition and Communication* 52, no. 1 (2000): 129–32.

Baraka, Amiri. "The Language of Defiance." *Black Issues Book Review*, September–October 2001: 28.

———. *See also* Jones, Leroi.

Baugh, John. *Beyond Ebonics: Linguistic Pride and Racial Prejudice*. Oxford: Oxford University Press, 2000.

———. *Out of the Mouths of Slaves: African American Language and Educational Malpractice*. Austin: University of Texas Press, 1999.

"Big L: R.I.P. 1974–1999." *The Source,* June 2000: 206–7.

Bizzell, Patricia, and Bruce Herzberg. "Henry Louis Gates, Jr." In *The Rhetorical Tradition: Readings from Classical Times to the Present.* Boston: Bedford Books of St. Martin's, 1990.

———, eds. *The Rhetorical Tradition: Readings from Classical Times to the Present.* 2nd ed. Boston: Bedford Books of St. Martin's, 2001.

Boyd, Todd. *The New H.N.I.C.: The Death of Civil Rights and the Reign of Hip Hop.* New York: New York University Press, 2003.

Brooks, Cleanth. *The Language of the American South.* Athens: University of Georgia Press, 1985.

Brooks, Gwendolyn. "We Real Cool." 1960. Reprinted in *The Norton Anthology of African-American Literature,* edited by Henry Louis Gates, Jr., and Nellie McKay, 1591. New York: Norton, 1998.

Brown, Cecil. *The Life and Loves of Mr. Jiveass Nigger.* 1969. Reprint, New York: Ecco, 1991.

———. *Stagolee Shot Billy.* Cambridge, MA: Harvard University Press, 2003.

Brown, Hubert Rap. *Die Nigger Die!* New York: Dial, 1969.

Burke, Kenneth. *Language as Symbolic Action: Essays on Life, Literature, and Method.* Berkeley: University of California Press, 1966.

Burke, Miguel. "Pimpology 101." *The Source,* May 1998: 104–8.

Campbell, Kermit E. "Contact Zone Theory." In *Theorizing Composition: A Critical Sourcebook of Theory and Scholarship in Contemporary Composition Studies,* edited by Mary Kennedy, 50–52. Westport, CT: Greenwood, 1998.

———. "'Real Niggaz's Don't Die': African American Students Speaking Themselves into Their Writing." In *Writing in Multicultural Settings,* edited by Carol Severino, Juan Guerra, and Johnnella Butler, 67–78. New York: MLA, 1997.

———. "The Rhetoric of Black English Vernacular: A Study of the Oral and Written Discourse Practices of African American Male College Students." Ph.D. diss., Ohio State University, 1993.

———. "*The Signifying Monkey* Revisited: Vernacular Discourse and African American Personal Narratives." *Journal of Advanced Composition* 14, no. 2 (1994): 463–73.

Canagarajah, A. Suresh. "Safe Houses in the Contact Zone: Coping Strategies of African-American Students in the Academy." *College Composition and Communication* 48, no. 2 (1997): 173–96.

Clark, Al C. *Crime Partners.* Los Angeles: Holloway House, 1974.

———. *Cry Revenge!* Los Angeles: Holloway House, 1974.

———. *Death List.* Los Angeles: Holloway House, 1974.

———. *Kenyatta's Escape.* Los Angeles: Holloway House, 1974.

———. *See also* Goines, Donald.

Cook, Dara. "The Aesthetics of Rap." *Black Issues Book Review,* March–April 2000: 22–27.

Cook, William W. "Writing in the Spaces Left." *College Composition and Communication* 44, no. 1 (1993): 9–25.

Cooper, Clarence, Jr. 1962, 1963. *Black! Three Short Novels.* Reprint, New York: Norton, 1997.

———. *The Farm.* 1967. Reprint, New York: Norton, 1998.

———. *The Scene.* 1960. Reprint, New York: Norton, 1996.

———. *The Syndicate.* 1960. Reprint, Edinburgh, Scotland: Payback, 1998.

———. *Weed.* 1961. Reprint, Edinburgh, Scotland: Payback, 1998.

Cosby, Bill. "Elements of Igno-Ebonics Style." *The Wall Street Journal,* January 10, 1997: A11.

Cross, Brian. *It's Not About a Salary: Rap, Race, and Resistance in Los Angeles.* London: Verso, 1993.

Davis, Anthony. "The New Sons of Iceberg Slim." *Black Issues Book Review,* September–October 2001: 56–57.

DeCurtis, Anthony. "Word." In *The Vibe History of Hip Hop,* edited by Alan Light, 91–99. New York: Three Rivers, 1999.

Diawara, Manthia. "The Song of the Griot." *Transition* 74 (1998): 16–31.

Dimitriadis, Greg. *Performing Identity/Performing Culture: Hip Hop as Text, Pedagogy, and Lived Practice.* New York: Peter Lang, 2001.

Dyson, Michael Eric. *Between God and Gangsta Rap: Bearing Witness to Black Culture.* Oxford: Oxford University Press, 1996.

———. *Holler If You Hear Me: Searching for Tupac Shakur.* New York: Basic Civitas, 2001.

———. *Reflecting Black: African-American Cultural Criticism.* Minneapolis: University of Minnesota Press, 1993.

Edwards, Viv, and Thomas Sienkewicz. *Oral Cultures Past and Present: Rappin' and Homer.* Oxford, UK: Basil Blackwell, 1990.

Ellison, Ralph. "Going to the Territory." In *Going to the Territory,* 120–44. New York: Vintage, 1986.

Farrell, Thomas J. "Literacy, the Basics, and All That Jazz." In *A Sourcebook for Basic Writing Teachers,* edited by Theresa Enos, 27–44. New York: Random House, 1987.

Fernando, S. H., Jr. *The New Beats: Exploring the Music, Culture, and Attitudes of Hip-hop.* New York: Anchor, 1994.

Gates, Henry Louis, Jr. *The Signifying Monkey: A Theory of African-American Literary Criticism.* Oxford: Oxford University Press, 1988.

Gee, James Paul. "Orality and Literacy: From *The Savage Mind* to *Ways with Words.*" *TESOL Quarterly* 20, no. 4 (1986): 719–46.

George, Nelson. *Hip Hop America.* New York: Viking, 1998.

Goines, Donald. *Black Gangster.* Los Angeles: Holloway House, 1972.

———. *Black Girl Lost.* Los Angeles: Holloway House, 1973.

———. *Daddy Cool.* Los Angeles: Holloway House, 1974.

———. *Dopefiend: The Story of a Black Junkie.* Los Angeles: Holloway House, 1971.

———. *Eldorado Red.* Los Angeles: Holloway House, 1974.

———. *Inner City Hoodlum.* Los Angeles: Holloway House, 1975.

———. *Kenyatta's Last Hit.* Los Angeles: Holloway House, 1975.

———. *Never Die Alone.* Los Angeles: Holloway House, 1974.

———. *Street Players.* Los Angeles: Holloway House, 1972.

————. *Swamp Man*. Los Angeles: Holloway House, 1974.

————. *White Man's Justice, Black Man's Grief*. Los Angeles: Holloway House, 1973.

————. *Whoreson: The Story of a Ghetto Pimp*. Los Angeles: Holloway House, 1972.

————. *See also* Clark, Al C.

Goode, Greg. "From *Dopefiend* to *Kenyatta's Last Hit:* The Angry Black Crime Novels of Donald Goines." *MELUS* 11, no. 3 (1984): 41–48.

Hager, Steve. *Hip Hop: The Illustrated History of Breakdancing, Rap Music, and Graffiti*. New York: St. Martin's, 1984.

Hale, Thomas. *Scribe, Griot, and Novelist: Narrative Interpreters of the Songhay Empire*. Gainesville: University of Florida Press, 1990.

Hannerz, Ulf. *Soulside*. New York: Columbia University Press, 1969.

Harris, Carter. "Eazy-E." In *The Vibe History of Hip Hop*, edited by Alan Light, 254–56. New York: Three Rivers, 1999.

Herbert, Wray. "The Making of a Hip-hop Intellectual: Deconstructing the Puzzle of Race and Identity." *U.S. News & World Report*, November 4, 1996: 48–49.

Himes, Chester. *Cast the First Stone*. New York: Signet, 1952.

————."His Last Day." 1933. Reprinted in *The Black Scholar: Journal of Black Studies and Research* 28, no. 1 (1998): 10–18.

————. *Yesterday Will Make You Cry*. New York: Norton, 1999.

Holmes, David. "Fighting Back by *Writing* Black: Beyond Racially Reductive Composition Theory." In *Race, Rhetoric, and Composition*, edited by Keith Gilyard, 53–66. Portsmouth, NH: Boynton/Cook, 1999.

Hrbek, I., ed. *Africa from the Seventh to the Eleventh Century*. Vol. 3 of *UNESCO General History of Africa*. London: James Currey, 1988.

Hudson, Julius. "The Hustling Ethic." In *Rappin' and Stylin' Out: Communication in Urban Black America*, edited by Thomas Kochman, 410–24. Urbana: University of Illinois Press, 1972.

Ice-T. *The Ice Opinion: Who Gives a Fuck?* New York: St. Martin's, 1994.

————. Introduction to *Doom Fox* by Iceberg Slim, v-x. New York: Grove, 1998.

Jackson, Bruce. *"Get Your Ass in the Water and Swim Like Me": Narrative Poetry from Black Oral Traditions*. Cambridge, MA: Harvard University Press, 1974.

Jackson, Scoop. "Play On." *Vibe*, April 1997: 96–101.

James, Darius. *That's Blaxploitation! Roots of the Baadasssss 'Tude*. New York: St. Martin's Griffin, 1995.

Jefferson, Roland S. *The School on 103rd Street*. 1976. Reprint, New York: Norton, 1997.

Jenkins, Sacha. "Short Stop." *Vibe*, April 1996: 63–64.

Johnson, Gregory. "Power of the Dollar." *The Source*, October 2002: 135–43, 186.

Jones, Leroi. *Blues People: Negro Music in White America and the Music that Developed from It*. New York: Morrow Quill, 1963.

———. *See also* Baraka, Amiri.

Jones, Rachel. "My Turn: Not White Just Right." *Newsweek,* February 10, 1997: 12–13.

———. "My Turn: What's Wrong with Black English." *Newsweek,* December 27, 1982: 7.

Ki-Zerbo, J., ed. *Methodology and African Prehistory.* Vol. 1 of *UNESCO General History of Africa.* London: James Currey, 1990.

Kochman, Thomas. "Rappin' in the Black Ghetto." *Trans-Action* 6 (1969): 26–34.

KRS-One. *Ruminations.* New York: Welcome Rain Publishers, 2003.

———. *Temple of Hip Hop.* http://www.templeofhiphop.org/.

Lassiter, Brian. "Talkin' Trash: Tracing Rap's Roots to the 'Signifying Monkey.'" *The Source,* June 1993: 22.

The Last Poets. *Vibes from the Scribes: Selected Poems.* Trenton, NJ: Africa World, 1992.

Lee, Carol D. *Signifying as a Scaffold for Literary Interpretation: The Pedagogical Implications of an African American Discourse Genre.* Urbana, IL: NCTE, 1993.

Levine, Lawrence. *Black Culture and Black Consciousness: Afro-American Folk Thought from Slavery to Freedom.* Oxford: Oxford University Press, 1977.

Lhamon, W. T., Jr. *Raising Cain: Blackface Performance from Jim Crow to Hip Hop.* Cambridge, MA: Harvard University Press, 1998.

Matthews, Adam. "Book of Rhymes." *XXL,* March 2003: 138.

McClendon, Garrard. *The African-American Guide to Better English: A Speaking and Writing Manual for African-Americans.* Culver, IN: Positive People, 1995.

McGregor, Tracii. "The Source's New World Hip-hop Dictionary." *The Source,* January 1998: 49.

McWhorter, John. "How Hip-Hop Holds Blacks Back." *City Journal,* Summer 2003. http://www.city-journal.org/html/13_3_how_hip_hop.html.

Major, Clarence, ed. *Juba to Jive: A Dictionary of African-American Slang.* New York: Penguin, 1994.

Mahiri, Jabari. *Shooting for Excellence: African American and Youth Culture in New Century Schools.* Urbana, IL: NCTE, 1998.

Medina, Tony, and Louis Reyes Rivera, eds. *Bum Rush the Page: A Def Poetry Jam.* New York: Three Rivers, 2001.

Mellix, Barbara. "From Outside, In." In *Our Times: Readings from Recent Periodicals,* edited by Robert Atwan, 171–80. New York: Bedford, 1989.

Mills, David. "The Gangsta Rapper: Violent Hero or Negative Role Model?" *The Source,* December 1990: 31–34, 36, 39–40.

Milner, Christina, and Richard Milner. *Black Players: The Secret World of Black Pimps.* Boston: Little, Brown, 1972.

Mitchell-Kernan, Claudia. *Language Behavior in a Black Urban Community.* Monographs of the Language–Behavior Research Laboratory No. 2, 1971 (revised edition 1974).

Moore, Jessica Care. *The Words Don't Fit in My Mouth*. Brooklyn, NY: Moore Black Press, 1997.

Morgan, Joan. *When Chickenheads Come Home to Roost: A Hip-Hop Feminist Breaks It Down*. New York: Touchstone, 1999.

Muckley, Peter. "Iceberg Slim: Robert Beck—A True Essay at a Biocriticism of an Ex-Outlaw Artist." *The Black Scholar: Journal of Black Studies and Research* 26, no. 1 (1996): 18–25.

Mufwene, Salikoko, John Rickford, Guy Bailey, and John Baugh. *African-American English: Structure, History and Use*. New York: Routledge, 1998.

"Murder Dog Magazine Presents E-40's Book of Slang Volume One." *Murder Dog* 10, no. 3 (2003): 72–73.

Niane, D. T. *Sundiata: An Epic of Old Mali*. Translated by G. D. Pickett. Essex, England: Longman, 1986. Translation of *Soundjata, ou l'Epopée Mandingue*. N.p.: Présence Africaine, 1960.

Newton, Huey P. "He Won't Bleed Me: A Revolutionary Analysis of *Sweet Sweetback's Baadasssss Song*." In *To Die for the People: The Writings of Huey P. Newton*, edited by Toni Morrison, 112–47. New York: Writers and Readers, 1995.

Nietzsche, Friedrich. *Friedrich Nietzsche on Rhetoric and Language*. Edited by Sander L. Gilman, Carole Blair, and David J. Parent. Oxford: Oxford University Press, 1989.

Nuriddin, Jalal, and Suliaman El Hadi. *The Last Poets: Vibes from the Scribes*. Trenton, NJ: Africa World, 1992.

O'Hagan, Sean. "Bardcore!" *New Musical Express* 6 (1985): 6–7.

Ong, Walter. "Literacy and Orality in Our Times." In *A Sourcebook for Basic Writing Teachers*, edited by Theresa Enos, 45–55. New York: Random House, 1987.

Parker, Mr. "Home Grown Love." *The Source*, November 2000: 169–71.

Pelton, Robert. *The Trickster in West Africa: A Study of Mythic Irony and Sacred Delight*. Berkeley: University of California Press, 1980.

Perry, Charles. *Portrait of a Young Man Drowning*. 1962. Reprint, New York: Norton, 1996.

Perry, Theresa, and Lisa Delpit. *The Real Ebonics Debate: Language and the Education of African American Children*. Boston: Beacon, 1998.

Pharr, Robert Deane. *The Book of Numbers*. 1969. Reprint, Charlottesville: University of Virginia Press, 2001.

———. *Giveadamn Brown*. 1978. Reprint, New York: Norton, 1997.

———. *S.R.O.* 1971. Reprint, New York: Norton, 1998.

———. *The Soul Murder Case: A Confession of the Victim*. New York: Avon, 1975.

———. *The Welfare Bitch*. N.p., c. 1975.

Potter, Russell. *Spectacular Vernaculars: Hip-hop and the Politics of Postmodernism*. Albany: State University of New York Press, 1995.

Pratt, Mary Louise. "Arts of the Contact Zone." *MLA Profession* (1991): 33–40.

Randall, Dudley, ed. *The Black Poets*. New York: Bantam, 1985.

Rice, Ed. "King of Slanguage." *The Source,* November 1999: 149–52.

Rickford, John. *African American Vernacular English: Features, Evolution, Educational Implications.* Malden, MA: Blackwell, 1999.

Rickford, John, and Russell Rickford. *Spoken Soul: The Story of Black English.* New York: John Wiley, 2000.

Roberts, John W. *From Trickster to Badman: The Black Folk Hero in Slavery and Freedom.* Philadelphia: University of Pennsylvania Press, 1989.

Rodriguez, Carlito. "The Boys of Summer." *The Source,* July 2001: 34.

———. "Gift of Gab." *The Source,* January 1998: 48.

Rose, Tricia. *Black Noise: Rap Music and Black Culture in Contemporary America.* Hanover, NH: Wesleyan University Press, 1994.

Royster, Jacqueline Jones. "When the First Voice You Hear Is Not Your Own." *College Composition and Communication* 47, no. 1 (1996): 29–40.

Royster, Jacqueline Jones, and Jean Williams. "History in the Spaces Left: African American Presence and Narratives of Composition Studies." *College Composition and Communication* 50, no. 4 (1999): 563–84.

———. "Reading Past Resistance: A Response to Valerie Balester." *College Composition and Communication* 52, no. 1 (2000): 133–42.

Salaam, Kalamu ya. "Wordsmiths for Your Shelf." *Black Issues Book Review,* March–April 2000: 48–49.

Samuels, Allison, N'Gai Croal, and David Gates. "Battle for the Soul of Hip-Hop." *Newsweek,* October 9, 2000: 60–65.

Scott-Heron, Gil. *Now and Then: The Poems of Gil Scott-Heron.* Edinburgh, Scotland: Payback, 2000.

Seale, Bobby. *Seize the Time: The Story of the Black Panther Party and Huey P. Newton.* 1970. Reprint, Baltimore: Black Classic, 1991.

Safire, William. "The Rap on Hip-hop." In *Rap on Rap: Straight-up Talk on Hip-hop Culture,* edited by Adam Sexton, 39–42. New York: Delta, 1995.

Shabazz, David, and Julian Shabazz. *Dolemite: The Story of Rudy Ray Moore.* Clinton, SC: Awesome Records, 1996.

Simmons, Herbert. *Corner Boy.* 1957. New York: Norton, 1996.

Sirc, Geoffrey. "Never Mind the Sex Pistols, Where's 2Pac?" *College Composition and Communication* 49, no. 1 (1998): 104–8.

Slim, Iceberg [Robert Beck]. *Airtight Willie & Me: The Story of Six Incredible Players.* Los Angeles: Holloway House, 1979.

———. *Death Wish: A Story of the Mafia.* Los Angeles: Holloway House, 1977.

———. *Doom Fox.* New York: Grove, 1998.

———. *Long White Con: The Biggest Score of His Life.* Los Angeles: Holloway House, 1977.

———. *Mama Black Widow: A Tragic, Bitter Family Portrait.* Los Angeles: Holloway House, 1969.

———. *The Naked Soul of Iceberg Slim: Robert Beck's Real Story.* Los

Angeles: Holloway House, 1971.

——. *Pimp: The Story of My Life.* Los Angeles: Holloway House, 1967.

——. *Trick Baby: The Story of a White Negro.* Los Angeles: Holloway House, 1967.

Small, Michael. *Break It Down: The Inside Story from the New Leaders of Rap.* New York: Citadel, 1992.

Smith, Vern E. *The Jones Men.* 1974. Reprint, New York: Norton, 1998.

Smitherman, Geneva. *Black Talk: Words and Phrases from the Hood to the Amen Corner.* Boston: Houghton Mifflin, 1994.

——. *Talkin and Testifyin: The Language of Black America.* Boston: Houghton Mifflin, 1977.

——. *Talkin That Talk: Language, Culture and Education in African America.* New York: Routledge, 2000.

Sparks, Allister. *The Mind of South Africa: The Story of the Rise and Fall Apartheid.* London: Mandarin, 1991.

Straight From the Projects: Rappers that Live the Lyrics. DVD by Image Entertainment. Advertisement. *Murder Dog* 11, no. 1.

Stanley, Lawrence, and Jefferson Morley, eds. *Rap: The Lyrics.* New York: Penguin, 1992.

Stone, Eddie. *Donald Writes No More: A Biography of Donald Goines.* Los Angeles: Holloway House, 1974, 1988.

Strunk, William, Jr., and E. B. White. *The Elements of Style,* 3rd ed. New York: Macmillan, 1979.

TAsHa. Letter to the editor. *XXL,* January–February 2002: 24.

Tate, Greg. *Flyboy in the Buttermilk: Essays on Contemporary America.* New York: Fireside, 1992.

Toop, David. *The Rap Attack: African Jive to New York Hip Hop.* N.p.: South End, 1984.

——. *Rap Attack 2: African Rap to Global Hip Hop.* London: Serpent's Tail, 1991.

Touré. "Gay Rappers: Too Real for Hip-Hop." *New York Times,* April 20, 2003: 1, 29.

Villanueva, Victor, Jr. *Bootstraps: From an American Academic of Color.* Urbana, IL: NCTE, 1993.

Voss, Karen. "Sugar Daddies." *Filmmaker,* February–April 1999: 64–67.

Welch, Kathleen. *Electric Rhetoric: Classical Rhetoric, Oralism, and a New Literacy.* Cambridge, MA: MIT Press, 1999.

Wepman, Dennis, Ronald Newman, and Murray Binderman. *The Life: The Lore and Folk Poetry of the Black Hustler.* Los Angeles: Holloway House, 1976.

West, Cornel. *Race Matters.* Boston: Beacon, 1993.

Westbrook, Alonzo. *Hip Hoptionary: The Dictionary of Hip Hop Terminology.* New York: Broadway, 2002.

White, Armond. *Rebel for the Hell of It: The Life of Tupac Shakur.* New York: Thunder's Mouth, 1997.

Wideman, John Edgar. *Brothers and Keepers.* New York: Penguin, 1984.

Williams, Frank. "Shorty the Pimp." *The Source,* August 1999: 179–82.

Williams, Robert L., ed. *Ebonics: The True Language of Black Folks.* St. Louis: Institute of Black Studies, 1975.

Williams, Saul. *She.* New York: Washington Square, 1999.

Wilson, Eliot. "Stillstupid." *XXL,* January–February 2002: 16.

Wimsatt, William Upski. *Bomb the Suburbs.* New York: Soft Skull, 1994.

X, Malcolm, and Alex Haley. *The Autobiography of Malcolm X.* New York: Ballantine, 1964.

Discography

Above the Law. *Black Mafia Life*. Warner Bros., 1992.

Adler, Bill. "Producer's Notes." *Flippin' the Script: Rap Meets Poetry*. Mercury, 1996.

Ant Banks. "Packin' a Gun." *Menace II Society*. Zomba, 1992.

Banner, David. "Like a Pimp." *Rap City*. BET, c. 2003.

Big L. "Ebonics." *The Big Picture*. Priority, 2000.

Big Pun. "Still Not a Player." *Capital Punishment*. BMG, 1998.

Bizzy Bone. "Thugz Cry." *Heaven'z Movie*. Relativity, 1998.

Blow, Kurtis. "The Breaks." 1980. Re-release, *The Sugar Hill Story Old School Rap*. Sequel, 1992.

Blowfly [Clarence Reid]. "Blowfly's Rapp." *Blowfly's Party*. Hot Productions, 1996.

Boogie Down Productions. "9mm Goes Bang." *Criminal Minded*. 1987. Re-release, S.H.R., 1991.

Brer Soul [Melvin Van Peebles]. *As Serious As a Heart Attack*. A&M, n.d.

———. *Brer Soul*. A&M, [c. 1969].

———. *What the . . . You Mean I Can't Sing*. Atlantic, 1974.

Brown, Oscar, Jr. "But I Was Cool." *Sin and Soul*. Columbia, 1960.

C-Murder. *Bossalinie*. Priority, 1999.

Common. "The 6th Sense." *Like Water for Chocolate*. MCA, 2000.

Copulatin' Blues Volume One. Stash Records, 1976.

Cortez, Jayne. *Celebrations and Solitudes*. N.p., 1974.

———. "Endangered Species List Blues." *Our Souls Have Grown Deep Like the Rivers*. Rhino Entertainment, 2000.

Crouch, Stanley. *Ain't No Ambulance for Niggers Tonight*. N.p., n.d.

Dirty. "Hit Da Floe." *The Pimp & Da Gangsta*. Universal, 2001.

———. "Yean Heard." *The Pimp & Da Gangsta*. Universal, 2001.

DMX. "Intro." *It's Dark and Hell Is Hot*. Def Jam, 1998.

———. "Who We Be." *The Great Depression*. Island/Def Jam, 2001.

Do or Die. *Headz or Tailz*. Virgin, 1998.

The Dogs. "Your Mama's on Crack Rock." 1991. Re-release, *Down South DJ's*. Joey Boy, 2000.

Dr. Dre. *The Chronic*. Priority, 1992.

———. "Deeez Nuuuts." *The Chronic*. Priority, 1992.

———. "Deep Cover." *Deep Cover: Music from the Original Motion Picture*. Capitol, 1992.

———. "Lil' Ghetto Boy." *The Chronic*. Priority, 1992.

———. "Nuthin But a 'G' Thang." *The Chronic*. Priority, 1992.

E-40. *Tha Hall of Game*. Zomba, 1996.

Eightball and MJG. *Lyrics of a Pimp: Strictly for da Undaground!* TAM, 1997.

Eve. "Let Me Blow Your Mind." *Rap City*. BET, 2001.

———. "Love Is Blind." *Rap City*. BET, 1999.

Fat Joe. *Don Cartagena*. Atlantic, 1998.

Foxy Brown. *Broken Silence*. Island/Def Jam, 2001.

Flippin' the Script: Rap Music Meets Poetry. Mercury Records, 1996.

Gaye, Marvin. "Save the Children." *What's Going On*. Motown, 1971.

The Geto Boys. "Let a Ho Be a Ho." *The Geto Boys*. Def American, 1990.

Giovanni, Nikki. "Ego Tripping." *Truth Is On Its Way*. Collectables, 1993.

———. *Like a Ripple on a Pond*. 1972. Re-release, Collectables, 1993.

Goodie Mob. "Free." *Soul Food*. Arista, 1995.

———. "Soul Food." *Soul Food*. Arista, 1995.

Grandmaster Flash and the Furious Five. "Freedom." 1980. Re-release, *The Sugar Hill Story Old School Rap*. Sequel, 1992.

———. "The Message." 1982. Re-release, *The Sugar Hill Story Old School Rap*. Sequel, 1992.

Hayes, Isaac. "By the Time I Get to Phoenix." *Hot Buttered Soul*. 1969. Re-release, Stax, 1987.

Hayes, Isaac, and Millie Jackson. *Royal Rappin's*. 1979. Re-release, Southbound, 1992.

Hentoff, Nate. "Gil Scott-Heron: An Introduction." Liner notes for *Small Talk at 125th and Lenox* by Gil Scott-Heron. BMG, 1970.

Hughes, Langston. *Weary Blues*. 1958. Re-release, Polygram, 1990.

Hutch, Willie. *Foxy Brown: Soundtrack*. 1974. Re-release, Motown, 1996.

Slim, Iceberg [Robert Beck]. *Reflections*. 1975. Re-release, Infinite Zero, 1994.

Ice Cube. Acknowledgments for *The Predator*. Priority, 1992.

———. *Amerikkka's Most Wanted*. Priority, 1990.

———. "Pushin' Weight." *Rap City*. BET, c. 1999.

———. "True to the Game." *Death Certificate*. Priority, 1991.

———. "We Be Clubbin'." *The Players Club: Soundtrack*. A&M, 1998.

———. "What Can I Do?" *Lethal Injection*. Priority, 1993.

Ice-T. "6 'N the Mornin'." *Rhyme Pays*. Sire, 1987.

———. "Somebody Gotta Do It (Pimpin' Ain't Easy)." *Rhyme Pays*. Sire, 1987.

Ja Rule. "Worldwide Gangsta." *Pain Is Love*. Island/Def Jam, 2001.

James, Rick. "Player's Way." *Urban Rapsody*. Mercury, 1997.

Jay-Z. "Ain't No Nigga." *Reasonable Doubt*. Priority, 1996.

———. "Big Pimpin'." *Vol. 3 . . . Life and Times of S. Carter*. Roc-A-Fella Records, 1999.

———. "Can I Live." *Reasonable Doubt*. Priority, 1996.

————. "Can't Knock the Hustle." *Reasonable Doubt*. Priority, 1996.

————. "Izzo (H.O.V.A.)." *The Blueprint*. Island/Def Jam, 2001.

————. "Who You Wit II." *In My Lifetime, Vol. 1*. Roc-A-Fella, 1997.

Jones, Leroi [Amiri Baraka]. *Black & Beautiful. . . . Soul & Madness*. Jihad Productions, n.d.

————. *Sonny's Time Now*. Jihad Productions, n.d.

Jordan, Louis. "Open the Door Richard." 1947. Re-release, *Five Guys Named Moe*. MCA, 1992.

Juvenile. "Ha." *400 Degreez*. Universal, 1998.

Kain. *The Blue Guerrilla*. Collectables, 1990.

Kane, Big Daddy. "Big Daddy Kane Vs. Dolemite." *Taste of Chocolate*. Reprise, 1990.

The Last Poets. "E Pluribus Unum." *Chatisement*. 1971 or 1973. Re-release, M.I.L., 1997.

————. Liner notes for *The Last Poets*. Douglas 3, 1969.

————. *Poetry Is Black*. Collectables, 2002.

Lee, Don L. [Haki Madhubuti]. *Rappin' & Readin'*. Broadside Voices LP-BR-1, n.d.

Lightnin' Rod. *Hustlers Convention*. 1972. Re-release, Celluloid, 1990.

Lil' Keke. "Southside." *The Commission*. Island, 1998.

Lil' Troy. "Wanna Be a Baller." *Sittin' Fat Down South*. Universal, 1999.

Ludacris. "Area Codes." Word of Mouf. Def Jam, 2001.

————. "What's Your Fantasy." *Back for the First Time*. Island/Def Jam, 2000.

Ludacris, and Jermaine Dupri. "Welcome to Atlanta." *Rap City*. BET, c. 2001.

Makaveli. *The Don Killuminati: The 7 Day Theory*. Uni Distribution, 1996.

————. *See also* Shakur, Tupac.

Master P. *Da Last Don*. Priority, 1998.

————. "Ghetto D." *Ghetto D*. Priority, 1997.

Mayfield, Curtis. "Freddie's Dead." Liner notes for *Superfly: Soundtrack*. 1972. Re-release, Curtom Records, 1997.

Mia X. *Good Girl Gone Bad*. Priority, 1995.

Mingus, Charles. *Symposium on Jazz*. Bethlehem Records, 1958.

Moore, Rudy Ray. *Beatnik Scene*. N.p., 1963 or 1964.

————. *Below the Belt*. N.p., 1961.

————. *Eat Out More Often*. 1970. Re-release, CIE, 1988.

————. *Let's All Come Together*. N.p., 1961.

M.O.P. "Ante Up." *Warriorz*. Loud Records, 2000.

Mosby, Rebekah. "Stepping into the Rivers of Poetry: The Word's Power in the 20th Century." Liner notes for *Our Souls Have Grown Deep Like the Rivers* by Jayne Cortez. Rhino Entertainment, 2000.

Mystikal. "Shake Ya Ass." *Let's Get Ready*. Zomba, 2000.

Nappy Roots. "Po' Folks." *Rap City*. BET, c. 2002.

A Nation of Poets. N.p., 1990.

Native Sun. *Eargasms*. Ozone Music, 1999.

Nelly. "Country Grammar." *Country Grammar*. Universal, 2000.

———. "Pimp Juice." *Nellyville*. Universal, 2002.

Notorious B.I.G. "Everyday Struggle." *Ready to Die*. Arista, 1994.

———. "Gimme the Loot." *Ready to Die*. Arista, 1994.

———. "Juicy." *Ready to Die*. Arista, 1994.

———. "Warning." *Ready to Die*. Arista, 1994.

N.W.A. "Boyz in the Hood." *Straight Outta Compton*. Priority, 1988.

———. "F—— the Police." *Straight Outta Compton*. Priority, 1988

———. "Gangsta Gangsta." *Straight Outta Compton*. Priority, 1988.

———. "Niggaz 4 Life." *Niggaz4Life*. Priority, 1991.

———. "Straight Outta Compton." *Straight Outta Compton*. Priority, 1988.

The Original Last Poets. "Die Nigger!!!" *The Original Last Poets from the Hit Movie* Right On! c. 1970. Re-release, Collectables, 1994.

Outkast. "Player's Ball (original)." *Southernplayalisticadillacmuzik*. Arista, 1993.

———. "The Way You Move." *Rap City*. BET, 2003.

P. Diddy. "Bad Boy for Life." *Rap City*. BET, 2001.

Parliament. "Chocolate City." *Parliament Greatest Hits*. Polygram, 1984.

———. "P Funk (Wants to Get Funked Up)." *Parliament Greatest Hits*. Polygram, 1984.

Public Enemy. "He Got Game." *He Got Game: Soundtrack*. Def Jam Records, 1998.

Rakim. "It's Been a Long Time." *The 18th Letter*. Universal, 1997.

Rappin' 4-Tay. *Introduction to Mackin'*. Celeb Entertainment, 1999.

Richie Rich. "Real Pimp." *Seasoned Veteran*. Def Jam Records, 1996.

Robinson, Wanda. *Black Ivory*. Magi, n.d.

Scarface. "The Pimp." *Mr. Scarface Is Back*. EMI, 1991.

Scott-Heron, Gil. "No Knock." *Free Will*. BMG, 1972.

———. "The Revolution Will Not Be Televised." *Small Talk at 125th and Lenox*. BMG, 1970.

The Sequence. "Funk You Up." 1980. Re-release, *The Sugar Hill Story Old School Rap*. Sequel, 1992.

Sermon, Erick. "Music." *What's the Worst That Could Happen? Soundtrack*. Uni/Interscope, 2001.

Shakur, Tupac. "Cradle to the Grave." *Thug Life: Volume 1*. Atlantic Recording, 1994.

———. "If I Die 2Nite." *Me against the World*. Atlantic Recording, 1995.

———. "Pain." *Above the Rim: The Soundtrack*. Atlantic Recording, 1994.

———. "Shorty Wanna Be a Thug." *All Eyez on Me*. Death Row/Interscope, 1995, 1996.

———. "So Many Tears." *Me against the World*. Atlantic Recording, 1995.

———. "2 of Amerikaz Most Wanted." *All Eyez on Me*. Death Row/Interscope, 1995, 1996.

———. *See also* Makaveli.

Shepp, Archie. *Live in San Francisco*. 1966. Re-release, Grp Records, 1998.

———. "Malcolm, Malcolm-Semper Malcolm." *Fire Music*. 1965. Re-release, MCA, 1995.

Shyne. "Gangsta Prayer." *Shyne*. Arista, 2000.

SirMixaLot. *Chief Boot Knocka*. American, 1994.

———. *Mack Daddy*. Def American, 1991.

SmootheDaHustler. "hustlin'." *Once upon a Time in America*. Profile, 1996.

Snoop (Doggy) Dogg. *Tha Doggfather*. Uni Distribution, 1996.

———. *Doggstyle*. Atlantic, 1993.

Styles. *A Gangster and a Gentleman*. Universal, 2002.

Sugarhill Gang. "Rapper's Delight." 1979. Re-release, *The Sugar Hill Story Old School Rap*. Sequel, 1992.

Three 6 Mafia. "Sippin' on Some Syrup." *When the Smoke Clears*. Loud, 2000.

Too Short. "Ain't No Bitches." *Can't Stay Away: Spittin' Game Since 1985*. Zomba, 1999.

———. *Born to Mack*. RCA, 1988.

———. *Cocktails*. Zomba, 1995.

———. *Don't Stop Rapping*. N.p., 1983.

———. *Get In Where You Fit In*. Zomba, 1993.

———. *Gettin' It (Album Number Ten)*. Zomba, 1996.

———. *Life Is . . . Too Short*. RCA, 1988.

———. "Pimpology." *Short Dog's in the House*. RCA, 1990.

———. *Shorty the Pimp*. Zomba, 1992.

———. *You Nasty*. Zomba, 2000.

Trick Daddy. "I'm a Thug." *Rap City*. BET, 2001.

———. "Nann Nigga." *www.thug.com*. Warlock, 1998.

———. *www.thug.com*. Warlock, 1998.

Tru. *Da Crime Family*. Priority, 1999.

Van Peebles, Melvin. *As Serious as a Heart Attack*. N.p., n.d.

———. *Brer Soul*. N.p., n.d.

———. Liner notes for *What the . . . You Mean I Can't Sing?!* 1973. Re-release, Runt LLC, 2003.

———. *Sweet Sweetback's Baadasssss Song: The Soundtrack*. 1971. Re-release, Ace, 1997.

The Watts Prophets. *The Black Voices: On the Street in Watts*. 1971. Re-release, Acid Jazz, 1997.

———. "A Pimp." *Rappin' Black in a White World*. ALA, 1971. Re-release, Acid Jazz, 1997.

———. *When the 90's Came*. Acid Jazz, 1997.

West, Cornel. *Sketches of My Culture*. Artemis, 2001.

Williams, Saul. *Amethyst Rock*. Universal, 2001.

Willie D. "Clean Up Man." *I'm Goin' Out Lika Soldier*. Priority, 1992.

Womack, Bobby, and Peace. "Across 110th Street." 1972. Re-release, *Super Bad on Celluloid: Music from '70s Black Cinema*. Universal, 1998.

X, Malcolm. "Message to the Grassroots." Recorded August 1963. Re-release, A-1 Records, 1992.

50 Cent. "P.I.M.P." *Get Rich or Die Tryin'*. Shady/Aftermath/Interscope, 2003.

Videography

"Acting White: Hurtful Accusation among Black Students." Narrated by
    Charles Gibson. *20/20.* WABC, New York, June 7, 1999.
American Beauty. Directed by Sam Mendes. Dreamworks, 1999.
American Pimp. Directed by the Hughes Brothers. MGM, 1999.
Baby Boy. Directed by John Singleton. Columbia Pictures, 2001.
Black Caesar. Directed by Larry Cohen. 1973. Re-release, Orion, 1988.
Boyz N the Hood. Directed by John Singleton. Columbia Pictures, 1991.
The Corner. Directed by Charles Dutton. HBO, May 1, 2000.
Dead Presidents. Directed by the Hughes Brothers. Hollywood Pictures,
    1995.
Dolemite. Directed by D'Urville Martin. 1976. Re-release, Xenon, 1987.
Foxy Brown. Directed by Jack Hill. 1974. Re-release, Orion, 1988.
Gangstresses. Directed by Harry Davis. Ground Zero Entertainment, 2000.
Girls! Girls! Girls! Directed by Norman Taurog. Performed by Elvis Presley.
    Fox Home, 1962.
Hookers at the Point. Directed by Brent Owens. America Undercover.
    HBO, c. 1997. Re-release, Miti Home Video, 2002.
I'll Make Me a World. By Henry Hampton. PBS, February 1–3, 1999.
The Mack. Directed by Michael Campus. Harbor Productions, 1973.
Menace II Society. Directed by the Hughes Brothers. New Line, 1993.
Monkey Hustle. Directed by Arthur Marks. American International, 1976.
New Jack City. Directed by Mario Van Peebles. Warner Bros., 1991.
Pimps Up, Hos Down. Directed by Brent Owens. America Undercover.
    HBO, 1998.
Pulp Fiction. Directed by Quentin Tarantino. Miramax, 1994.
Shaft. Directed by Gordon Parks, Jr. Metro-Goldwyn-Mayer, 1971.
The Show. Directed by Brian Robbins. Rhyser, 1995.
Slam. Directed by Marc Levin. Offline Entertainment, 1998.
South Central. Directed by Steve Anderson. Warner Bros., 1992.
Superfly. Directed by Gorden Parks, Jr. Warner Bros., 1972.
Sweet Sweetback's Badasssss Song. Directed by Melvin Van Peebles.
    Magnum, 1971.
Thug Life in DC. Directed by Marc Levin. America Undercover. HBO,
    1998.

The Wedding Singer. Directed by Frank Coraci. New Line, 1999.

Willie Dynamite. Directed by Gilbert Moses III. 1974. Re-release, Universal Studios, 2000.

Index

Above the Law, 116
Abrahams, Roger, 34, 37–38, 63, 66
academic/professional voice, 3
acapella groups, 51
"Acting White: Hurtful Accusation
    among Black Students" (20/20
    TV program), 12
Adler, Bill, 53
affirmative action, 4, 12, 144
Africa, sub-Saharan: griot tradition
    in, 30–33, 37, 51; migrations in,
    25–26
African Americans, 10, 149;
    bidialectal, 13; black radio
    stations, 77; Ebonics debate
    and, 1; folklore and, 69, 70–71,
    79; ghetto silent majority,
    94, 102; inner-city youth, 2,
    7; intellectuals, 132; literary
    scholars, 2, 24, 54; in pulp
    fiction, 96; rapping among, 35;
    suburban middle class, 102–3;
    upwardly mobile, 16
African American students, 123–27,
    149–50, 152; contact zone and,
    133–49; rapping by, 128–31;
    redemption of the oral and,
    144–49; storytelling exercises
    and, 138–42; transculturation
    and, 142–44
African American Vernacular English
    (AAVE), 1–3, 7, 125, 126, 130;
    arts of contact zone and, 134;
    discursive practices, 15, 35;

ghetto realist fiction and, 97; in
    Hip-hop magazines, 145–46;
    mainstream academic discourses
    and, 143; oral tradition and,
    14; poetic voice, 13; rapping,
    38; rhetorical tradition and, 24;
    southern, 18–19; toasting and,
    34
African National Congress, 25
Afrocentrism, 30, 39
Airtight Willie & Me (Iceberg Slim),
    98
Akinyele, 50
aliases, 141
Allen, Richard, 24
American dream, 75, 99, 100, 106,
    114
Al-Amin, Jamil Abdullah, 27
Ananse, 64
Angelou, Maya, 5, 6–7, 11, 14
Ant Banks, 66
Anzaldua, Gloria, 9, 143
Aristotle, 112
army songs, 51
Ashanti, 82
As Serious as a Heart Attack (Van
    Peebles), 42
assimilationism, 13, 16
Autobiography of Malcolm X, The
    (Malcolm X), 56
autoethnography, 133–34, 140

Ba, A. Hampaté, 30, 51–52
baby boomer generation, 16, 99

181

Permissions Acknowledgments

195